# THE WAY OF DEEP MAGICK

# THE WAY OF DEEP MAGICK
## Aleister Crowley, Simon Iff and the New Aeon

*Ian Rees*

**AEON**

First published in 2024 by
Aeon Books

British Library Cataloguing in Publication Data

A C.I.P. for this book is available from the British Library

ISBN-13: 978-1-80152-146-8

Typeset by Medlar Publishing Solutions Pvt Ltd, India

www.aeonbooks.co.uk

*This book is dedicated to Aly, the most magical person in my life; to Steve who carries the flame onwards and above all to the Priest who wears the mask of Anubis.*

# CONTENTS

# FOREWORD: OPENING THE WAY

Magick is a tradition where we seek to serve the universe and not ourselves. That the author has used the work of Aleister Crowley to reveal this truth may seem unlikely to many readers, but nevertheless, that is precisely what this book does.

From the outset, I just want to say how very difficult I have always found Aleister Crowley as an individual, and how conflicted I felt to be presented with a book that is based upon the ideas behind his magical work. I also know that I am not alone in holding that view. But, having read and greatly enjoyed the author's previous book, *The Tree of Life and Death*, which lives beside my bed for consultation months after its publication, I realised that the present book was a complement to it, and so I read onwards.

No-one arrives fully-armed as a magician at the outset: this is a long journey which includes the overcoming of habitual patterns, such as self-wilfulness and self-indulgence—accusations of which have been often levelled at Crowley—but I think very few magical practitioners have had Crowley's singleness of purpose or his willingness to strip down his soul to become of service to the sacred calling of magick. He was undoubtedly one of the pioneers of practical magick in an era that was striving to reclaim ancient traditions as signposts to deep, effective magical work. Alas, this process of recovery had many casualties at the time, as some students of magick and their teachers became bogged down in the peripherals of magical work, where robes, degrees, personalities, and titles tended to predominate over the dedicated self-clarification and reformation that is required of the Neophyte.

With his incisive intellect, his driven enquiry into the ancient traditions, and his short fuse for grandiose nonsense, Crowley finally decided to leave the Magical Order of the Golden Dawn; the seeds of his divine discontent with his teachers were crystallised for him at his first initiation which had revealed to him "the secrets of the Hebrew Alphabet"—of which he was already cognisant. Breaking free, he subsequently continued upon his own path of discovery, creating a new vocabulary and building an array of images that better suited his own approach to magick.

Any student of magick knows that the impatience of the young Neophyte tends to outrun the orderly practice of the more mature teacher, and so it has always been. Crowley jumped out of his formal training, immediately immersing himself into the deepest of experimental studies, often not sparing his own body and safety, in order to come to the deeper secrets of magick. The results of these experiences and his innovative researches are precisely the areas which become instructive to us.

Fortunately, our guide in this book has himself been in training for over fifty years and he was also a young man once, more fortunate in many ways than Crowley, in that he found wise and ethical teachers who provided a firm foundation. One of these teachers we share, for I also trained in the school that W. E. Butler founded. In this book, Ian Rees makes sense of Crowley's work by casting the light of his own magical training upon it, as a practitioner of the Western Mysteries and the Qabalistic tradition. Under the author's guidance, we are expertly led to the sources of Crowley's inspiration—the texts and inscriptions of ancient Egypt, which formed the foundation and developmental focus of his magical life, particularly those of the Stele of Revealing, which opened the way. It is so that we can understand that Crowley's dictum of "do what thou wilt shall be the whole of the law" is not an invitation to do exactly what we like, nor even a self-deterministic way of ignoring the rest of the world, but rather we can see that the "Thou" in this saying points to the eternal intelligence of the universe to which the magician is dedicated. Many readers may also have missed the full saying: "Do what thou wilt shall be the whole of the Law, Love is the Law, Love under Will", which makes the meaning much clearer.

The assembly of the Body of Light, the working self-image of the magician, is the fruit of faithful practice, for it requires that the practitioner comes face to face with the angelic guardian and teacher of the soul. Crowley had learned the Bornless Ritual from his Golden Dawn teachers, but he also drew upon the medieval working ascribed to Abramelin the Mage; through the rite of the Knowledge and Conversation of the Holy Guardian Angel, Crowley sought to unite heaven and earth—the central premise of all magical work—by a continuous ongoing dialogue with his own guardian.

Lest Crowley's own system seem alienating, the author shows that its revelations are corroboratively found in other approaches to spiritual realisation. He draws upon the parallels offered by the *vicara* or "self-enquiry" of the Advaita Master, Ramana Maharshi, as well as finding the pathways in the *Tao Te Ching*, which was followed by the author's other main teacher, Tom Oloman, as well as by Crowley himself, so the reader is offered several pathways by which to approach the mystery.

Within this book is both the necessary background and a practical workbook to begin to approach a study of deep magick. We are led through several of Crowley's magical formulas and rituals in ways that return us to an essential connection between heaven and earth. Throughout, there are helpful diagrams, glyphs, and illustrations to support our understanding. Also, as fiction often unfolds more simply and directly what magical instruction can sometimes obscure, throughout we are given the illuminating template of Crowley's magical novel, *Moonchild*, which exemplifies his own teachings through the character of Simon Iff, and his magical colleagues who lead us into the way of understanding.

Finally, by devoted practice and sincere intent, by means of continued meditation, we are led into the realisation that "Every woman and man is a star", whereby the divine life becomes our own life, where the illumination that we have sought becomes also the light which shines from us. This is the true embodiment of magical presence where divine will and love flow through us, and where we pass from living in a fragmented world into the fullest life that a human being can achieve.

In the final analysis, the outrageousness of Crowley's public reputation can be seen as merely a carapace that veils a steady stripping away of ego, and a loving surrender into the deep ocean of being. By spurning the crippling restraints of narrow Victorian mores, by leaving behind the hypocrisies and contradictions of occult legacies, Crowley stepped into the liberation that the ancient traditions of enlightenment might offer. By following his idiosyncratic way, he became a pioneer of magick for the twentieth century and beyond.

Now, as I have gained newfound respect for Aleister Crowley and a better understanding of his work from the reading of this excellent book, I hope that you may also be led to open your own book of life, and find the star that forever shines above it.

*Caitlín Matthews,*
*Oxford, January 2024.*

# INTRODUCTION

This book is based around a simple-sounding but difficult question: "What is the point of studying and practising the Qabalah and where does this practice take us as human beings?"

I have studied and practised this tradition for fifty-three years, and have been fortunate to have worked with some remarkable teachers, but that question is ever before me. It challenges and refreshes my understanding and relationship with the Qabalah and asks me to be ready to jettison everything I know in favour of entering into mystery and enquiry.

My principal teachers, W. E. (Ernest) Butler and Tom Oloman, held this attitude to be central; Ernest, in particular, would remind us that the greater the circle of light and knowing around us, the greater the darkness and not-knowing; while Tom held knowing very lightly, often forgetting the names of very basic aspects of the Qabalah, which would frustrate the young fundamentalist Qabalist that I was in those days.

Aleister Crowley's formulation of Qabalistic study, combining the method of science with the aim of religion, is also central to this understanding. He took the tradition of the Tree of Life, stripped it back to the number mysticism it arose from, and combined it with a new formulation of ancient Egyptian lore and the Eastern traditions of Taoism, Yoga, and Buddhism. In his novel *Moonchild* (1929) he looks at one of the principal issues the Qabalah addresses, namely our potential to become lost in our own desires and in the images of ourselves and the world that we create. The novel describes a magical operation of creating a child imbued with the powers of the moon, and through this Crowley shows us how our desire to create can either bind us in delusion or awaken us into a new and deeper life. A subplot of the book is the relationship between Cyril Grey, a young magician filled with the mystique of being a magical being, and Simon Iff, his master. Simon Iff practises the way of the Tao and demonstrates a deep magick which is silent and mysterious and profoundly non-dual.

Aleister Crowley's work is controversial, attracting both deification and demonisation. Ernest Butler thought his work was valuable for experienced Qabalists, while Tom had no time for him. When I was an adolescent Qabalist I loved the flamboyant aspects of his personality—the Cyril Grey in him—but, as I outgrew my own need to pose and shock, felt repelled by much of Crowley's personality. It is only over the last fifteen years that I have looked more deeply into his work, seeing the face of Simon Iff within it. In some ways, Crowley was a forerunner of the social media and celebrity age, courting publicity and acquiring labels such as "The Wickedest Man in the World" and "The Great Beast" that have never gone away, and myths about him abound. One of the persistent myths is that he died penniless, alone and confused, and that his last words were: "I am perplexed". There is no reliable source for this. In actuality, the last years of his life, from January 1945 to December 1947, were spent in Netherwood, a comfortable retirement home near Hastings on the English south coast, where he actively organised his papers and completed his final work, *Magick without Tears* (1954).

Crowley like Ernest Butler and Tom Oloman based his inner work around the Qabalistic diagram called the Tree of Life, which Ernest Butler described as: "the key glyph around which all the other associated symbolism of the western training is centred, the mighty all-embracing glyph of the universe and the soul of man" (Butler, 1978, p. 17) and went on to say: "it is a method of using the mind in a practical and constantly widening consideration of the nature of the universe and the soul of man"(Butler, 1978, p. 22). This image of ten spheres

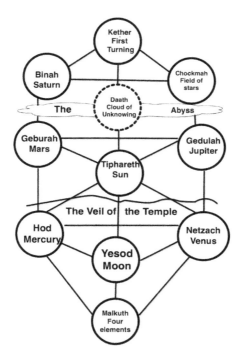

(referred to as *sephiroth*, plural, and *sephira*, singular) and twenty-two connecting paths is envisaged as a great tree, growing out of the earth, and embracing the moon, planets, sun, and stars.

These ten sephiroth and the mysterious extra sephira of Daath are used in the Qabalah as a master mandala and mirror to represent the deep image of the universe and the soul so that, for example, the sephira Malkuth represents the qualities of matter as conveyed by the medieval elements of earth, fire, air, and water, and also represents those qualities within our bodies, such as the groundedness of our body, our energy, our body and mind's ability to move fluidly, and our capacity to expand into space and receive newness.

Yesod, the foundation of life, is related to the moon and represents the underneath of things, the subtle tides of life and our unconscious, the great pool of images and energy that our image of self and universe is drawn from. Similarly, the sephira Hod and the planet Mercury refer to all things mercurial: communication; the cleverness and inventiveness of the universe and, within us, these qualities in our minds; our ability to think and communicate thought; our capacity to generate ideas and link them together.

Netzach is Venus: universal eroticism; the capacity of the universe to unite and generate life while, in the psyche, it represents our emotions.

Tiphareth, the solar centre, represents centrality, balance, and the capacity to mediate, and relates to our capacity to become present and maintain a sense of awareness.

Geburah, the sphere of Mars, relates to will and clarity and boundary, while Gedulah corresponds to compassion, love, and growth.

The mysterious sphere of Daath represents the doorway to non-dual life and the mystery of not-knowing, while Chockmah, Binah, and Kether represent the roots of the universe and the roots of the soul: non-dual will, non-dual love, and non-dual awareness.

In the practice of the Qabalah there are three major developmental points:

- The entrance into Malkuth and working with the triangle of Yesod, Hod, and Netzach, which involves our ability to be present in our bodies and to work with the tangle of thought, emotion, and sub-liminal image that constitutes our inner dialogue or commentary on our lives. This requires us to work with what the Qabalah calls the *Qliphoth*, the obscurations which restrict our awareness, perceptions, and will. The word "Qliphoth" (קליפות) has the meaning of "a husk" or "shell" which covers and restricts growth and, while this first stage is the place where we first meet these forms, they are worked with throughout the developmental process.
- The movement from this triangle into the mediating awareness of Tiphareth and the ability to work with the principles of will and love, so as to open our capacity to think, feel, and act into a much deeper sense of self and universe.
- The movement from the middle triangle into the mystery of the sephira Daath and the capacity to embody the non-dual mystery of will, love, and awareness of the supernal sephiroth (i.e. Binah, Chockmah, and Kether) as the roots of all.

We can ascribe these three steps (respectively) to the ancient Egyptian forms of (1) the Eloquent Peasant, a man of the land who spoke for Maat, the justice and balance that keeps the world working in harmony;

(2) the Good Shepherd, the principle of sovereignty that works with the principles of severity and mercy to ensure that Maat manifests; and (3) the Silent Sage, or the Geru Maa: the person so steeped in the quality of Maat that their being and nature radiates it to all, and effortlessly brings all into a sense of peace and growth. In essence, the three steps ask us to become present in our bodies, and to clarify our internal dialogue so that we can enter into the lived experience of active presence and sovereignty, in such a way that we are the anchor and transmission point for the non-dual love, will, and awareness that is always emerging from the deep places of the soul and the universe.

There are two further steps that the Geru Maa can make in order to complete their work in which the deep will of the universe and the creative awareness of the universe are successively incorporated. In Egyptian tradition this refers to: (1) the role of the Chief Lector Priest who is the chief magician and is responsible for the practice of will and magick; and (2) the position of Pharaoh who is the primary priest and representative of the divine. The word "Pharaoh" comes from the hieroglyphs for "Great House":

The upper hieroglyph, *Per*, is a house, and the lower, *Aa*, is a great column, hence Pharaoh is the container of the divine and represents the pillar that upholds the universe.

These five steps of awareness are paralleled in the Hermetic Qabalah by the esoteric grades of the Neophyte, centred in Malkuth and connecting to Yesod, Hod, and Netzach; the Minor Adept, centred in Tiphareth and connected to Geburah, Gedulah, and Daath; the Master of the Temple, centred in Binah; the Magus, centred in Chockmah; and the Ipsissimus, centred in Kether. These grades are, in turn, a reflection of the parts of the soul given in Qabalistic psychology:

- *Nephesch* (נפש). This is normally referred to as the animal soul but is the reactive, entangled part of our nature, the conditioned image of self and universe held in Yesod, which involves the mental aspect of the Hod and the feeling nature of Netzach.

- *Ruach* (רוח). This is the sense of mediating, reflective presence focused in Tiphareth, linking the dualistic will and rigour of Geburah and the dualistic love and expansiveness of Gedulah with the non-dual supernals and our mind, feelings, and self-image.
- *Neshamah* (נשמה). This is the presence of Binah, the non-dual maternal principle that generates all form, the non-dual intuition whose quality it is to embrace deeply all manifest forms with a quality of love that deeply understands their particularity.
- *Chiah* (חיה). This is the non-dual will, the creative principle that creates duality, and the generative vector that causes movement and new life.
- *Yechidah* (יחידה). This is the single point of awareness, the position or fulcrum point around which all revolves.

Conventionally these esoteric grades are thought of as achievements and assumptions are made that these deeper states are not available to people who have not reached the grade, and that a grade—once reached—is permanent. In actuality the real situation is much less linear than this. In any one moment we may experience any of the aspects of the soul, but the question is where we can we sustain our awareness. The Sufi tradition has a useful way of looking at this issue in that it distinguishes between states and stations. States are moments of awareness, while stations are the capacity to enter into and sustain ourselves within a particular aspect of soul at will. The ability to rest in the station of the *Ruach*, Neshamah, and the deeper stages depends upon significant inner work to successively incorporate these deeper qualities within us. It is also the case that where we normally have access to a station of the soul, particular difficulties can diminish our capacity to enter into that state and the capacity to enter a deeper stage does not preclude the necessity to continue to work on the earlier stages.

In the Hermetic Qabalah these stages are further subdivided into ten to correspond with the ten sephiroth.

If we consider the etymology of the esoteric grades we may discover something about their function. The word "Neophyte" comes originally from the ancient Greek and has the meaning of a young plant just placed in the soil. Its fundamental function is therefore to root itself and to grow. In this case it is planted in Malkuth and the

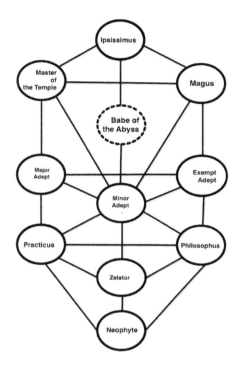

conditions for its growth are determined by its interaction with the bottom triangle of Yesod, Hod, and Netzach. Its rooting practice is to keep interrupting the momentum of the inner dialogue of thought, emotion, and memory image, so as to open our senses to the inner and outer awareness. Jesus's parable of the sower and the seed applies here:

> A farmer went out to sow his seed. As he was scattering the seed, some fell along the path, and the birds came and ate it up. Some fell on rocky places, where it did not have much soil. It sprang up quickly, because the soil was shallow. But when the sun came up, the plants were scorched, and they withered because they had no root. Other seed fell among thorns, which grew up and choked the plants. Still other seed fell on good soil, where it produced a crop—a hundred, sixty or thirty times what was sown. Whoever has ears, let them hear. (Matthew 13: 1–9)

The capacity to be sufficiently rooted in Malkuth and not choked by the profusion of forms from the internal dialogue is essential to this stage of development. In the Hermetic grade system this stage is subdivided into Zelator, Practicus, and Philosophus. Zelator, which is applied to Yesod, is derived from the Latin *zelo*, which means "to love ardently", and relates to the passionate commitment needed to keep working with the aspects of Yesod that cause us to lose awareness. Practicus is applied to Hod and comes from the ancient Greek *praktikós*, which has the meaning of "carrying out the practice of business". In this case the business is of becoming an occultist and of understanding (in theory, at least) the whys and wherefore of being one. The deeper meaning is that of understanding the functioning of the mind, and the way that chains of thought generate the sense of world and self. Philosophus, which is applied to Netzach, comes from the Greek *philósophos* (φιλόσοφος) and means "lover of wisdom". The task here relates to the redirection of the desires of Netzach into the desire to be successful in achieving the great work of deepening awareness. All three of these grades can be seen as particular aspects of the Neophyte's task of rooting and growing as a new plant.

The next stage is that of Adept where the focus of awareness is in Tiphareth and the work is to link the middle and lower triangles of the tree with Malkuth. The word "Adept" has its etymology from the Latin *adeptus*, meaning "one who has attained or reached something". The traditional Hermetic grades at this level are described as Minor Adept, Major Adept, and Exempt Adept, linked successively with Tiphareth, Geburah, and Gedulah. The attainment of the Minor Adept is to have achieved the Knowledge and Conversation of the Holy Guardian Angel sufficiently so as to be able to maintain the sense of reflective presence. The attainments of the Major and Exempt status refer to the mastery of the processes of banishing, invocation, and uniting love and will in the operation Crowley describes as "the Mass of the Holy Ghost" and lays out in detail in his novel *Moonchild*.

Prior to the third stage there is a transitional stage, which is the experience of Daath, a surrendering and stripping away of the skill and security of the Adept stage, becoming what Crowley describes as a Babe of the Abyss, in which we simply rest in the presence of the unknown and allow ourselves to be reshaped by the deeper soul.

The third stage, which is concerned with the supernal roots of soul and universe begins with the grade of *Magister Templi* or "Master of the Temple". The word *magister* comes from the Latin and means "teacher", whereas "temple" comes from the Latin *templum*, meaning "to clear a consecrated space". *Magus* comes from an old Persian word, meaning "magick", while "Ipsissimus" comes from the Latin *ipse*, which means "self"—the suffix *issimus* is a superlative which amplifies the meaning of *ipse* into the sense of being fully and completely yourself. Esoterically, it has a connection with the term *Asar un nefer*, which means being an Osiris made beautiful by being self-justified. This third stage perfects our capacity to understand and love, to will, and simply to be.

These topics are studied deeply in Aleister Crowley's writings, but on looking into this we are immediately confronted with the dynamic of the icon and the idol of Crowley himself. We can become trapped in the convolutions of his personality, either through adulation or demonisation, or we can look into what he was pointing us to which, in essence, is a revision of the Qabalah, linking it back to deep roots in Ancient Egypt and forwards into a quantum and fractal understanding of the life of the soul and the life of the universe.

The particular focus of this book is on exploring the process of moving from the unconscious incompetence of the Neophyte stage to the conscious competence of the Adept and then entering the unconscious competence of Mastery.

Crowley, in his novel *Moonchild* (1929), shows us this process and gives us the image of Simon Iff as the master magician whose being is based in stillness and the work of the Tao and who is contrasted with the figure of Cyril Grey, his student and protégé.

It is the viewpoint of the deep magician that we see Simon Iff enacting when he quotes from Crowley's inspirational poem, *The Book of the Heart Girt with the Serpent* (3: 21–26)

> I, and Me, and Mine were sitting with lutes in the market-place
> of the great city, the city of the violets and the roses.
> The night fell, and the music of the lutes was stilled.
> The tempest arose, and the music of the lutes was stilled.
> The hour passed, and the music of the lutes was stilled.
> But Thou art Eternity and Space; Thou art Matter and Motion;
> and Thou art the negation of all these things.
> For there is no symbol of Thee. (Crowley, 2015, p. 111)

This verse shows the shifting from the sense of the untrained human mind into the starry consciousness of the deep magician: the sense of I, me, and mine are reorganised by attuning to the deeper, stellar awareness; the rising of the night represents the sense of doubt; the tempest, the rising of reactivity of thought, feeling, and bodily sensation; and the passing of time, the weariness that separates us from the music manifesting from the core of our being. As we align with the deeper presence, we dissolve the network of attachments that maintain I, me, and mine and discover the sense of ourselves described as "Thou". This is the process of moving from the stage of the Neophyte to the Adept. The immersion in this deeper awareness and the entrance into the understanding of the Geru Maa or Master of the Temple is shown in another holy book, *Liber Liberi Vel Lapidis Lazuli* (5: 1–5) in the following verse:

> O my beautiful God! I swim in Thy heart like a trout in the mountain torrent.
> I leap from pool to pool in my joy; I am goodly with brown and gold and silver.
> Why, I am lovelier than the russet autumn woods at the first snowfall.
> And the crystal cave of my thought is lovelier than I. (Crowley, 2015, p. 155)

Then from this place of deep alignment, another verse from *The Book of the Heart Girt with the Serpent* (3: 27) applies:

> If I say Come up upon the mountains! the celestial waters flow at my word. But thou art the Water beyond the waters. (Crowley, 2015, p. 111)

This is the place of profound union and deep resonance with the All. This act of causing the celestial waters to flow is the step beyond the Geru Maa—the Magus or Chief Magician—while the "Thou" who is the "Water beyond the waters" refers to the Ipsissimus state of Kether.

My teacher Ernest Butler's sense of this practice of deep magick was expressed in his experience of being a Christed human being. He used an alchemical formula that he called "the flyer must descend into the sea", which involved the immersion in the great sea of Binah through which he entered the state of being the Geru Maa or

Master of the Temple. His further work with the resurrection Body of Light that follows the descent embodied the stages of the Magus and Ipsissimus. My other teacher, Tom Olomon, expressed this process in a practice of uniting the letters of the Name (יהוה) and the further stages of working with the lamp of darkness and the mirrored womb.

This deeper stage of practice is also addressed in a medieval Qabalistic school, the thirteenth-century Iyyun Circle, or Circle of Contemplation, which demonstrates a simplicity of practice and an ability to work with flow and contra-flow and unite opposites and contraries. Their work was organised around the Name (יהוה) and they envisaged the universe as a fountain of light and darkness, or as a book of contemplations, all of which arise from the single flame of the Yod (י) that appears from the infinite void. In one of their principal texts, *The Fountain of Wisdom*, we are told:

> This book is *The Fountain of Wisdom* that Michael gave to Pe'eli and Pe'eli to Moses. Moses revealed it for the enlightenment of [subsequent] generations. When David understood the nature of its knowledge he exclaimed, "I shall acknowledge my gratitude to You, Lord, with all my heart. I shall honor Your Name forever" (Ps. 86: 12).
>
> These are the *tikkun*, combination, utterance, sum, and computation of the explication of the Ineffable Name—unique in the branches of the root of vocalization that is magnified in the thirteen types of transformation.
>
> How is the *tikkun* [accomplished]? It derives the word through the utterance and the utterance through the word; the *tikkun* through the combination and the combination through the *tikkun*, the sum through the computation and the computation through the sum—until all the words are positioned in the font of the flame and the flame in the font—until there is no measuring or quantifying the light that is hidden in the superabundance of the secret darkness. (Verman, 1992, pp. 50–51)

In this context the word *tikkun* means "enquiry" or "uncovering the fundamental elements of self and universe", and this is the work of the Neophyte; the combination, sum, utterance, and computation is the work of the Adept; the explication of the Name, the work of the Master.

The cryptic-seeming words of *The Fountain of Wisdom* are entirely concerned with the unfolding creative play of the divine and the act of *tikkun*, utterance and explication, is both the action of uncovering the roots of that play and restoring us from being lost in that play to being an active participant in and with it.

# FOUNDATIONS OF THE WAY—THE WORK OF THE NEOPHYTE

The work of the Neophyte, as the name of "new plant" implies, is the need to root and grow; the roots of the work are found in understanding with mind, heart, and body the elements of the tradition that we are seeking to incarnate within us. Just like a plant, we must root ourselves in the soil of the tradition and nourish ourselves on its contents using it as a mirror to expose the patterns within us that restrict our growth. Our connection with the deeper aspects of the soul and the universe is held within the image of self and universe that we have constructed through the decisions of our lives, and this image is maintained through our subliminal dialogue of thought, feeling, and memory image. It is through our immersion in the material of the tradition and becoming a follower of the tradition that the deeper soul can communicate to us using the images and exercises of the Way to adjust our habitual patterns so that our awareness opens to new possibilities. We are continually seeking to move from the fragmented and qliphothic world that we have shaped for ourselves into the experience of Malkuth—the living body in the living world—and from that fulcrum disrupting the internal dialogue that keeps us trapped.

The chapters in the first section are designed to enable this task.

# CHAPTER 1

# Meeting Aleister Crowley

Aleister Crowley remains a mysterious figure in the shadows of western culture, in his lifetime he was called "The Wickedest Man in the World" and demonised by the British press; his picture appears on the Beatles Sgt. Peppers Lonely Hearts Club Band album and Tobias Churton, Crowley's biographer, tells us that in 2002 a BBC poll placed him seventy-third in a list of the "100 Greatest Britons" (Churton, 2011, p. 3). His ideas and practices continue to appear in many different places; a number of academic studies of his life and work have appeared that take him and his ideas seriously seriously (Evans, 2007, Mistlberger, 2010; Bogdan, 2012); significant recording artists such as David Bowie and Jimmy Page have acknowledged him as having influenced the development of their music, while the philosopher John Moore considers him in relation to the development of philosophical thought (Moore, 2009). It is, however, the art and practice of magick that was his life's study and work and it is this central core that we will consider in this book.

I first encountered Aleister Crowley when I was fifteen. It was 1970 and, courtesy of Swansea Library, I read *The Great Beast* by John Symonds (1973) and *The Confessions of Aleister Crowley: An*

*Autohagiography* (1971). It was heady stuff for an adolescent boy living in a small village in South Wales. While there wasn't much rock
and roll in the books, there was plenty of sex and drugs to be getting
on with. I didn't know it then, but it was the beginning of a relationship with Crowley that fifty-two years later leads me to writing
a book about him. I have at various times been fascinated by him,
repelled by him, awed, annoyed, admiring, and judgemental of him.
My teacher Ernest Butler regarded him as an important Qabalist but
felt that his work should be studied by experienced occultists, not
beginners. Tom Oloman had no time for him at all and felt that he
lacked balance.

In my late teens and early twenties I enjoyed the rebellious aspects of
Crowley and my teachers' caution and disapproval were, if anything,
a spur to my interest in him. As I have become older, I have come to
believe that many of the aspects of his personality I once found excit-
ing were the least interesting aspects of his nature and that within
the colour, pomp, and ceremony of the events of his life is something
altogether stiller, deeper, and more potent.

Crowley was born in 1875 and became a member of the Hermetic
Order of the Golden Dawn in 1898. One of the interesting features of his
early inner development was his ability to internalise inner practices.
He was a student of a Golden Dawn Adept called Allan Bennett who
had studied Buddhist tradition and later moved to Ceylon and became a
Theravadin monk, taking the name Ananda Metteyya. Aleister Crowley
was also a dedicated mountaineer, and when he climbed with Oscar
Eckenstein in Mexico, in 1900, Eckenstein explained to Crowley that he
was making no progress in his inner life through the ritual methods of
the Golden Dawn:

> Eckenstein turned on me and gave me the worst quarter of an hour
> of my life. He summed up my magical situation and told me that my
> troubles were due to my inability to control my thoughts. He said:
> "Give up your Magick, with all its romantic fascinations and deceit-
> ful delights. Promise to do this for a time and I will teach you how
> to master your mind." He spoke with the absolute authority which
> comes from profound and perfect knowledge. And, as I sat and
> listened, I found my faith fixed by the force of facts. I wondered
> and worshipped. (Crowley, 1971, p. 211)

Eckenstein taught him the art of concentration, focus, and visualisation that is the true foundation of magick. He began by teaching him to visualise simple objects, then moving objects—such as a pendulum—in order to discover how to sustain attention and stop the form from distorting, changing, or vanishing. Next he involved the senses of hearing, smelling, tasting, and touching, creating a multi-dimensional image and deepening the capacity of his concentration and imagination to generate and sustain a living inner world. The capacity to focus attention and work with will that he developed through these practices lead him to feel that Eckenstein deeply understood the maxim: "For pure will, unassuaged of purpose, delivered from the lust of result, is every way perfect" (I: 44). Much later in his life he came to believe that Eckenstein was an Ipsissimus, the highest grade of initiate, and what the Eastern Advaita tradition would call a *jivanmukta*—a living being who is free from the play of the opposites and whose will is identified with the divine will.

Later, he visited Allan Bennett in Ceylon and deepened his understanding of the practice of training the mind. Bennett taught him that the substance of the mind is based upon elements called *sankharas* or "tendencies", which are constellations of thought, feeling, and intention. The capacity of focusing will that he learned from Eckenstein he now developed through the Buddhist practice of right concentration or *samma samadhi*. Allan Bennett tells us:

> If we consider the action of a great and complex engine—such a machine as drives a steamship through the water—we shall see that there is, first and foremost, one central and all operating source of energy: in this case the steam which is generated in the boilers. This energy in itself is neither good nor bad—it is simply *Power*; and whether that power does the useful work of moving the ship, or the bad work of breaking loose and destroying and spoiling the ship, and scalding men to death, and so on, all depends upon the correct and coordinated operation of all the various parts of that complex machinery. If the slide-valves of the great cylinders open a little too soon and so admit the steam before the proper time, much power will be lost in overcoming the resistance of the steam itself. If they remain open too long, the expansive force of the steam will be wasted, and so again power will be lost; and if they open

too late, much of the momentum of the engine will be used up in moving uselessly the great mass of machinery. And so it is with every part of the engine. In every part the prime mover is that concentrated expansive energy of the steam; but that energy must be applied in each divers piece of mechanism in exactly the right way, at exactly the right time; otherwise the machine will not work at all, or much of the energy of the steam will be wasted in overcoming its own opposing force.

So it is with this subtle machinery of the mind—a mechanism infinitely more complex, capable of far more power for good or for evil, than the most marvellous of man's mechanical achievements, than the most powerful engine ever made by human hands […]

The name of that power is Mental Concentration; and there is nothing in this world, whether for good or for evil, but is wrought by its application. It weaves upon the loom of time the fabric of men's characters and destinies […]

It is by the power of this Samādhi or Mental Concentration that the baby learns to walk; it is by its power that Newton weighed the suns and worlds […]

If the Sankhāras act well together, if their varying functions are well coordinated, then that man has great power, either for good or for evil. When you see one of weak mind and will, you may be sure that the actions of his Sankhāras are working one against another; and so the central power, this power of Samādhi, is wasted in one part of the mind in overcoming its own energy in another. (Bennett, 1911)

It is this early training of the mind, will, and imagination that is the basis of Crowley's understanding of the true will and the practice of magick and which emerges as the new, barebones version of the Qabalah found in the inspirational text, *The Book of the Law* (1904). There are two key principles that run through all of his work: an ongoing process that he calls the Knowledge and Conversation of the Holy Guardian Angel, which assists the second principle of the emergence of the true will. This sober, inner training of focusing the mind, will, and imagination is held in counterpoint with a powerful devotional imagination that he called "inflaming with prayer" and produces an ongoing colloquy with the angel, which begins in Malkuth and ends in Kether.

In his novel *Diary of a Drug Fiend* (1922), Crowley explores the nature of the relationship with both the true will and the angel through the figure of Peter Pendragon, a veteran First World War pilot who has come into a large inheritance and is suffering from depression and loss of direction. He meets, falls in love with, and marries Louise Laleham, a student of the philosopher occultist Basil King Lamus, and the two of them embark on a sustained drug binge across Europe. The majority of the book, which is based on Crowley's own struggles with heroin, is concerned with applying the discipline of magick to free them from their addiction and enable the emergence of their true wills. In this process, Peter Pendragon realises:

> I did not exist at all, in any ordinary sense of the word. I was a mathematical expression in a complex scheme of geometry. My equilibrium was maintained by innumerable other forces in the same system, and what I called myself was in some mysterious way charged with a duty of manipulating the other forces, and these evaded me. When I strove to grasp them, they disappeared. My functions seemed to be to simplify complex expressions, and then to build up new complexes from the elements so isolated as to create simulacra of my own expression in other forms. (Crowley, 1922, p. 341)

It also contains an account of Louise inviting and communing with her Holy Guardian Angel who appears to her as Keletiel, a white-winged figure in blues and greens with a gold sapphire studded diadem that bears her name. This figure appears to her inner vision in many different forms and is a focus of inspiration and teaching for her. In this story, the magician is Basil Lamus, the teacher of the true will, who frees them from their addictions, addresses Peter's feelings of depression and loss of direction, and Louise's sense of meaninglessness. We are told of Lamus: "The secret of his power is that he doesn't exist for himself. His force flows through him unhindered" (Crowley, 1922, p. 356).

We witness the emergence of Louise and Peter's true will. In Peter's case, he discovers that his true will is to be an engineer as he creates in his mind a plan for constructing a helicopter. Louise discovers that her true will is to be his helper and companion and they both discover that it is their true will to be together and to assist each other. They then find that:

> Our union destroyed our sense of separateness from the universe of which we were part; the sun, the sky, the sea, the earth, partook with us of that ineffable sacrament. (Crowley, 1922, p. 357)

And:

> [D]eep eternal peace sat like a dove, a triple tongue of flame upon our souls, which were one soul for ever. Each of our lives was one, individual, and eternal, but each possessed its necessary and intimate relation with the other, and both with the whole universe. (Crowley, 1922, p. 367)

Crowley's novel *Moonchild* (1929) continues these themes, but looks much more deeply into the practice of magick. On the surface it is an adventure story about the right-hand path Adepts Cyril Grey and Simon Iff who are performing a magical operation of sex magick with the assistance of Lisa la Giuffria to incarnate a soul that will be an avatar of the moon. Opposing them are the Black Lodge, headed by Douglas (a very thinly veiled reference to Samuel McGregor Mathers, Head of the Golden Dawn) and his disciples Arthwaite (Arthur Edward Waite) and Gates (W. B. Yeats).

On a deeper level, *Moonchild* addresses the lunar sphere of Yesod on the Tree of Life and the magical art itself. Simon Iff and Cyril Grey are presented as two images of the magician—Cyril as the obvious image; Simon as the true image—while Douglas and his companions are presented as images of black magicians—that is, those who are dedicated to separation and the worlds of the Qliphoth.

The tarot trump the Magician shows us an ambiguity implicit in this figure. The traditional title of the card is *Le Bateleur*—the wielder of the wand or baton that conjures images of activity and movement, the conducting of orchestras, pointing the way, the casting of spells, etc. Here we are shown an image that depicts the mystery of movement and direction, and the unification or division of the will. It can also represent trickery, deception, and illusion—the aping of the true magician who works with the living image and the divine play.

· LE   BATELEVP ·

In the image above we can see the wielding of the baton, the table that is the field of attention, and the hat that conceals the lemniscate ∞ which, as the symbol of infinity, represents the mysterious presence of the angel enfolding into the form and practice of the magician.

The relationship between the will and the imagination, between truth and illusion, is explored in depth in *Moonchild* and takes us into the heart of the sephira Yesod. This sephira is aligned with the moon and called "the treasure house of images". Here are the subliminal images that influence our thinking, feeling, and action, which live in what might be termed "the inner sea". It is also described as the place of mixed waters, both sweet and bitter. It is a reflection within us of the great non-dual sea of Binah, which is the place where non-dual love exercises its creativity, and causes all forms to come into being. Cyril Grey is the magician operating in the triangle of Yesod, Hod, and Netzach (or image, thought, and feeling) while Simon Iff sits firmly in Binah, the place of non-dual love and spontaneous action. Crowley's sense of the imagination being rooted in the non-dual love of Binah causes him to define the two major forces of his magick as will and love, where love's capacity for growth and for embracing all possible forms includes imagination and transcends it. Just as Yesod is the foundation of the known sense of psyche and universe, the mysterious sphere of Daath is the foundation of and doorway to the experience of being the Geru Maa, the Master of the Temple.

In the novel, Simon Iff shows us Daath in action, while his pupil Cyril Grey gives us the Yesodic image of the magician. He is enigmatic and does strange things—he attracts our attention whereas Simon Iff is a very ordinary seeming old man. Yet it is Simon Iff who, early in the story, deals with the appearance of "the Thing in the Garden", a demonic entity. We learn that Cyril would have banished the thing with pentagrams and high ritual, whereas Simon simply connects to it and draws it into himself through the inner practice of working with love and will.

Similarly, Simon Iff uses the image of a cone descending into a bowl of water to explain the art of deep magick and of the interlocking nature of the planes of the universe. He asks us to imagine that we are dwellers on the surface of the water, as two-dimensional beings, and to consider our experience as the cone descends. He notes that we would first experience the sense of a point, and then of increasing circles, if the cone descends vertically; or ellipses if the cone descends at an angle, one way producing parabolas and the other hyperbolas; and were the cone to be instead an irregular body, then a variety of unusual and unrelatable forms would be perceived. It is the capacity to embrace the deeper dimension, in this case the third dimension, that enables us to perceive the experience as a whole rather than as disconnected units. He next asks us to transfer this perception from two dimensions to three, four, or more, and suggests that the whole art of magick can be found in this analogy (Crowley, 1929, pp. 60–64).

What he is describing in this homely analogy is the Knowledge and Conversation of the Holy Guardian Angel. The bowl of water represents the pool of Yesod, the foundation place of our psyche, and the focal point of the inner dialogue of thought, feeling, and image (Hod, Netzach, and

Yesod on the Tree of Life), while the cone is the descending presence of the Holy Guardian Angel manifesting within that pool (Tiphareth, and the higher spheres of the tree). He is pointing to the necessity to consider the events of our lives as connected to this deeper process, which he also describes as the unfolding of the true will. In the analogy the difficulty of those who are operating from the two-dimensional place is they cannot perceive the connected nature of the experience, so, too, he invites us to consider that the apparently disconnected events of our lives may have a deeper coherence and purpose.

The combination of this teaching with his resolution of the issue of the Thing in the Garden gives us an insight into a deeper and more potent form of magick than the forms espoused by Cyril Grey. Indeed, Cyril's journey in this book is, like Shakespeare's Prospero, an abjurement or renunciation of the rough magick he has hitherto promulgated and practised. We can see this in Crowley's distinction between the way of Simon Iff, as the balanced magician, and the way of Douglas, the magician working for separation, illustrated in the following paragraph:

> Now Simple Simon, at this time, did not know Douglas for the enemy General; but he was in the closest possible magical touch with him. For he had absorbed the Thing in the garden into himself and that Thing had been a part of Douglas. So he set himself to the complete assimilation of that Thing; he made certain that it should be part of himself for ever. His method of doing this was as simple as usual. He went over the Universe in his mind, and set himself to reconcile all contradictions in a higher Unity. Beginning with such gross things as the colours of the spectrum, which are only partialities of white light, he resolved everything that came into his mind until he reached such abstractions as matter and motion, being and form; and by this process worked himself up into a state of mind which was capable of grasping those sublime ideas which unite even these ultimate antinomies. That was all. Douglas, still in magical touch with that "watcher," could feel it being slowly digested, so to say, by some other magician. This (incidentally) is the final fate of all black magicians, to be torn piecemeal, for lack of the love which grows by giving itself to the beloved, again and again, until its "I" is continuous with existence itself. "Whoso loveth his life shall lose it" is the corresponding scriptural phrase. So Douglas, who might at that moment have saved himself by resignation, was too blind to see the way—an acquired blindness resulting from repeated acts

whose essence was the denial of the unity of himself with the rest of the universe. And so he fought desperately against the assimilation of his "watcher." "It's mine, not yours!" he raged. To the steady and continuous affirmation of true unity in all diversity which Simon Iff was making, he opposed the affirmation of duality. The result was that his whole mind was aflame with the passion of contrasting things, of playing forces off against each other. When it came to practical decisions he divided his forces, and deliberately created jealousy and hatred where co-operation and loyalty should have been the first and last consideration. Yet Simon Iff had used no spell but Love. (Crowley, 1929, p. 155)

There is a way in which the two novels give us insight into the two key aspects of will and love that underlie all of Crowley's teachings. The earlier novel *Diary of a Drug Fiend* (1922) focuses on the principle of will and the communion with the angel and the love relationship of Peter and Louise as aspects of that will, thus giving us the classic Crowleyan formula of "Love is the Law, Love under Will" while *Moonchild* (1929) focuses on the performance of magick and the uniting of will and love in the act of creation.

*Moonchild* shows us the two aspects of Aleister Crowley: the outer, egotistical, self-proclaimed messiah who has been extensively commented on and is alternately demonised and deified (even by himself) but, beneath this, a deep will and love that can show us wonderful things. In this process we are freed from our addictions, through the guidance of the angel and the arising of true will. By uniting love and will in the practice of magick, Simon Iff shows us the manifestation of the true moonchild—the icon made flesh. In this moment, Daath and Yesod are perfectly aligned, and the world and self we know die and a new self and world comes into being.

This principle of the new world appearing is shown in Crowley's work as the idea of the "aeons", periods of time in which particular models of spirituality and inner practice predominate and that determine the ways in which spiritual and moral progress can be made. He was strongly influenced by J.G. Frazer's *The Golden Bough* (1890) and a way of thinking about religious tradition that saw it as developmental—in concert with Darwin's evolutionary theory and Freud's notion of the development of the psyche. Crowley suggested that from prehistory human beings lived and worked under what he described as "the Aeon of Isis", in which society was matriarchal; the primary divinity was the great goddess and human beings lived in unconscious harmony with nature. This was replaced by "the Aeon of Osiris" and the rise of the male god, a dying and risen god, such as Osiris, Dionysus, and, of course, Christ. This he linked to the development of the ego and a vision of life in which the spiritual was exalted above the earth and spiritual progress was dependent upon a cataclysmic process of dying and being brought into a new life. Crowley saw himself as inviting in the new "Aeon of Horus", the aeon of the crowned and conquering child, and the appearance of a formula of spirituality in which human consciousness shifts from being earth-centred to being solar, becoming a star in the body of infinite space.

A deceptively simple practice concerning this new consciousness was described by Crowley's magical son, Frater Achad, in 1919. He learned this from Sister Hilarion, a Thelemite Adept, and it consists of—each night, as we go to sleep—consciously laying down all the shadows and difficulties of the day and, as we wake, uprising with the sun and living in the sunlight. Here we release and let go of the events that have impacted us and take the point of view of the ever-shining sun, projecting light into our environment, and thus enacting the verse from *The Book of the Law*: "Every man and every woman is a star" (I: 3).

This simple-seeming practice connects us with ideas such as the true will and the Star-Sponge vision, which we will explore later in the book, as well as the deep simplicity of immersing ourselves in the flow of the Tao and being a vehicle for it. We are shining because it is our nature to shine and our shape is the shape that naturally arises from the flow of life that passes through us.

# CHAPTER 2

# Ernest Butler and the Body of Light

My first encounter with Ernest Butler was through a book of his called *Apprenticed to Magic* (1962). It was 1971, and I found the book through a magazine called *Exchange and Mart*, which was mainly concerned with selling second-hand cars, but at the back it had a section where booksellers advertised their catalogues and one of these was the Aquarian Press. The book is a series of letters written by a Qabalist teacher to a student about the practice of the art of magick. It was straightforward, clear, and suggested that if you wanted to use the methods of the book you should buy and contemplate Dion Fortune's *The Mystical Qabalah* (1976), Paul Foster Case's *The Tarot: A Key to the Wisdom of the Ages* (1947), and acquire the Waite–Smith tarot deck. What made this book special for me was that it is very practical, beginning with relaxation exercises, taking the reader through a version of Qabalistic yoga, and teaching the principles of ritual. I shortly acquired his other books: *The Magician: His Training and Work* (1959); *Magic: Its Ritual, Power and Purpose* (1952); and *Magic and the Qabalah* (1964). This little library was and still is, in many ways, the foundation of my occult work, and I wholeheartedly followed the practices he described. During this time I came across a discrete and private book service called

Helios Books (in those days buying occult books was not greatly dissimilar from buying pornography—very much an underground activity) and to my delight I discovered that they were offering a training course called "The Helios Course in the Practical Qabalah". I was even more delighted when I discovered that the course was written and supervised by W. E. Butler in person. As I was only eighteen, and the admission age for such a course in those far-off days was twenty-one, I had to argue my corner to be let in. They allowed me to join and, in addition to Mr Butler's guidance, I was given a personal tutor called Tom Oloman of which more later. The Helios Course later became "The Servants of the Light School of Occult Science" and was the receptacle into which Ernest Butler poured his considerable learning and understanding of the way of the Qabalah.

While Ernest Butler had been a member of the Society of the Inner Light under Dion Fortune, his principal teacher was Robert King, a liberal Catholic bishop, a spiritualist medium, and theosophist—although when Ernest knew him, he was working solely with small groups and teaching the Christian Qabalah.

Ernest Butler 1898–1978

Robert King 1869–1954

It was through Robert King that Ernest first experienced the inner worlds, which he described in this way:

[H]e one day finds that he is no longer in the inert physical body, which he sees resting on the bed or couch before him. Like Tennyson's "Ancient Sage", the mortal limit of the self has been loosed, and the student stands, fully conscious in the Body of Light.

This is a tremendous experience, and the present writer well remembers the time, now some forty years ago, when, under the guidance of his teacher, he first stood forth in the Body of Light, and gazed on his earthly form lying in deep trance on the couch. Whoever has this experience *knows* in a mode of absolute knowledge, that he is not the physical body with which he has for so long identified himself. It is possibly one of the greatest experiences which can happen to man, and perhaps the novelist, Lord Bulwer Lytton, was thinking of this in his book *Zanoni*, when he makes the Rosicrucian adept Mejnour remark, "Man's first initiation is in trance". (Butler, 1959, p. 116)

Robert King derived his teaching from an inner plane teacher who presented himself as a priest from ancient Alexandria, and who referred to himself as "The Opener of the Ways" or "the Priest who wears the Mask of Anubis". Through his work with Robert King, Ernest came into relationship with this inner teacher and, subsequently, Tom Oloman; and much later I came into relationship with him also.

This inner teacher drew on the sense of Alexandria as the ancient city where the East met the West. In this new iteration of work he placed at its centre the ancient Egyptian tradition of working with the living image, and the daily process of following the course of the sun, down into the underworld, to be renewed in the waters of the beginning and reborn into in the new day. The Opener of the Ways drew on the image of the Tree of Life and the Arthurian myths, while insisting that the root of the school, like the roots of the Qabalah, are in the traditions of ancient Egypt. He used the image of the spiritual sun as an image of the divine root of our being. The name of the training group, "The Helios Course in the Practical Qabalah", hinted at these solar roots: Helios is the ancient Greek name for the sun god; and while, at one level, this was simply practical (because it was hosted by the Helios Book service), it was reiterated when the group became "The Servants of the Light" with its acronym "SOL" (the Roman name for the sun god).

The course was organised upon the image of the Round Table, situated in a Grail Castle, each room of which was one of the sephiroth of the Tree of Life. The castle was accessed by the use of a phrase:

> *Now do I descend into the inner sea, whose waters rise and fall within my soul. Let the inner elements be subdued and still as I immerse myself within the living waters and, emerging therefrom, unfold from latent stress to potent image the symbol of the King's High Table.*

The effect of contemplating this phrase is to produce a sense of immersion in the waters and the arising of the image of a Round Table in a great hall, situated within a castle on a mound in the Arthurian landscape. Within the castle and landscape is a fusion of Egyptian, Arthurian, and Qabalistic imagery. At the end of the meditation the form is absorbed back into the body, to remain latent until called out again. The contemplation verse was linked to an alchemical phrase that Ernest would often use: "The flyer must descend into the sea", by which he meant that the surface personality must descend into the depths, moving from the formed, known self into the fluidity and foundations of our being that the Qabalists called Yesod and, even beyond Yesod, into the mystery of Daath. Through Daath, the deep sea of Binah, the supernal mother, is accessed and through the process of *solve et coagula* or "dissolution and recreation" we emerge in a new and renewed form.

This continual practice of alignment with the process of the sun and the descent into the deep waters, and the return therefrom, gradually bring about a transformation of our sense of self and universe that mirrors the inner aspect of the Egyptian process of mummification. The inner inspirer of this whole process therefore presented himself as a priest of Anubis, superintending the process of death and resurrection.

Ernest's deeper work concerned the development of the magical personality and the manifestation of the Body of Light. His contemplations focused on the phrase from Genesis: *yehi or* (יהי עור), "let there be light", and the beginning of the Gospel of John:

> In the beginning was the Word, and the Word was with God, and the Word was God. He was with God in the beginning. Through him all things were made; without him nothing was made that has been made. In him was life, and that life was the light of all mankind. The light shines in the darkness, and the darkness has not overcome it. (John 1: 1–5)

Ernest taught this process, meditatively inviting us to travel backwards in time and space until we find ourselves in the deep darkness that precedes manifestation, asking us to contemplate the three veils of the unmanifest, beginning with the deepest veil of אין or Ain (which means "no-thing"), then אין סוף, Ain Soph, which means "the limitless", and then אין סוף אור, Ain Soph Aur, which means "the limitless light". From this sense of unmanifest but limitless light he would then contemplate *yehi or*, seeing this as the will of the divine artist manifesting through the contemplator. He described this centre of creative will as a fountain or whirlpool of light, pouring out of the primordial point at the centre of our being, causing the shaping of self and universe and containing within it all the possible forms of existence that will be. He would then invite us to contemplate the name of God associated with Kether, אהיה אשר אהיה, "I am the ever-becoming one; I will be that which I will be". He saw this as the divine imagination in action, the name אהיה indicating the activity of imagining ("I will be") אשר ("that", or the imagined); and the repetition of אהיה causing us to return to the place of beginning again. We were encouraged to see our own acts of will and imagination as reflections of that divine process and were given this phrase to contemplate.

> We ask you to keep this idea of the Divine Imagining and Its reflection in Space in mind, for it is a key point in the whole of this teaching. (Rees, 1973)

The reflection in space of the divine imagination was linked for him with working with the light of creation and the appearance of the Body of Light within the temple of the universe. He connected this to his understanding of the resurrection body of Christ and to a certain tradition concerning the Apostle John, which named him as the Christomorph— that is, one formed in the image of the Christ and therefore a transmitter of the Christ light and a Christ-bearer. There is an ancient Christian tradition that says the reason Judas identifies Jesus with a kiss in the moment of betrayal is because Jesus was a shapeshifter and no-one knew his true shape; if Judas had given a verbal description of Jesus to the arresters then he would have switched his appearance. This is linked to another tradition of the image of Christ on a square of cloth called "the Mandylion" or "image of Edessa", which is the prototype of all icons. The living image of the Christ is the transmitter of the potent redeeming Christ-light. Ernest's sense of the difference between the ordinary personality and the "magical personality" is that the latter is built in the image of Christ and, like Christ, is fluid, shapeshifting, and enables the passage of the creative light through it.

Ernest Butler's own personal sense of the Christ was indicated for him in the image of the Fool in the tarot. In one of his contemplations on this figure we find him describing the Fool as the form the divine presence takes when, as the cosmic artist, it steps into creation. His contemplations are based upon the Waite–Smith Fool and he describes the consciousness that arises from this image as perpetually youthful and green with new life. Ernest continually suggested that we should identify with this figure, feeling the power, potency, freshness, and vulnerability of this form passing through our own and expanding our awareness into new and unknown dimensions. This he held in tension with the sense of the dark mother who is found in the centre of matter and who is responsible for the form that holds that Christ presence.

His continual immersion in the deep sea of the mother, the dissolving of the known form and the receiving of the Christ-Fool was his constant and deepest practice. His work on the Body of Light was for him a form of redemptive prayer and blessing. He received the pain and struggles of his own life and of the whole world through the manifestation of that light by responding to it and offering healing.

# CHAPTER 3

# Tom Oloman and the Path of the Name

I met Tom when I joined the Helios course. My studies were overseen by Ernest Butler and he assigned Tom to be my personal supervisor. I have never forgotten my first meeting with Tom. I was born and brought up in a small village in the Swansea valley. It was 1973 and this was my first long journey by train on my own. The experience was given added charge by my parents' total opposition to my involvement in the occult in general, and with Tom and Ernest in particular. I recall running to catch the train with my father bellowing after me, "Why do you want to go and see those madmen?"

The journey from South Wales to Wickham Bishops in Essex is not far but, in the much less connected world of the 1970s, felt like an enormous adventure, and so it proved to be. Eventually I arrived by taxi (my first ever solo taxi ride) at a beautiful redbrick cottage and found myself greeting a short, bespectacled man with white, swept-back hair who asked me to call him "Tom" rather than Mr Oloman. From then, I would visit him every two to three months and, in between, we would communicate by letter as, step by step, he taught me the Qabalah using Ernest Butler's course as the framework.

Tom Oloman and I in 1983

Tom died in 1994, at the age of eighty, and I feel sure would not be pleased at having his name linked with Aleister Crowley because he felt strongly that Crowley had an unbalanced personality. Oddly though, when we move beyond the more obvious aspects of both men's personalities and into their practice of the art of the Qabalah there is much they had in common—in a very particular way, they practised a way of magick that was simple but of infinite depth.

Tom lived very quietly with his partner Peter, and when I met him was completing his career as a primary school teacher in the village of Maldon, but his life underwent many changes. He was born in 1914, was innately religious, and became a Methodist minister in the North of England, was married and had a child, but always felt that there was something important missing from his life. In his late twenties he discovered he was gay so he told his wife, family, and church, and was disowned by all of them and never saw his daughter again. At a time when most gay men were deep in the closet, Tom came out to those he cared about even though he knew the consequences for him would be terrible. He moved to London and started living in Soho where he created a rather more bohemian life for himself than he could ever have experienced in the North of England. He was involved as a caseworker for the Charity Organisation Society, one of the groups out of which social work arose in Britain. His interest in spiritualty deepened and he studied and practised the Qabalah initially with a group called

"The Dawn" (no relationship to the Golden Dawn) and then, later, with Ernest Butler. During the Second World War, he was a conscientious objector, a stance that brought a great deal of criticism his way. After the war, he trained as a primary school teacher and, after teaching in London, for years he and his partner lived at Wickham Bishops in Essex.

In his quiet and private way, he was a radical man with great energy. At seventy he learned to drive a car, having previously driven a motor scooter, and greatly enjoyed driving around the lanes of Essex at high speed. He was radical too in his practice of Qabalah, having essentialised his approach to a daily practice of linking with the flow of life, absorbing disturbance, and bringing blessing, balance, and light into the world.

For many years he used the image below as a focus for contemplation. One of his students drew it for him and he allowed the Servants of the Light to use it for their in-house magazine, *Round Merlin's Table*. He used it as a way of summarising his work on the Qabalah and the Arthurian tradition. Seated around the table are the four holy living creatures of the Qabalah: the man, the bull, the eagle, and the lion. The table is edged with intertwined dragons and each of the symbols are related to the development of the flow of energy and the bringing together of opposites. At the centre is the circled cross that became the heart of all his contemplations.

Later, as he developed his work around the traditions of the healing name, he used the much simpler mandala of יהשוה (*YHShVH*) shown below.

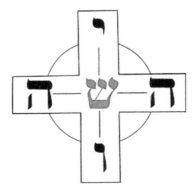

The roots of the path of the name that Tom followed are described powerfully In Rabbi Lawrence Kushner's novel *Kabbalah: A Love Story* (2006). This introduces us to Rabbi Kalman Stern, a widower who, on a visit to Safed in Israel, visits the ancient Yose Benaiah Synagogue and has a conversation with an old Moroccan-looking caretaker who tells him that Yose Benaiah was a mysterious third-century Talmudic teacher who visited Abraham's burial cave. Guarding the cave was Abraham's servant, Eliezer, who told Yose that he could not enter because Abraham and Sarah were making love in eternity. Rabbi Kalman notices a pile of old Hebrew books in poor repair on a table in an alcove and sees a very old copy of the *Zohar* from 1647 in poor repair. He wants to buy it, but is given it freely as it has no cover and its binding is just about holding together. Many years later he is showing the old *Zohar* to a student and reads with her the opening verse:

> IN THE BEGINNING [...] The beginning of the Holy One's inter-pretation was the scoring of a glyph in the supernal purity, a dark spark, a hardened flash of light. It issued from what is beyond com-prehension, from the secret of the One without End [...] Beyond that point nothing can be known. (Kushner, 2006, p. 11)

By chance he discovers a page that has become lodged in the remains of the book's binding. Like the *Zohar*, it is in Aramaic:

Now I understand. *Botzina d'qardinuta* is the seed point of the beginning, and *alma d'ah-tay* is the mother womb of being. *Botzina d'qardinuta*, he is the flash of light. *Alma d'ah-tay*, she is the unattainable and infinite womb. But these two must become one. You are the darkness; I am the spark. *Botzina d'qardinuta* and *alma d'ah-tay*. (Kushner, 2006, p. 16)

The novel explores the mystery of the spark of darkness and the mirror-shining womb at a number of levels: in Rabbi Kalman Stern's romantic relationship with a physicist; in the teacher–pupil relationship between the medieval Qabalist Moshe ben Shem Tov and the wife of a Jewish Spanish aristocrat; and through the understanding of the dynamics of the divine nature. Kushner's novel, through these subplots, takes us into a contemplation of the what the Qabalists call the *partzufim*, or "faces of the divine", and into a deeply connected erotic vision of the universe in which veiling and unveiling, meeting and parting, uniting and separating, are aspects of a great unfolding.

The *partzufim* are a spiritual form that arises from the contemplation of the divine name יהזה and represent an intensification as well as a simplification of Qabalistic practice. The single point above the *yod* (י), which is Kether, is said to be the face of the Ancient One, sometimes called *Arikh Anpin*, "the Great or Long Face", the place of pure light and mercy. From this point arise the figures of *Abba*, the archetypal father, linked to the letter yod and Chockmah; and *Imma*, the archetypal mother, linked to the letter *heh* (ה) and Binah. They give rise to an aspect of the divine linked to the letter *vav* (ו), called *Zeir Anpin*, "the Small Face" and "the Son", an image of the divine that is wrathful and dynamic, connected to the sephiroth Gedulah, Geburah, Tiphareth, Netzach, Hod, and Yesod. The final face is called *Nukbah*, the Bride, linked to Malkuth and the letter *heh* final (ה). The notion of the faces dates back to the kohanic blessing practice that we find described in the Book of Numbers:

And the LORD spoke unto Moses, saying:
"Speak unto Aaron and unto his sons, saying: On this wise ye shall bless the children of Israel; ye shall say unto them:
The LORD bless thee, and keep thee;
The LORD make His face to shine upon thee, and be gracious unto thee;

The LORD lift up His countenance upon thee, and give thee peace.

So shall they put My name upon the children of Israel, and I will bless them." (Numbers 6: 22–27)

Where we find the word "LORD", in the original Hebrew the name written is יהוה and the placing of "My Name" in the verse refers to the experience of being made one with the divine in that the name יהוה is placed upon us so that we become *B'Tzelem Elohim*, the living image of the divine.

In the making of the blessing, the Kohanim hold their hands in the gesture shown below:

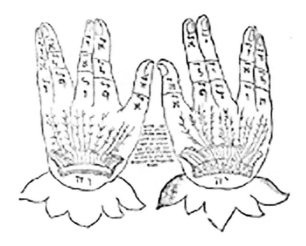

Here we see the hands making the shape of the letter שׁ (*shin*) which represents the *Ruach ha Qodesh*, "the divine breath", that harmonises and unites opposites. The blessing is also said to align the divine faces so that there is flow and contraflow. The marriage of Abba and Imma is paralleled by the marriage of the Small Face and the Bride; in this way the name is united and the sense of the resonance of the non-dual creative energy of the divine is everywhere present.

Tom Oloman condensed the blessing into the simple phrase "face beholds face" in which he dissolved his own sense of identity using the ladder of the name, יהוה, beginning with the contemplation of his body and the world perceived by his senses as ה and Bride, which he brought into the presence of the ו and the Small Face, the sense of the divine at the centre of his being; then, in an act of profound surrender, he would give himself into the sense of the mystery of Binah, ה, the silent non-dual mirror-womb of love, *alma d'ah-tay*, that sustains his form, and the dark spark of *botsina d'qardinuta*, which is the root of will and Chockmah, י, entering at last into the single point of Kether that is the face of the Ancient One, or "the Great Face" that is beyond the play of the opposites. This practice, which Ernest Butler calls the "the flyer descending into the sea" is also the communion with *botsina d'qarduta*, the lamp of adamantine darkness, and *alma d'ah-tay*, the mirror-womb. The practice of working with these profoundly paradoxical images takes us into the wellspring of the supernal triangle. The place that is entered in this act is described by the Iyyun Circle as follows:

> The light that is darkened from illuminating is hidden and impossible to know. Accordingly, it is called darkening darkness, not because it resembles murk, but because no creature can look at it. Even the angels seated in the front row of the kingdom of heaven lack the power to look at it. It is like a human who cannot look at the eye of the harsh sun. However, all lights emerge from it, therefore it is only called darkening darkness because it is exalted, hidden, and concealed from perception. (Verman, 1992, p. 59)

Crowley described this communion as the crossing of the abyss and dwelling in the city of the pyramids; as involving the surrender of the known identity. He stated that only Nemo ("no man") can cross the abyss (Crowley, 1972, p. 140). We are told in the *Zohar*: "Of that Glory is written *Through it no man passed, there no human dwelled*" (Matt, 2009, p. 556). The deep surrender that Crowley shows us in his image of Simon Iff was that same surrender Tom practised as he became no-man, dissolving name and form into the presence of the adamantine darkness.

From this place of silence, mystery, and profound inward-turning, and having united the faces of the divine, he would chant the name יהשוה (*YHShVH*), seeing this as the descent of the *Ruach Elohim* through his body into the universe, connecting him with each and all. This was his principal contemplative practice and, as he met the events of his day, he experienced each as a particular instance of face meeting face in an act of alchemical love. For example, on going for a walk and coming across a rabbit that had been run over by a car, he would make himself one with the rabbit and its death and bless it. Similarly, he would commune with the trees, flowers, and the sense of the world that he was embedded in, seeing every incident as a particular dealing of God with his soul. This practice was his version of the Knowledge and Conversation of the Holy Guardian Angel and each encounter deepened his knowledge and understanding of the unfolding mystery of his life.

In his final five years he worked with a form of Qabalah that drew on the image of a white monk whose face was like a mirror, the name *YHShVh*, and the conjunction of four tarot cards: the Fool, the World, the Devil, and the Lovers, which we will consider later. He also studied the *I Ching* as a way of deepening his understanding of the conjunction of opposites and the process of change.

# CHAPTER 4

# The Egyptian Background

The roots of Aleister Crowley's work, like the roots of the Qabalah, are in ancient Egypt. Late in 1903 he and his wife Rose were in Egypt on honeymoon and, as a romantic gesture, they had dinner beside the Great Pyramid. On finishing their meal they entered the pyramid and went to the king's chamber. There, Crowley decided to demonstrate his magical skills and performed a second-century CE Graeco-Egyptian ritual called "the Headless" or "Bornless" Ritual as part of the romance of the evening. To his surprise, he experienced the chamber as being filled by a clear light that made the candlelight seem dirty. He was able to read the ritual by means of the ethereal light. This ritual would come to be central to his later magical work but, at this stage in his development, while he was impressed by the phenomena he put it behind him and the couple carried on with their honeymoon and went to Ceylon. In April, 1904, they returned to Cairo, and in another act of ritual magick he decided to evoke sylphs, spirits of the air, for Rose. She went into trance and exclaimed: "They are waiting for you!" subsequently telling Crowley that Horus was the one waiting and it was all about Osiris and the child. Although apparently previously knowing nothing about Egyptian mythology, Rose was able to describe the attributes of Horus and took Crowley to the Boulak Museum and an ancient Egyptian grave marker, or "stele", belonging to a priest of Montu named Ankh af na Khonsu of the twenty-fifth or twenty-sixth dynasty. Crowley came to believe that he was the reincarnation of this priest and that there was a direct relationship between his work in that life and his work currently. Moreover, he believed that the priest was part of a movement recreating the mystery traditions of Egypt and that same impulse was now working in him.

The Stele of Revealing

This stele, and others like it, act as doorways into the inner world, aiding the dead to visit the world of the living, and to which the living come to commune with the blessed dead. If we consider the image of the stele above, we will see that on the right-hand side of the picture is the dead priest, Ankh af na Khonsu, making an offering to the hawk-headed god Ra Harakhty, while at the top of the stele, wrapped around the whole periphery of it, is the goddess Nuit, the goddess of the stars. Immediately beneath her is the winged sun disk.

Having proved her bona fides in this way, Rose went on to give Crowley instructions for invoking Horus and told him that these were coming from an inner being named "Aiwass" who was the messenger of Horus. We will discuss the nature of Aiwass in a later chapter, but it is interesting to consider his name in Hebrew letters: עיוז (ayin, yod, vav, zain).

The letter *ayin* was anciently depicted as a circle and connected to the awareness arising out of the void, or perception. The letter *yod* is a pointing hand or the will. The letter *vav* is a nail or peg that joins things together, and *zain* is a plough or mattock (later a sword) that cuts or separates. Here is a messenger, then, whose name suggests working with perception and will and joining together and separating.

The process that occurred between Crowley and Rose concluded with Crowley receiving the three chapters of *The Book of the Law* on the 8, 9, and 10 April 1904. We will look at its content in detail later, but what is described is the inter-relationship of the figures found on the stele: Nuit, goddess of the stars who, amongst other things, represents the principle of infinity and infinite points of view; Hadit, the winged sun, who represents the star at the heart of our own being and our own particular expression of infinity; Ra Harakhty (Ra Hoor Khuit), a fusion of the creator god, Ra, and Horus, seen as the god of the horizon (or *akhet*) that represents the moment of sunrise and the creation of the new day, new life, and new aeon. There is a further, hidden figure: Hoor Paar Kraat or Horus, the child, as named by Rose in her inspired utterance. This stele and the inspired text that arose from it becomes the basis of Crowley's later work and magick.

The Stele of Revealing dates to the period of the Kushite kings, or the black pharaohs. Kush is situated in modern-day Sudan and the conquest of Egypt by the Kushites led to the renewal of ancient Egyptian culture because the Kushites were worshippers of Amun Ra and deeply dedicated to Egyptian religion. The shared religion between Egypt and Kush made this a particular time of the flowering of Egyptian culture as well as the incorporation of ideas from ancient Nubia within Egyptian thought and practice.

Stele of Revealing reverse

The birthplace of the chief god, Amun, was at Jebel Barkal in ancient Kush, shown in the photograph below.

Jebel Barkal and Temple of Amun Ra

Here we see the great rock outcrop of Jebel Barkal with the ruins of the temple of Amun at its base. The outcrop was regarded as the primal mound that arose at the beginning of time. On the left side of the rock is a formation that the ancient Egyptians believed to be the primal serpent, the uraeus that protects the universe.

One of the great Kushite priests, also based in Thebes, a priest of Montu and a contemporary of Ankh af na Khonsu was Padiamenope. His is the largest tomb found in the Valley of the Kings, known as "Theban tomb TT33". Padiamenope was a friend of Pharaoh Taharqa and bore the title of "Chief Lector Priest", which, at that time, was tantamount to being called "Chief Magician". The plan of his tomb (below) at its first level shows us a series of courts getting smaller, which successively depict the outer life of Padiamenope, his relationship with his religious duties and the gods, his journey through the netherworld, and, finally, into the presence of Osiris, the god of death and resurrection.

Tomb of Padiamenope, first level

The entrance to the tomb is a classic Kushite open sun court and funerary chapel where the living can visit the dead and commune with them.

Kushite sun court

The open sun court leads to a series of covered courts describing the process of descent into the *duat*, or underworld, also seen as the body of Nuit, the goddess of the stars. They end in a false door with the image of Osiris at its centre. The perspective of the door gives the impression of receding into an infinite distance towards the point of origination. Here we are very close to the idea of Hadit in Crowley's philosophy; Osiris represents the renewal of life and the geometry of the door suggests that all converges on Osiris as the generative single point. The combination of the sun court with the underworld mysteries of Osiris is fundamental to Egyptian tradition and elaborated further in the rest of the tomb.

Osiris door, outer

Osiris door, inner

As we move past the Osiris door, the passage then turns right, descends a level, and becomes a temple library: a replica of a nineteenth dynasty tomb with the funerary texts of that era is found on this level. This, in turn, leads to a chamber in which the Old Kingdom Pyramid Texts are preserved.

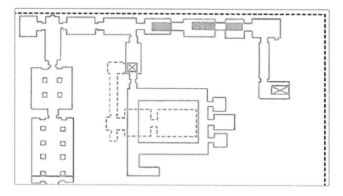

Tomb of Padiamenope: second, third, and fourth levels

There is a third, deeper layer with a replica of the tomb of Osiris at its centre surrounded by chambers inscribed with the Books of the Netherworld. This leads to the fourth and deepest level of the tomb where we find Padiamenope's burial place, situated directly underneath the tomb of Osiris and therefore symbolically within the waters of Nun, the place of the origins of life. This is indicated by a dotted line in the diagram.

At the entrance to the tomb of Osiris is the following inscription:

> O living ones
> O those who are upon the Earth
> Those who are born and those who will be born (in the future) [...]
> Those who walk through the necropolis in order to entertain oneself [...]
> May they enter to this tomb
> In order that they may see what is in it
> Amun-Re, Lord of the thrones of the Two Lands is living for you,
> If you adore the god recite the offering formula in order to make this monument complete
> May you make grow that which decays. (Pischikova et al., 2014, pp. 220–221)

The offering formula is the practice of communion between the worshipper and the living image of the divine. It is the formula that we find depicted on the Stele of Revealing and is the Egyptian version of the process of "face beholds face". Here we see the mutual reflection of Nuit and Hadit; Ra Harakhty and Ankh af na Khonsu. This shows us the polarity of infinity and the single point, the sun god and the moon priest and the mystery of the crowned and conquering child. This can be seen also as the descent of the name יהזה (YHVH) in which י and ה represent Hadit and Nuit, ו is Ra Harakhty, and ה is Ankh af na Khonsu or the appearance of the personal self and universe out of the creative play of the divine.

# CHAPTER 5

# Yesod, Daath, and *The Book of Gates*

If, following *The Fountain of Wisdom*, we inquire more deeply into this mystery of the appearance of the self and universe we will find some help in the Ancient Egyptian Book of the Netherworld, called *The Book of Gates*. This gives us a fusion of the mysteries of Amun Ra, the sun god, with the Osirian underworld mysteries, and is concerned with the foundational dynamics of the universe. The text depicts the descent of the sun (beginning at sunsey) into the *duat* or underworld within the body of Nuit; the journey through the twelve hours of the night; and the emergence at sunrise of the reborn sun and the new day. The journey begins with the initiate identifying themselves with Amun Ra and being within the ship of Ra. At the prow of the ship is Sia, who represents perception, and in the stern, working the rudder, is Heka, the principle of magick, who represents will. In this first hour the initiate takes the form of Khephera, the dung beetle, who represents the principle of eternal recreation and the deep will that enables the cycles of day and night to keep moving. The initiate enters the inner desert between the Nile (the world of the living) and the western mountains (the world of the dead). Here, she or he contemplates two staffs set on either side: the jackal-headed staff of Anpu, the guide of the dead; and the ram-headed staff of Ra, which both represent, respectively, the opposites of death and life.

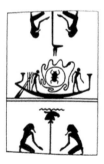

This contemplation of the opposites of life and death; the world of the living and the world of the dead; the creative life of Ra and the destructive energy of Set; are all needed in the underworld journey to come. The next step is the encounter with the serpent guardian of the inner desert in order to begin the process of descent into the *duat*.

The Serpent Guardian

The serpent image is ubiquitous in *The Book of Gates*. In each of the hours of the night there is a gateway, guarded by a serpent, who challenges the passing and generates an alchemical process appropriate to that hour. The spiral serpent, Mehen, who surrounds Khephera, is one of the major protective forces that enables the initiation, whereas Apep, the agent of inertia who opposes life, is also imaged as a serpent. The snake represents that fluid principle of life that, later, the alchemists would call the *prima materia* or "the secret mercury". It is none other than the imagination but means infinitely more than our current conceptions of this because, in Egyptian dialect, it describes the dynamics of the divine play and our relationship to it. It asks us to consider that our deepest nature is that of the creator god Amun Ra, and that our imaginations arise from and are the divine play that creates the worlds. The implication of this is that the act of perception arises from this divine, creative power, so that the seer and the seen are joined together in a non-dual conversation of creation, maintenance, and destruction, which the Advaita seers would have considered the faces of Brahma, the creator god, but here this conversation is envisaged as the journey through the night that creates the new day.

The journey is overseen by the goddess Renenutet, the goddess of the harvest, sometimes called "the serpent with breasts", the mentor, guide, and nourisher of the initiates who are the harvest of *The Book of Gates* and rise with the new sun into the new day.

Renenutet

As we pass the serpent guardian of the first gate we stand in the boat as the ram-headed Amun Ra, in a shrine protected by the spiralling serpent Mehen. An upright serpent stands before us as we hold the *was* ("power", "dominion") sceptre of will in our right hand and the *ankh* that represents life and love in our left. As in the first hour, in the prow of the boat is Sia, or perception, and in the stern, holding the rudder of the boat, is Heka, representing magick and will. The form that we take is referred to literally as "the meat of Ra", indicating that we stand as the incarnate form of Ra, the creative principle. This is depicted below.

The Boat of Amun Ra (from the tomb of Seti I)

The initiate who has become connected with the star in the centre of their being now descends into the body of Nuit, the infinite sea of stars, in order to be renewed. The straight and the spiral serpents are both protection and challenge as we descend into the hours of the night in order to find balance, to return to the beginnings of life and arise again made new and refreshed by immersion in the waters of Nun.

The boat of Amun Ra, which we see marked with the eye of Horus, represents the vehicle within which our consciousness is housed and is both our physical body and our Body of Light and awareness. Our task is to shine the light of presence through each of the divisions of the night and to keep moving so that the processes of creation both inwardly and outwardly continue to flow forward. We are opposed in this work by the serpent Apep, the opponent of Ra, who represents the energies of inertia and who seeks to stop the progress of the boat and, in so doing, causes all life to stop. Below, we see a picture of a servant of Ra working against Apep.

Challenging Apep

On entering the *duat* we are presented with images organised in three registers. The boat of Ra proceeds along the underworld river in the middle register, towed by the initiates whose task it is to ensure that Ra journeys successfully through the hours of the night. Each hour presents a set of dualities and issues that have to be negotiated; for example, in the first hour the blessed dead and followers of Maat are shown in the upper register, and the followers of Apep are shown in the lower register. Each hour culminates in a meeting and communion with a guardian serpent who guards the gate into the next hour.

At the entrance to the sixth hour of the night we encounter Osiris, the god of the dead, and must stand before him as a living form of scales.

The judgement of Osiris from *The Book of Gates*

This is the demonstration that the initiate has thoroughly embodied Maat, truth and balance, and is become one that can speak with a just voice or *maat kheru*. Having passed through the test of the scales, the mystery of the union of Amun Ra and Osiris is enacted in the midst of the waters of Nun, the primal sea from which all emerges. This mystery is not depicted in the imagery as it is too sacred but is hinted at by figures whose arms cannot be seen, whose activities therefore are mysterious: reapers of barley (Osiris is the barley god of the renewal of life) and a series of mummies, who are depicted sleeping on couches and about to awaken.

In arising from the depths, we encounter a series of posts, called "the geb posts", which are staffs topped with the head of a jackal, each having two men tied to them, supervised by a watching, mummiform figure, all of which is watched over by a figure holding the *was* sceptre of power and the *ankh* of life.

Geb Post

The seven jackal-headed posts represent seven aspects of created forms that restrict us and are the roots of what, later, in Christianity, became known as "the seven deadly sins" and in the Qabalah the Qliphoth. Each post has a pair of bound captives that represent an aspect of the energy of Apep and a mummiform figure that represents the antidote to that opposing force. *The Book of Gates* is famously cryptic and the titles here need considerable unpacking but, in the first post, we are confronted with those who are the enemies of Ra and a mummiform that is called "Grasper". The second post is called "enemies of Atum" and the mummy is "the Masher" ("the one who brews beer"). The third post is given to the enemies of Khephera and the mummy is "the Violent One". The fourth is the enemies of Shu and the mummy is called "the Terrible One". The fifth is the enemies of Geb, and the mummy is "the One Who Makes Straight". The sixth is the enemies of Osiris, and the mummy is "the Thresher". The seventh is the enemies of Horus, and the mummy is "the One of the Awesome Face".

Superficially, this gives us a list of the servants of Apep who oppose the journey of Ra and a set of antidotes but, if we inquire more deeply into the pattern that is being shown here, we will find there is much more. Firstly, this pattern appears at the point at which the new energy and new creation starts to emerge, and what is being described are the aspects of the universe and ourselves that seek to prevent that ascent and emergence of new life.

If we take a deeper look at the geb posts we see that they begin with the enemies of Ra, who is signified as the sun disc and the sun-crowned falcon, bearing the *ankh*, the energy of life and love, and the *was* wand of will.

Ra

The enemy of Ra is Apep, the anti-life principle of inertia, shown here as a serpent with a head of flint pierced by five knives that hold and bind his energy.

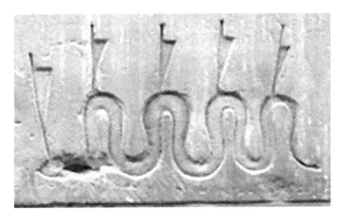

Apep

This is what is meant by the ability to "grasp" or "hold", so that the energy of inertia is restricted and redirected in the service of life. It is very noticeable in Egyptian tradition that Apep is never entirely destroyed; he is seized and held, for he is the counterweight that enables forward motion.

The next post is the enemies of Atum, whose name is thought to have been derived from the verb *tm*, which means "to complete" or "to finish", and hence the adversary seeks to stop the process of completion. This is challenged by the ability to mash beer, as would a brewer, referencing the process of death and resurrection of the barley god Osiris. The capacity to create new life is the important quality here, rather than to rest in the shadow of completion and believe we are finished.

This is followed by the enemies of Khephera, who, as the dung beetle, represents the energy that in the midst of the night moves the new sun up to the horizon. Therefore, its enemies represent the opposition of the process of self-generation or development. They are countered by "the Violent One", or the capacity to defend boundary and not be invaded.

Next are the enemies of Shu, the god who creates space and stillness and whose name comes from the verb *sw*, which means "to rise up" or "emptiness". The antidote here is embracing the sense of terror and awe that arises in the face of emptiness and the understanding that there is space for all conditions and beings.

We then come to the enemies of Geb—from *gbb*, "the earth"—the fullness of the creative energy. Here, the antidote is straightness and correction, so that the energy does not overflow but moves in creative channels, like the irrigation channels of the Nile.

Next we encounter that which would oppose Osiris or Asar whose name in hieroglyphics is shown thus:

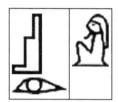

Here we are given the conjunction of eye and the throne, with the god determinative just behind them. This is the older title of the god Osiris, "Seat of the Eye", the sense of an enthroned awareness that sees through all and can create all; the eye in Egypt had both a creative and destructive function. This capacity is shown through the experience of threshing: seeing through the husks to find the grain; or recognising the Qliphoth to discover the light beneath and constantly recreating the balance of Maat.

Finally, we come to the enemies of Horus or *hrw*, "the falcon", also called "the distant one" because he sees from up on high. As with Ra, his enemy is Apep, the snake, who would stifle the new life at birth. The quality that challenges this is to allow the shining face, which is the divine quality within us, to shine forth with authority. This is the quality we find much later in the Kohanic blessing, which invokes the lifting up of the divine face.

To truly be Simon Iff, we must find a way to untangle ourselves from the convolutions and distortions of the serpent Apep through being able to grasp the energy of distortion, hold it fast, and become at one with it. We must be able to work with inertia in the service of the deeper, creative life; to understand and work with the catalytic function of brewing and constant generation; to work constructively with boundary and patient persistence; possess the capacity to generate space and make space for all; to channel the vastness of the life force moving through us into constructive channels; to continually pierce the husks of resistance with awareness; to lift up the shining face and practise the mystery of the blessing of face beholds face.

In each of these processes, aspects of Apep are worked with and harnessed in the service of the life and love of awareness but, if they are not resolved, they remain as trapped and separated aspects of ourselves and the universe that have taken on their own life. Within us they are what Jung described as "complexes" of memory, thought, and emotion that influence our sense of self and world, and which the Advaita and Buddhist traditions would call *sankharas*, the tendencies that bind us. As aspects of the universe they function as demonic presences that suck the life out of situations and create conflict and chaos.

The image of the geb posts shows us how these disturbed forms function: they are the result of unassimilated opposites, so they are represented as tied back-to-back around the geb post, which denotes a moment in time and space when the opposites are encountered. For example, this may represent a moment in our life when we are confronted by a dilemma that we cannot resolve—such as the desire for mother love yet the desire to be autonomous, as a small child. If this is resolved in the sense of "face beholding face" then we discover that we can be both loved and free, but, if not, a vortex of energy based upon the unresolved dilemma is created that comes into play whenever the sense of intimacy arises, which may cause us to sacrifice our autonomy or avoid intimacy. In objective terms this can apply to powerful cultural moments, such as a national defeat or collapse, which might give rise to vortices of betrayal and trapped rage. The jackal head of the staff reminds us of the work of the god Anubis as "the Opener of the Way" and as the enabler of the resurrection of the trapped form. The mummiform figure who superintends each post likewise represents the possibility of transformation, and its hidden arms remind us that this is a mysterious process.

Later, in Christian traditions, these seven principles become identified as the seven deadly *logismoi* or "sins". The original idea of the sins is a complex of thought, emotion, and sensation that deadens the energy of life. For example, we could say that the sin of *acedia*, or deep depression, is one of the enemies of Ra the source of life; the sin of lust or *luxuria* is the opposer of Geb, the power of growth, which needs to be contained and directed; the sin of wrath is the enemy of Khephera and self-generation; whilst the enemy of Atum is sadness; avarice, the enemy of Shu; gluttony, the enemy of Osiris; and pride, the enemy of Horus.

We might encapsulate these obstacles and antidotes thus:

| Obstacle | Antidote |
| --- | --- |
| Entropy (Enemy of Ra). | Holding and containing. |
| Giving up before completion (Enemy of Atum). | Mashing (completing fermentation). |
| Invasion (Enemy of Khephera). | Defending boundary. |
| Terror of emptiness (Enemy of Shu). | Trusting emptiness. |
| Overflowing, proliferation (Enemy of Geb). | Straightness, simplicity. |
| Fantasy, illusion (Enemy of Osiris). | Threshing, seeing through. |
| Hiding (Enemy of Horus). | Shining. |

We use the keywords of *ra, tm, kephri, sw, gbb, asar,* and *hrw,* and the images of the geb staffs as ways of tapping into the configurations of our life energy and the energies of the universe through the power of awareness, so that both principle and opposition are brought into balance as face beholds face.

This is the process we see described in *Moonchild* (Crowley, 1929, pp. 64–67), when Simon Iff absorbs "the Thing in the Garden" using no spell but love. The key to this we find in the verses from *The Book of the Heart Girt with the Serpent* (3: 21–26) in which we dissolve the bonds of I, me, and mine, and open to the immersion in the deep life of the universe. Then, as the representative of that deep life and joy, we resolve the dilemmas of the geb posts that keep us and the universe out of alignment.

This fusion of the opposites of life and death, immersion in the waters of the beginning, and the movement through the obstacles of the geb posts results in the progress upwards through the remaining hours of the night towards the horizon of the new day. Just before the moment of daybreak, *The Book of Gates* presents a line of seated goddess figures.

The Justified Ones

These are "the justified ones", holding a star in their hands and seated on a serpent that upholds them. This is the image of one who has the capacity to work creatively with the energies of Ra and Apep; who has worked with the geb posts. Their inner form is shown as a goddess seated on a serpent throne and holding a star in her hand.

The Servant of the Star and the Snake

Curiously, because Crowley never saw *The Book of Gates*, those who complete Crowley's training system are called "the Servants of the Star and the Snake" and—whatever their sex—are regarded as feminine because they are generators of life. The capacity to work with the star of will at the heart of our being, and to be upheld by the creative serpent of deep love or desire is the process we will return to time and again in this book. The question that we will continue to contemplate is whether our moment-by-moment will and desire is in alignment with deep will and working in combination with the principle Crowley called "love under Will". If it is, then the forms we generate are icons that transmit the creative light of the divine self. If it is not, we create idols that block that light and bind us into a more limited sense of self and universe.

*The Book of Gates* concludes with the emergence of the new sun into the new day in which the world is recreated. This creative light is seen as the new-born child Horus.

The Child Horus

This is the image of what Crowley calls "the crowned and conquering child", emerging into the new day able to step on crocodiles and hold snakes and scorpions without injury.

The extraordinary tomb of the priest Padiamenope preserves not just this remarkable book but a summary of all the wisdom of ancient Egypt, inscribed in the most durable material then available and hidden deep in the earth. This is not just for those of the priesthood who contemplated the mysteries with him in his time but, as his inscription makes clear, for those of us who will be born in the future and who walk through the necropolis for entertainment and pleasure. We are invited to see what is there, to make offering, and to renew what has been destroyed. There is a way in which Crowley's work does this also, in working with these ancient forms in a new way so that, like the concluding image of

*The Book of Gates*, we are seated on the sacred snake that upholds us and we hold the star of our being in our hands.

This descent into the underworld (which is simultaneously the field of the stars) described in *The Book of Gates* is indicated in the Tree of Life by the relationship of the sephiroth Yesod and Daath. Yesod, the foundation of things, represents the underpinnings of the visible world and has the title of "the machinery of the universe". As we descend we begin to move from solidity to fluidity, and start to experience what in Eastern tradition is called *maya*, "illusion", or *lila*, "divine play", in which things are not what they seem. We enter this play of colour and illusion that shapes everything in the name of the creator, becoming the "meat" or embodiment of Amun Ra and letting the light of awareness shine into the hidden places. We work with the ubiquitous serpent that is creator, destroyer, sexuality, and life energy, which can manifest in many forms as we work with this divine play. Central to this work is the transformation of idols that obstruct the hidden light into icons that transmit it and, in that process, the opaque and mechanistic aspects of Yesod become Daath, the sephira that expresses the mystery of non-duality.

*The Book of Gates* gives us a context within which to understand Crowley's work, which is profoundly different from the masonic-based Golden Dawn system he was trained in. We will consider Crowley's *The Book of the Law* (1904) in greater detail, but we can see already how its key images and ideas resonate with those of the Kushite revival. The principles of the infinite points of view of Nuit and the single point of Hadit that emerge as both "the silent child" and "the crowned and conquering child", who brings all opposites together, as described in *The Book of the Law* are intrinsic to the ancient initiatory text, *The Book of Gates*. The boat of Ra brings together the principles of will and perception and the interactions in the twelve hours of the night give us an understanding of the underside of creation and our own psyche. We are shown also the dynamics of creation in which intention and perception and the crossing of the horizon causes the collapse of wave forms of multiple possibilities into the actuality of particle reality. We will explore this in the view of the universe offered by quantum physics, the unusual barebones version of Qabalah that Crowley called "the Naples arrangement", and in the mysterious flow of the Tao.

CHAPTER 6

# Simon Iff, the 0 = 2 Equation, and the Naples Arrangement

Crowley's holy book *Liber Liberi vel Lapidus Lazuli* is described as "the birth words of a Master of the Temple" (Crowley, 2015, p. 135) and offers us a profoundly interconnected and responsive vision of the universe. It begins in the Prologue with an experience of loneliness and separation, that evokes a vision of Pan as the All, filling our senses and the centre of our being and taking us into the abyss of annihilation that brings the loneliness to an end. In chapter 1 Verse 25 of the text we are told, "I based all on one, one on naught" (Crowley, 2015, p. 137), which shows us firstly the interconnectedness of the universe ("all on one") and the ground of non-dual mystery which generates all phenomena ("one on naught"). From this statement, and the method it is based on, Crowley derives the formula 0 = 2 which describes the relationship between the non-dual ground 0 and the changing, moving, dualistic universe 2(+1 −1).

There are three key images in the text that indicate this new world: a white cat, an oak tree, and a temple of stones shaped as a vulva.

> Then I perceived Thee, O my God, sitting like a white cat upon the trellis-work of the arbour; and the hum of the spinning worlds was but Thy pleasure.

> O white cat, the sparks fly from Thy fur! Thou dost crackle with splitting the worlds.
>
> I have seen more of Thee in the white cat than I saw in the Vision of Aeons. (4: 31–33) (Crowley, 2015, p. 151)

The cat gives us the experience of an arising phenomenon—as he contemplates the cat, through it, he perceives the dynamic background of the universe. This experience of perceiving the stillness of the cat and the crackling impermanence of the sparks reveals movement through time and the splitting of worlds, as probabilities multiply and new branches of space, time, and event become available.

This movement in time is extended into space in these verses:

> Thou wast a priestess, O my God, among the Druids; and we knew the powers of the oak.
>
> We made us a temple of stones in the shape of the Universe, even as thou didst wear openly and I concealed. (6: 1–2) (Crowley, 2015, p. 159)

We are given the oak tree as an image of the universe seeing it as a living interconnected being and are also told that the shape of the Universe is a Yoni or Vesica Piscis (Crowley, 1996, p. 244) and thus formed from overlapping of fields of influence, even as the *vesica* is formed from two overlapping circles. This, together with the eternal stillness of the cat and its ephemeral, fiery sparks opens us to a new understanding of space, time and event and the way in which we and the universe relate together.

A key aspect of Crowley's work, which relates to this understanding, is presented in what he calls "the Star-Sponge vision":

> I was on a retirement in a cottage overlooking Lake Pasquaney in New Hampshire. I lost consciousness of everything but a universal space in which were innumerable bright points, and I realized this as a physical representation of the universe, in what I may call its essential structure. I exclaimed, "Nothingness with twinkles!" I concentrated upon this vision, with the result that the void space which had been the principal element of it diminished in importance; space appeared to be ablaze, yet the radiant points were not confused, and I thereupon completed my sentence with the exclamation, "but what twinkles!"
>
> The next stage of this vision led to an identification of the blazing points with the stars of the firmament, with ideas, souls, etc.

I perceived also that each star was connected by a ray of light with each other star. In the world of ideas each thought possessed a necessary relation with each other thought; each such relation is of course a thought in itself; each such ray is itself a star. It is here that the logical difficulty first presents itself. The seer has a direct perception of infinite series. Logically, therefore, it would appear as if the entire space must be filled up with a homogeneous blaze of light. This however is not the case. The space is completely full and yet the monads which fill it are perfectly distinct. The ordinary reader might well exclaim that such statements exhibit symptoms of mental confusion.

A further development of the vision brought to the conscious-ness that the structure of the universe was highly organized, that certain stars were of greater magnitude and brilliancy than the rest.

While at Montauk, I had put my sleeping bag to dry in the sun. When I went to take it in, I remarked, laughingly, "Your bedtime, Master Bag" as if it were a small boy and I its nurse. This was entirely frivolous; but the thought flashed into my mind that after all the bag was in one sense a part of myself. The two ideas came together with a snap, and I understood the machinery of a man's delusion that he is a teapot.

From this I came to another discovery: I perceived why platitudes were stupid. The reason was that they represented the summing up of trains of thought, each of which was superb in every detail at one time. A platitude was like a wife after a few years; she has lost none of her charms, and yet one prefers some perfectly worthless woman.

It would be quite impracticable to go fully into the subject of this vision of the Star-Sponge. It must suffice to reiterate that it has been the basis of most of my work for the last five years, and to remind the reader that the essential form of it is "Nothingness with twinkles". (Crowley, 1971, p. 810)

This image of the universe is, of course, literally true in that the universe is composed of stars organised in galaxies that generate all the elements of the universe and, through their vast gravitational forces, create spacetime. Crowley is using it here as an image of the All, just as in *Liber Liberi Lapidis Lazuli* he is relating to the divinity of the all and seeing this pattern as fractal, existing at all levels of being. It is present in human relationships, in our relationship with external objects, and within our psyche, such as in the relationship between thoughts.

The image of the oak and the Star-Sponge vision give us a sense of the universe as one deeply interconnected organism at all its levels, while the *vesica* brings us into a sense of twoness, which brings us to the $0 = 2$ equation that is at the heart of Qabalistic cosmology.

Put at its simplest, the deep root of things is envisaged as infinity without characteristics, no-thing, *ain* (אין), and as it comes into manifestation it becomes the simple point of Kether, the unity of the one, but as such involves a paradox for there is now a relationship between the point and its background, and hence there is an implicit twoness that comes into activity as the process of creation proceeds and yet remains deeply one organism. This can be symbolised by the $0 = 2$ equation in which $0 = +1 -1$. Within this simple formulation is the whole process of creation and destruction, separation, and unification, and any other series of opposites.

This led Crowley to formulate a version of the Tree of Life he called "the Naples arrangement", so-called because he was living there when he formulated it.

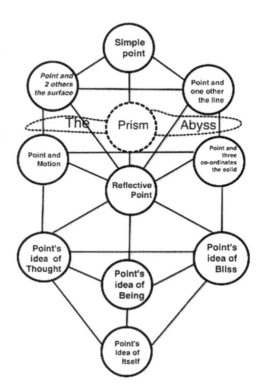

This is an essentialised form of the tree based upon the Star-Sponge vision and the 0 = 2 equation. Thus, from the background of the 0 arises the single generative point, the one, of Kether, which generates the vector of the line, becoming the two of Chockmah, which, with the addition of a third term becomes the surface and the number three of Binah. By passing through the prism of Daath and crossing the abyss between the ideal and the actual we enter into solidity, the dimension of space, and the number four of Gedulah, which, through the principle of motion brings in the dimension of time in the five of Geburah. This in turn leads to the arising of the mediating point operating within space and time, and between the ideal and the actual—the six of Tiphareth. As the mediating point becomes generative within space-time, it manifests its idea of the feeling of bliss, the seven of Netzach; its idea of thought, the eight of Hod; and its idea of being, the nine of Yesod; and then finally its idea of itself, based upon the interaction of thought, bliss, and being, in the ten of Malkuth.

Each point of the universe that emerges into time and space manifests its own Tree of Life and each tree, like each point, is connected to every other tree. If we take Crowley's images of the Star-Sponge vision, the oak tree, and the *vesica*, we come into a profoundly interactive network of life in which each point is both profoundly itself and profoundly in relationship, and so each phenomenon is both simply itself and a moment in a multi-level generative dialogue that multiplies the possibilities available to the universe. So, experiencing the white cat and the sparks flying from its fur is an act of noticing the arising of the particular as a process of appearance and movement that gives us access to the dynamic background its particularity arises from. This is true of each particular arising, and each apparent form, and is a continuation of the experience of being met by Pan, the All, through all six senses.

As we increasingly enter into this experience of dialogue and emergence, like Simon Iff, the bonds of I, me, and mine are replaced by the direct sense of being the unfolding point whose will gives us vector and direction and whose love has the capacity to dialogue and combine without losing our particularity. It is then we discover the deeper identity that *The Book of the Heart Girt with the Serpent* reminds us of (3: 25):

> Thou art Eternity and Space; Thou art Matter and Motion; and
> Thou art the negation of all these things. (Crowley, 2015, p. 111)

This is the 0 = 2 equation made flesh. Through this deeper, more fluid identity we are able to participate in the life of the universe more fully as indicated in the following verses from *Liber Liberi vel Lapidus Lazuli* (5: 1–6), "O my beautiful God! I swim in thy heart like a trout in the mountain torrent. I leap from pool to pool in my joy; I am goodly with brown and gold and silver. Why I am lovelier than the russet autumn woods at the first snowfall. And the crystal cave of my thought is lovelier than I" (Crowley, 2015, p. 155).

This is also the practice of face beholds face, in which the divine faces coincide and enable the manifestation of the blessing that generates the new day, the new world, and the new life. As we have seen this new and deeper life is said by Crowley to be the birth words of a Magister Templi (or "Master of the Temple"), his term for the ancient Egyptian title Geru Maa, or "silent sage". In the New Kingdom book, *The Instruction of Amenomope*, we find that the Geru Maa is steeped in the quality of *maat*, or dynamic balance, contrasted with the unrestrained human being who is very much caught up in the dynamics of I, me, and mine, and thus unable to participate in the deeper music of the universe that Crowley calls the music of the lutes in the great city of the violets and roses.

> Now the unrestrained [*smm*] man in the temple,
> He is like a tree growing in the garden,
> In a brief moment, its leaves fall off.
> It reaches its end in the woodshop
> It is floated far from its place.
> And fire becomes its burial ground.
> Now the self-mastered person [Geru Maa] sets himself apart.
> He is like a tree grown in a meadow.
> It grows green, it doubles its harvest.
> It stands before its owner.
> Its fruit is sweet; its shade is pleasant.
> And it reaches its end among other trees. (Karenga, 2004, pp. 98–99)

The image of the fruitful tree amongst other trees, providing greenness, fruit, and shelter, and of being in living dialogue with the universe, as opposed to the tree without leaves or new life, shows us the end result of clinging to I, me, and mine. We become a thing, an encapsulated object, rather than a generative subject, as a result of our pulling away from the multi-levelled dialogue. This is a similar image to that given by the Taoist Master Chuang Tzu (Watson, 2013, pp. 30–31), when he contrasts the importance of being a twisted and useless oak rather than being a tree that produces useful planks, by which he means the ability to embrace and manifest our particular and unique nature, our true will, as opposed to becoming a useful but inert object based upon mechanistic reactivity.

It is this danger that Simon Iff points at when he suggests that the fall of night, or the arising of a tempest, or the passage of time, can still the music of the lutes in how moments of darkness and difficulty, or strong reactions, or just the passage of time can cause us to lose faith in the deep dialogue and collapse into the apparent comfort of I, me, and mine. The geb posts of *The Book of Gates* also give us a framework for working with this potential collapse in its suggestions of holding fast, of being like brewer's yeast, of persisting to completion, of defending boundary, working with simplicity and straightness, taking the stance of being the seat of the eye, and adopting the practice of face beholds face.

The Naples arrangement gives us a form of the Tree of Life that is both simple and radical, taking it from a medieval vision of the cosmos into an immediate, moment-by-moment process of participation in the unfolding creativity of the universe. It invites us into the choice of being the living tree that is an integral part of the forest of eternity and infinity, or else ending in the woodshop.

# CHAPTER 7

# The Book of the Law

Central to Crowley's work is the inspirational text that arose from his visit to Egypt: *Liber AL vel Legis* or *The Book of the Law*. Before we look at the contents of the book it is useful to look at the title. Initially it was entitled "*Liber L*" where L is the Hebrew letter *lamed* (ל), "the ox-goad". This letter in the version of the Tree of Life that Crowley practised is applied to the path between Geburah and Tiphareth, or between the principle of motion or will and self-reflection, mediation, and balance. This path has the tarot trump Justice associated with it, which invokes the principle of the scales and of dynamic balance. When he created the Thoth tarot, Crowley renamed it "Adjustment", and the image he used for this trump was the goddess Maat, portrayed in greens and blues as a masked figure, up on the points of her toes like a ballet dancer, holding a sword with the weighing scales arising out of her body.

He later redefined the title of *The Book of the Law* to "*Liber AL*", *aleph lamed* (אל), combining the letter *aleph*, "the ox", with the ox-goad. *AL* is an ancient, Qabalistic god-name that conveys the image of the ox prodded by the ox-goad, which suggests the image of the ox walking in a circle, bringing water out of the ground, and hence bringing about creation. It is a name that combines opposites: the straightness and focus of the *lamed* combined with the openness and circularity of the *aleph*.

The *aleph* is applied to the path between Kether and Chockmah, connecting the primal point with the principle of reflection and deep will. The associated tarot trump is the Fool, which Crowley envisaged as a Dionysian and green fool of pure spontaneity, leaping towards us out of the card, which is filled with bright colour. Combining the Fool with Adjustment gives us a sense of opposites in union: creative chaos with focus and discipline. *The Book of the Law* is an invitation, therefore, to embody these principles in our life and practice. The "Law" of the title is in the same sense of the "laws" of physics and chemistry, rather than in the sense of human law—i.e. what is revealed here is the way things are, rather than an injunction to believe.

The two key statements that guide us in exploring this text are:

1. "Every man and every woman is a star" (I: 3). This takes us back to the sunlight practice that underlies the whole process of this book you are reading, as well as reminding us of the Star-Sponge vision.
2. "Do what thou wilt shall be the whole of the Law" (I: 40). The key word here is "thou" and we are reminded of Simon Iff's suggestion to abandon I, me, and mine in favour of the "Thou" that is eternity, space, matter, motion, and "the Negation of all these things" (Crowley, 2015, p. 111). Where that will arises from in us is a central question and one that *The Book of the Law* seeks to address.

*The Book of the Law* arises out of the Stele of Revealing and has three chapters, which relate to the three figures of the stele.

1. Nuit. The goddess representing the field of stars, Infinity, and the principle of love.

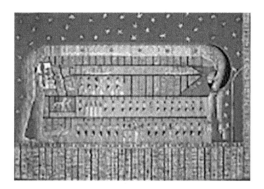

2. Hadit. The winged sun (sometimes called "Horus of Behedet"), the generative point, and embodying will.

3. Ra Hoor Khuit. The conjunction of Ra and Horus, also known as "Ra Harakhty", who creates the new day and is the conjunction of love and will.

In the first chapter we are told that Hadit ("Had") is the manifestation of Nuit; that this is the unveiling of the company of heaven; that every man and woman is a star; and that each number is infinite. This takes us immediately into Crowley's Star-Sponge vision and the Naples arrangement of the Tree of life. Nuit is infinite space, containing infinite points of view, and Hadit the single point of view that is the core of our experience. The mystery here is that each single point is the centre of the whole cosmology and is the generative source—hence, a star. Equally, each number is infinite: that is to say, a thing in itself, not merely part of a continuum that can be measured. For example, the quality that the number one possesses is Kether, the generative point of beginning, and when applied to another number imparts something of its quality to it. So, if we add one to eight it becomes nine and, in terms of the Naples arrangement, the simple point added to the point's idea of thought (Hod, eight) becomes the point's idea of being (Yesod, nine) as its nature has been nudged forward into a new category of generation. Each number then represents a whole set of possibilities, of alchemical marriages and separations as we add, subtract, multiply, and divide. This shows us the possibilities of the Naples arrangement in which the simplicity of the root numbers that describe the unfolding of the point can generate infinite possibilities.

Nuit goes on to ask for the help of the "warrior lord of Thebes" (I: 5) in her act of unveiling. Crowley believes this to be Ankh af na Khonsu, whom Crowley regarded as his own prior incarnation—although this seems unlikely as Ankh af na Khonsu was a priest, not a warrior. The reference is more likely to apply to the hawk-headed Theban war god, Montu, a form of Horus who makes himself manifest in the third chapter. Nuit asks the warrior lord to be Hadit, the generative secret centre.

We are next told that this book comes from Aiwass, who is the minister of Hoor Paar Kraat. Aiwass was believed by Crowley to be his Holy Guardian Angel and Hoor Paar Kraat is a form of the Egyptian term for Horus, the child. Next, Nuit tells us that "the Khabs is in the Khu, not the Khu in the Khabs" (I: 8), that her servants are "few & secret" and "shall rule the many & the known" (I: 10) and that "These are fools that men adore; both their Gods & their men are fools" (I: 11). We are then invited to take our fill of love under the stars.

Here we are given the basis of the cosmology of deep magick; of the practice of being a star and of the unity of love and will; but, in understanding it, and seeking to draw out the key themes of practice, it is important to the remember the title of the book and the combined images of the Fool and Adjustment tarot cards: the fusion of creative spontaneity and the balance and focus of Maat.

This first chapter shows us the infinite possibilities of Nuit, held in tension with the single point of view of Hadit, and takes us into the experience of unveiling. The removal of veils is the central aspect of the work because it is the removal of all that is inessential, which enables the deep roots of being to shine forth and act in their essential simplicity. "Unveiling" is connected in meaning to the word "apocalypse", from the Greek αποκάλυψη (apokalypsi, or "uncovering"). Unveiling is, therefore, an uncovering that is apocalyptic in its action in that it reveals a new world of thought, speech, and action. The invitation of the warrior lord of Thebes to help in this act of unveiling underlines its apocalyptic function, because Nuit asks him to be as Hadit, the centre of motion and generation. The figure of Aiwass as the messenger of Horus, the child, amplifies some of these themes. The silence of the child is the precursor to the manifestation of the new day and suggests the returning to the womb and to the essentials of life just prior to the new emergence. This is a regular theme in Egyptian tradition in that each night the sun god returns to the waters of Nun and is reborn in its depths.

The next image of the "Khabs" and the "Khu" is fundamental: the Khabs is the star within us, the centre of our being and the generative source that forms around the single point of view which is our fundamental essence. The Khu is the magical body that takes shape around this source point and which veils the potency of its light. Crowley refers to the uninitiated as "dark stars" (Crowley, 1974, p. 97), not because they are corrupted but because the outer form has become so complex; there are layers and layers of veils which obstruct the generative, transforming light. The verse concerning the "few & secret" and "the many & the known" (I: 10) refers to this dynamic; the many and the known are the many veils of our image of self and universe that constitute our normal sense of self. To relate to the few and the secret means to enter the process of unveiling; to enter into alignment with the silent, secret self that is the true ruler and centre of all our motion, and which we can consider as Horus the Child, manifesting as Ra Harakhty. Next there is a play on the image of the Fool in which we are told that what men adore is fools, and both the men that adore and their gods are fools (I: 11). This is both a deconstruction of conventional religious practice and a reminder of the Fool tarot trump. The fact that this is not a religious text is underlined later in the chapter when we are told that "with the God & the Adorer I am nothing: they do not see me" (I: 21).

The book moves onto a direct experience of Nuit and we are told that she is none and two (I: 28) and "divided for love's sake, for the chance of union" (I: 29). We are told that "The word of the Law is THELEMA" (or "will") (I: 39) and that "pure will, unassuaged of purpose, delivered from the lust of result, is every way perfect" (I: 44). The principle of love under will that is shown here is central to the practice of this art of deep magick, for the movement of the will is what enables the manifestation of duality and love is the motivation of that movement. In respect of this, we find Nuit telling us that Ankh af na Khonsu shall learn and teach the art of "the obeah and the wanga; the work of the wand and the work of the sword" (I: 37) and preside over the three ordeals. We are given three images for this: the man of Earth, the Lover, and the Hermit (I: 40). We are also told that all rituals, ordeals, words, and signs of previous understanding are now obsolete as Ra Hoor Khuit has taken his seat in the East (I: 49). The first chapter ends with an exhortation to invoke Nuit and to come unto her.

This is the blueprint for the practice of the deep magick of the way of Simon Iff. The apocalyptic experience of unveiling aligns us with the silent self that emerges out of the simple point of Hadit, the centre-point of the infinity of Nuit, as the wholeness of the universe expresses itself through the particular point of the star that is at the heart of our being. We, as Ankh af na Khonsu, and therefore as the one whose life is aligned with the hawk-headed child, contemplate the name that unites the macrocosm and microcosm and, working with love under will, we learn to practise magick. This deep magick is an expression of this principle of will and a consequence of the practice of the process of unveiling and the simplification of the veils that distort and block the will. As we increasingly come into relationship with the Khabs and allow ourselves to respond to the prompting of the silent self, so, then, we function as the magician because we enable motion and change. This is emphasised in the use of the words "obeah" and "wanga" (I: 37). "Obeah" is a form of sorcery intended to produce tangible effects while "wanga" is a charm, a bag, or other physical object that acts as a talisman which earths the work of the will. The moonchild of Crowley's novel is a wanga, a living form that acts as an avatar of the particular act of will that is being incarnated. The work is undertaken through the use of the wand, or the sword, and the principles of creation and destruction, and takes us through three ordeals represented by the images of the man of earth, lover, and hermit, which might remind us of the Egyptian images of the eloquent peasant, the shepherd sovereign, and the Geru Maa.

The second chapter takes us more deeply into this expression of will and magick, for it begins with the invocation of Hadit, the single generative point: the centre that is everywhere present, expressing itself as "the Magician and the Exorcist" (II: 7); "the axle of the wheel, and the cube in the circle" (II: 7). Hadit is then symbolised as Heru-pa-kraat and declares that it is not an object to be worshipped and asks us to identify with it and worship Nuit (Crowley, 1974, p. 188–189). He describes himself, as "the Snake that giveth Knowledge & Delight" (II: 22) and asks us to take wine and "strange drugs" (II: 22) in the act of worship. We are subsequently told that that if the snake lifts up his head he is one with Nuit, and if it droops its head and releases its venom it is one with the earth and there is rapture (II: 26). The snake, as we have seen in *The Book of Gates* is the active life energy, and the encouragement to take wine and strange drugs is a suggestion to activate our energy. The two postures, "raising up" or "drooping" the head of the serpent, relate to mystical union and working with duality.

This chapter continually asks us to overcome reason and to be one with the moving power of Hadit and goes on to indicate a whole series of rituals and feasts that are to be observed. "Rituals", here, are particular acts of will and imagination, while "feasts" represent the receiving of nourishment and of particular acts of love and union. We are told that there is "a feast for life and a greater feast for death" (II: 41), which Crowley interprets (Crowley, 1974, p. 211) as celebrating births and funerals. However, there is a deeper meaning, in that in every moment there is birth and death and our capacity to be with both is one of the key features of the deep magician. The tone of this chapter is that beneath the sorrow of life is the experience of life as ecstasy and that, if we penetrate the veil of sorrow, we enter into fullness of life and joy. The act of unveiling is once again mentioned in the image of the tearing down of the black "veil of sorrow" (II: 52), which is "the veil of the modest woman" (II: 52), the self-enclosed, unreachable stance. This is in contrast to the scarlet woman, described in III: 43, who is loud, adulterous, and shameless and who represents the capacity to receive all and give to all. The colour symbolism is interesting here in that the colour black is normally applied to the sphere of Binah, which is normally thought of as "the mother of sorrows"; the colour of her deepest function, however, is red and relates to the non-dual love that continually manifests and receives all the living forms of the universe.

We are also told that those who align with this work are "against the people" (II: 25), invoking once again the sense of the herd as those aspects of self and life that will not align with these deeper principles and instead operate from an unexamined reactivity. Use is made of the term "dogs" to describe those who are not able to reach this deeper alignment and we are told that for them there is death (II: 45). The dog image is particular here, as it is the reversal of the word "god" and what is being described in this book is our inner divinity; the dog, then, represents that which is opposite to this inner lucidity.

The star within us, in taking incarnation, manifests a body, mind, and psyche. In *Liber Aleph*, Crowley describes this as the "tabernacle" of the soul (Crowley, 2005, p. 192), which, as in the act of offering, is intended to be the mirror and vehicle of the interplay of Nuit and Hadit expressed through the dual mystery of Heru Ra Ha (the combination of the silent child and the crowned and conquering child, or Hoor Paar Kraat and Ra Hoor Khuit). This vehicle is shown on the Stele of Revealing and in *The Book of the Law* as the figure of the priest, Ankh af na Khonsu. This figure seen as the scribe (I: 36) and as the prophet of Heru Ra Ha (III: 38) is described as self-slain (III: 37), and as the living dead man continually manifests the energies of will and love and, in the next moment, returns to the source of life.

If this mirroring is interrupted there is a separation between the star and that which should be its vehicle. What can then happen, in both the living and the dead, is a situation where the conditioned sense of self then operates independently according to its immediate needs and desires. In place of the fusion of the opposites of life and death, expressed in the idea of Ankh af na Khonsu, the living dead man, there is a persistence in a death-like state of separation and encapsulation. This is the state the Qabalah describes as the Qlipoth, the shell that is no longer in dialogue, and this is what also is meant by the black veil of "the modest woman" (II: 52).

The third chapter is concerned with Ra Hoor Khuit or, more accurately, Heru Ra Ha, who is a synthesis of Ra Hoor Khuit (also known as Ra Harakhty) and Hoor Paar Kraat ("the silent child"). He is the projection of the solar will to create the new world. The chapter begins with an injunction to create an inner citadel that is protected and that in its secret place holds an image of the Stele of Revealing which, we are told, shall be our "Kiblah" (III: 10) or the place that indicates the direction of prayer. We are then shown the work of war and destruction, having been shown the work of love and union in the second chapter.

In the first verse we are told that Abrahadabra, the word that symbolises the fusion of the macrocosm with the microcosm, is "the reward of Ra Hoor Khu[i]t" (III: 1). Crowley tells us that the eleven letters of this word represent the fusion of five and six, or the pentagram and the hexagram. He shows us the conjunction as a diagram:

Qabalistically, the letters *aleph*, *bet*, and *resh* are the first letters of *abba* ("father"), *bou* ("son"), and *ruach* ("spirit"); or, respectively, Kether, Chockmah, and Binah. Crowley, through the numerical technique of gematria, calculated that the number of the letters of the pentagram when added is 12, and the number of the two triangles is 406. In gematria, if two words have the same number they are said to share an identity.

1. The word *HUA* (הוא), which stands for the macrocosmic divine presence, also has the number 12.
2. The word *AthH* (אתה), which means "you" or "thou", and can be seen as indicating our individual identity, and hence the microcosm, also has the number 406.

The interesting feature of this arrangement is that the pentagram is normally seen as the symbol of the microcosm, the individual human being, while the conjoined triangles are the symbol of the macrocosm, so here we are shown the fusion and mutual identity of both.

The word "Abrahadabra" is of course derived from "Abracadabra", the archetypal word of magick beloved of many a stage magician and repurposed by Crowley so that "HAD" is at its centre. Its ancient use is as a process of destruction and vanishing, and we may depict it thus:

**ABRACADABRA**

**ABRACADABR**

**ABRACADAB**

**ABRACADA**

**ABRACAD**

**ABRACA**

**ABRAC**

**ABRA**

**ABR**

**AB**

**A**

It was written on an amulet in this form, and used as a healing talisman, thought to make lethal diseases vanish. It is an example of the simplification or "unveiling" process spoken of in *The Book of the Law* (I: 5). It was used by the gnostic followers of Basilides of Alexandria and associated with the figure of Abraxas, a solar daimon with a cockerel's head and serpent limbs. Crowley might also have been attracted by the fact that the letters beginning and ending are "ABRA", because one of his major practices had been the prayer ritual called "the Abramelin operation", which he used to obtain the Knowledge and Conversation of his Holy Guardian Angel and, hence, brought together the microcosm and the macrocosm in the way that Abrahadabra represents.

In the training of the Qabalist there is a fundamental ritual called "the banishing ritual of the pentagram" which, like many of the fundamental exercises, is rarely given enough attention. Its function is to clear our energetic sphere of all that impedes our will. It, too, is an example of the process of unveiling and will be discussed later. It ends with the phrase: "About me flame the pentagrams, and behind me shines the six-fold star". The ritual creates a defended citadel around us and affirms the unity of macrocosm and microcosm, in keeping with the injunction beginning the third chapter of *The Book of the Law*.

The fusion of the five and the six can also mean the fusion of the energies of Geburah and Tiphareth, and the particular form of Horus addressed in this chapter is a fusion of the ancient sun god, Ra, with Horus, the war god. This is further underlined by Ankh af na Khonsu having been a priest of Montu, the hawk-headed war god and, hence, the third chapter is about the combination of fresh illumination with the destruction of that which prevents the new light from shining.

The book asks us to set up the image of the Stele of Revealing in our secret house, and says that the other images will cluster around the image of Heru Ra Ha (III: 22). It goes on to give us a sense of that initial image:

> I am the Hawk-Headed Lord of Silence & of Strength; my nemyss shrouds the night-blue sky.
> Hail! Ye twin warriors about the pillars of the world! For your time is nigh at hand.
> I am the Lord of the Double Wand of Power; the wand of the Force of Coph Nia—but my left hand is empty, for I have crushed an Universe; & nought remains. (III: 70–72)

The phrase "Coph Nia" is unknown but might relate to the Hebrew letter *coph* (ק), which means "the back of the head", and *nia* is the reverse of *ain* (אין), the Hebrew word for "nought" or "the void". The "Force of Coph Nia" (III: 72) might indicate the emergence of those energies, forms, and images that arise from the back of the head and indicate the god's capacities to work with dualities. Right at the end of the book we are told, "There is a splendour in my name hidden and glorious, as the sun of midnight is ever the son" (III: 74).

This is a reference to the beetle god, Khephera, whose name means "he who becomes", and this may link to an Eucharistic reference earlier in the book when we are asked to make cakes of cornmeal, honey, Abramelin oil, olive oil, and blood, which, if laid before Heru Ra Ha and prayed over, will become "full of beetles as it were and creeping things" (III: 25), which are named as our enemies and then fall before us. As we eat the cakes our personal power increases. This is possibly an indication of an inner process, as the cornmeal can represent body; the honey, the distillation of the spirit; wine, ecstasy; the oil, the anointing that manifests in prayer; and blood is our life principle. As we bring all this before the god in an act of prayer and offering, what emerges are beetles, which are examples of forms appearing from the back of the mind that have their own sense of becoming. They are, in effect, the idols we have created and, by naming them with clear and passionate aware-ness, they are dissolved and pass away. The result of this is that our true will and sense of personal power expands. Much of this third chapter is concerned with the destruction of forms that prevent the new light and power from emerging; thus, we find the hawk god pecking out the eyes of Jesus, flapping its wings in the face of Mohammed, clawing out the flesh of Buddhists, and demanding that Mary be torn upon wheels (III: 51–22). This is the destruction of any form that stops or distorts the emergence of the true will, for, we are told, "There is no law beyond Do what thou wilt" (III: 60).

The practice of the solar adorations referred to obliquely in the front text of the Stele of Revealing ("Make for me the path to the place in which Re, Atum, Khephri, and Hathor are therein") is asserted for we are told that there is a secret door made into the house of Ra and Tum, Ahathoor and Khephera (III: 38). Here we are brought back to the sunlight practice of being a star and letting our life shine, for these are the forms of the sun god at rising and setting, noon and midnight.

The third chapter and *The Book of the Law* end by bringing us back to the word Abrahadabra. We are told that the book is both "Written and Concealed" (Crowley, 2015, p. 92), and there are two mantric phrases: *Aum*, which is the ancient Indian mantra of creation, and the word *Ha*, which is an expulsion of breath and a word for the sun. They are also the first and last words of the Sanskrit alphabet, and therefore one way to translate them might be, "The Beginning and the End, the Eternal Breathing Sun".

# CHAPTER 8

# The Praxis of the Neophyte

There are of course many ways in which we can apply the material we have been contemplating, and there is a sense in which the major work is simply to immerse ourselves in the tradition and allow it to influence us at all the levels of our being. There are three major practices that bring together many of the major themes of deep magick.

1. The lesser banishing ritual of the pentagram.
2. The salutes of the sun.
3. The evening review.

### The Lesser Banishing Ritual of the Pentagram

The pentagram ritual is based in Malkuth and is designed to balance the elemental qualities within us. It has the effect of clearing our field of awareness and inviting in the life of the universe to nourish and refresh; in effect, to nourish the roots of our Tree of Life and encourage its growth. It is linked with the process in *The Book of the Law* of breaking down old forms and bringing in a new world. The pentagram is the star of will and has a fractal nature in that, at its centre, is a pentagon within which another pentagram can be traced, and thus it extends both into the infinitely small and the infinitely large.

Eliphas Levi tells us:

> The pentagram expresses the domination of the mind over the elements, and it is by this symbol that we enchain the demons of air, the spirits of fire, the specters of water, and the ghosts of the earth. Armed with this symbol and properly prepared, you can see the infinite by using that faculty which is like the eye of your soul, and you will have the legions of angels and columns of demons serve you. (Levi, 2017, p. 67)

In the pentagram ritual each of its points are seen as linked to an elemental quality.

The form of the pentagram that is most often used in the lesser banishing ritual begins in the lower left-hand or earth point and proceeds through spirit (top point), fire (lower right-hand point), air (upper left-hand), and water (upper right-hand), before sealing the knot back in the earth point. Finally, and perhaps most fundamentally of all, the pentagram represents a human being, with head and four limbs extended, depicting our particular nature as a living star.

The ritual, as we saw in Chapter 7, is an example of the formula of Abrahadabra and begins therefore with the contemplation of the sphere of the universe, seeing it as the sphere of infinite points of view that is Nuit. As we stand in this sphere, we contemplate our place at the centre, identifying our place as Hadit, the singular point, taking our stance as the magician and the exorcist. We are the axle of the wheel of the universe exercising the energies of will and love within the infinite variation of the interplay of the 0 = 2 equation.

We begin by performing the Qabalistic cross. Imagine a sphere of diamond-white light above our head. We touch our forehead with the dominant hand and say: *Ateh* (את) ("Ar-taay").

Aligning with the source of light and life, we bring our hand down the body to the solar plexus, imagining a river of diamond light flowing down the centre of the body into the ground, and say: *Malkuth* (מלכות) ("Mal-kooth").

Then we bring our hand to the right shoulder and imagine a sphere of intense, red energy. We say: *Ve Geburah* (ו גבורה) ("Vay-gebooraah").

Bringing our hand to the left shoulder, we imagine a river of diamond-white light flowing to it and forming a sphere of deep blue light. We say: *Ve Gedulah* (ו גדולה) ("Vay-gedoolaah").

Bringing our hands together, just above the solar plexus, we imagine a miniature sun shining there. We say: *Le Olam Amen* (ל עולם אמן) ("Ley-olaam arr-men"), imagining the sun shining more and more intensely as we fully extend our arms to form a cross of light and fire.

Beginning in the east, with forefinger and second finger extended we make the first banishing pentagram, drawing it as the endless knot, commencing at the left, earth point and moving clockwise through the shape, locking it back at the earth point. We visualise it in pure white light and energise it by thrusting our hand into its centre, vibrating *YHVH* (יהוה) ("Yod-hey-vow-hey"). Turning clockwise to the south, keeping our hand extended and visualising a line of light following our hand, we repeat the gesture and energise the form with the name: *Adonai* (אדני) ("Arr-doe-nye"). We next turn to the west, again draw a banishing earth pentagram, and chant: *Eheieh* (אהיה) ("Ey-hey-yeh"). Then we turn to the north, make the banishing earth pentagram, energising it with the name: *Agla* (אגלא) ("Arr-glar"). Finally, we complete the circle and link the line of light to the eastern pentagram. Letting our hand drop, we centre ourselves in the midst of circle and say: "Before me, Raphael (רפאל)". We visualise Raphael as a hooded figure and as the morning sun, in yellow and violet and the colours of dawn, bringing in the element of air, breath and beginnings.

Then, "Behind me, Gabriel (גבראל)", we say, visualising Gabriel in blue and orange, all the colours of the setting sun, in a hooded robe, bringing in the element of water and flow.

"On my right hand, Michael (מיחאל)", we say, visualising Michael in a hooded robe of red and gold, with fiery, solar radiance coming from their face as they bring in the element of fire.

"On my left hand, Auriel (אוראל)". We visualise Auriel in an indigo-black and green-hooded robe, with a great sense of stillness as they bring in the element of earth.

Feel the qualities of the invoked archangels as they fill the circle with their vast energies, and then we sense or visualise the interlinked triangles of the hexagram behind us: the upright triangle is of red fire, and the downward-facing of blue water, and we say: "About me flames the pentagrams, and behind me shines the six-rayed star". Sense the pentagrams and the hexagram flare into incandescence, and we are at one with the light.

Finally, perform the Qabalistic Cross again and close the working.

This ritual is given as initial training exercise for obvious reasons: it trains the mind and body of the worker and its initial effect is to produce a sphere of stillness and dynamic peace, although its deeper intention is a reconfiguration of self and world. The Qabalistic Cross begins by aligning ourselves, our deepest nature, and inviting the outflow of that nature into full manifestation. This axis is then brought into magical activity through the activation of Geburah and Gedulah and the solar equilibrium in Tiphareth. Having confirmed and expressed our identity as the mystical magician, we next inscribe the pentagrams, projecting that energy of love and will into the universe. The extent to which we understand the 0 = 2 equation and the generative nature of the pentagram determines what comes next, so that it is experienced not as a flat diagram but as a generative star of will. It begins with the banishing of the east and the invocation of the name YHVH (יהוה), thus stilling the east and the breath-energy of beginning, then, successively, the south and the energy of radiant sovereignty; the west and the principle of flow; and finally, the north and the principle of manifestation and fixation. This is the first part of the working, the casting out.

Then the four archangels are invoked into the empty space, bringing forward the breath of inspiration, the radiant fire and light of blessing, the purifying and flowing water, and the crystallisation and fixation of the deep earth. These qualities are invoked in relationship with the generative pentagram, and their energies reach us through it because they act as a lens between us and the archangel, which enables mutual alignment and augmentation. The infinite extension of the pentagram in both directions (inward and outward) indicates the amplification of the balanced energy of will and focus, which gives the ritual a profound flexibility and applicability. At this point in the working, the colour of the pentagram may reflect that associated with the archangel, in which case the eastern pentagram may become yellow, the southern red, the western blue, and the northern green.

Archangels are strange and vast beings. The word comes from two Greek words: *arche*, which means "the root of" or "the beginning" or "the chief", and *angelos*, which means "a messenger". The message they bring is the power of creation itself and thus, when invoked, they summon a new world into being. The ritual reaches its apogee with the uniting of the pentagram and the hexagram and the proclamation of the unity of both, which we find also in the Abrahadabra formula.

### The Salutes of the Sun

This is a prayer form that engages our attention at the key points of dawn, noon, sunset, and midnight, aligning us with the sun as the centre of life and light, using the ancient Egyptian forms of:

- Ra Harakhty. A fusion of Ra and Horus, representing the energy of dawn and the creation of the new day.
- Hathor. The goddess of love, fertility, and protection whose fiercer form is the lion-headed Sekhmet, goddess of magick and healing.
- Atum. The ancient sun god, often envisaged as an old man walking with a stick, gathering all into the stillness.
- Khephera. The beetle god who represents the midnight sun and the mystery of generation in the midst of darkness.

At Dawn we say:

> Hail to thee, the eternal spiritual sun who rises as Ra Harakhty, the manifester of the morning. Hail to thee who makes us stand upright.

At noon:

> Hail to thee, the eternal spiritual sun who stands as Hathor at noon—the nurturing lady of fire and light who is Sekhmet, radiant in power. Hail to thee, who makes our limbs strong.

At sunset:

> Hail to thee, the eternal spiritual sun who are Atum at sunset, gathering all into the blessed west. Hail to thee who gives us rest.

At night time:

> Hail unto thee, the eternal spiritual sun who art Khephera, the sun at midnight. Hail to thee who renews our souls.

The intention of this prayer form is to link us with the source of creative light, life, and power at regular intervals in the day. Here we employ the ability of the magical imagination to connect to the cycle of the sun and follow its sequence through the day so that the pattern of our day is linked to something bigger than our own daily life. The more vivid our imagining of these moments, the greater the sense of presence and power we touch. We increasingly live against the felt experience of the eternal spiritual sun that is the star at the heart of our own being. The use of the Egyptian god forms will help to deepen that experience.

### The Evening review

The night or evening salute is linked also to an exercise performed just before sleep in which we contemplate the events of the day backwards, using imagination to reverse time and to digest the events of the day. This is linked with Khephera's process of self-renewal. Again, this is a simple-seeming exercise but enables us to bring a profound sense of awareness into our daily activities. A deeper form of this practice is used in working with the supernal sephiroth, but this discipline, introduced here at the beginning of the way, creates the basis for that later work.

# DISCOVERING THE WAY—BECOMING ADEPT

Having become rooted in the tradition, and having worked sufficiently with the internal dialogue to see beyond it, we become capable of engaging in the more direct experience of communion with the deeper soul. This relies on a capacity to remain rooted in Malkuth and to direct our attention towards the still, silent voice of Tiphareth, navigating the stormy currents of thought, emotion, and sensation that arise when we do this. This is the process that Simon Iff describes in *Moonchild* when he speaks of the movement between "I, me, and mine" and the communion with "Thou" (Crowley, 1929, p. 66). All the work described in this section of the book arises out of this communion and is at its service.

CHAPTER 9

# The Knowledge and Conversation of the Holy Guardian Angel

C rowley called this work "The Knowledge and Conversation of the Holy Guardian Angel", basing his understanding of the process on a grimoire called *The Book of the Sacred Magic of Abra-Melin the Mage* (MacGregor-Mathers, 1976). This book, unlike many grimoires, is essentially a prayer operation of purification and devotion in which we address the divine and invite the presence of the angel that is our particular guardian and teacher to descend into us and commune with us. There are no prescribed forms of prayer for this, as the operation is considered to be an intimate and personal process that we will develop through our own artistry. The *Abramelin* book recommends using the psalms as models for this process, but Crowley used the Graeco-Egyptian ritual called "the Bornless Ritual", which he had learned from the Golden Dawn, as the basis of his work. So important was this to him that in his seminal book *Magick* he describes it thus:

> There is a single main definition of the object of all magical ritual. It is the uniting of the Microcosm with the Macrocosm. The Supreme and Complete Ritual is the Invocation of the Holy Guardian Angel. (Crowley, 1989, p. 151)

The classical ritual is performed for six months or eighteen months as an intense prayer practice, after which the angel descends and teaches the worker how to bind elemental and demonic energies to his or her will. My own experience of it, however, has been of a continuous process of deepening communion, which has accompanied me through my life and work. There are many places where Crowley looks into the relationship between the aspirant and the angel, but perhaps the most important is in the holy book he called *The Book of the Heart Girt with the Serpent*. The "Holy Books" are a series of inspirational works, like *The Book of the Law*, which fall into a category of his writings he considers to be directly written through him by Aiwass, his Holy Guardian Angel.

The book is organised under the symbols of the heart and the serpent. The heart in Ancient Egypt was called the *ab* and was considered to be our locus of consciousness and the centre point of our being. The serpent, as we have seen in *The Book of Gates*, represents the energy of will and imagination  and is the activity of the divine. The interplay between the heart and the serpent is an image of the relationship between the adept and the angel in an unfolding communion of call and response as the angel summons us into deeper awareness and we invite the angel to descend more and more deeply into the heart. Initially, we experience ourselves centred in Tiphareth, in the place of beauty and balance, and contemplate the angel wrapping around us as the fluidic, mercurial initiator.

The five chapters of *The Book of the Heart Girt with the Serpent* are based on the five parts of the soul. Chapter I is concerned with the *nephesch* and the element of earth; Chapter II the *ruach* and the element of air; III, the *neschamah* and the element of water; IV, the *chiah* and the element of fire; and V, the spirit and the *yechidah*. This is principally an instruction book to the Adept who has the capacity to touch the awareness of Tiphareth and, through, it has access to all states of the tree. The book unfolds the whole path to the Adept but we must remain aware that the view is from this particular station of the tree (i.e., Tiphareth).

In the first chapter we are introduced to the image of the heart with the snake wrapped around it; we are also given the image of the corpse of Osiris in his tomb, floating in the waters of the beginning—a vignette that evokes the central section of *The Book of Gates*, in the deepest part of the night, which involves the fusion of Ra and Osiris and the movement upwards to the sunrise and the creation of the new day and world. The chapter underscores this sense of beginning by the appearance of the beetle god Khephera who rolls the reborn sun into and through the horizon of the new day. We are shown in this the whole process of the work with the angel that is the continual act of resurrection and recreation. The poem goes on to give us an image of the angel as Adonai speaking to the scribe V.V.V.V.V. (this is the magical motto of Crowley as the Master of the Temple, *Vi veri vniversum vivus vici*, "By the force of Truth I, while living, have conquered the universe"), talking of the individual and intimate nature of this work, and saying that one scribe of the work writes in the colours "of mother of emerald, and of lapis-lazuli, and of turquoise" (1: 4) (Crowley, 2015, p. 96), while another uses "topaz, and of deep amethyst, and of gray sapphire, and of deep sapphire with a tinge as of blood" (1: 5) (Crowley, 2015, p. 96). We are told that the work is to ascend to Kether, the Crown, through the path of the arrow, passing through the moon and the sun, pursuing the way until the end of union with Kether is reached. We are then shown how the activity of the angel disrupts the patterned nature of the nephesch, using images such as acid cutting into steel, or cancer destroying the organic body, and that the angel shall not rest until it is all dissolved.

What is being addressed here is the fixity of the Yesodic sense of self and universe, and an image of the heart and serpent as almost inanimate, as if carved from stone; such is the density of the patterns that shape us. In a verse that echoes the writings of John of the Cross, we approach the angel in the night, stealing close and gripping the angel, crowning the angel with flowers and daring greatly to kiss the angel upon the lips. We learn that the angel has all along been seeking us and we have only needed to slow down and look in the right direction for the angel to find us. As a result of this, the heart is experienced as a heart of gold and the serpent as soft and sinuous and entwined about us. Our inner vehicle then has moved from a solid, fixed shape to be a vessel of quicksilver. We are asked to remain close to the angel and, from this place of communion, our viewpoint expands so that what would have seemed disaster or triumph become not events but aspects of the creative spectrum of life.

The image for this communion is a boat of mother of pearl riding on the river of life, which is seen as *amrit*, the elixir of the divine. All events are seen as shades of colour reflected in the mother of pearl: joy is a silver gleam, and woe a blue gleam. We start to gain here a sense of the divine play, *lila*, and realise that the journey of life is simply the journey of the Adept and the angel through eternity. Continually we are asked to simply participate in the communion with the angel, and to unify our experience and become committed to what we might call "one-ing": remaining the aware subject rather than scattering our intention and attention into the subject–object dualism that produced the inanimate heart and serpent. This is a constant communion, in which we continually direct what the writer of the Christian mystical text *The Cloud of Unknowing* (Anon, 1944, p. 17) calls the "*nakid entente*" of our being towards the angel. Crowley speaking as the Angel uses the verse, "The strong brown reaper swept his swathe and rejoiced. The wise man counted his muscles, and pondered, and understood not, and was sad" (1: 56) (Crowley, 2015, p. 100) to illustrate the difference between being in the communion with the angel and being out of communion. We are invited to "Reap thou, and rejoice!" (1: 56) (Crowley, 2015, p. 100) as the close communion and unification brings a sense of ecstasy and joy which is continually refined as the dialogue progresses. This new sense is continually refined, becoming deepened and expanded, for: "Bacchus grew old, and was Silenus; Pan was ever Pan for ever and ever more throughout the aeons" (1: 63) (Crowley, 2015, p. 101). Here, Bacchus represents the limited ecstasy of the nephesch which, like Silenus, decays, grows old, and loses freshness while Pan, as the infinite divine presence, remains ever fresh and new. This constant refinement of the dialogue is emphasised by the call of the angel: "Intoxicate the inmost, O my lover, not the outermost" (1: 64) (Crowley, 2015, p. 101), and the response of the Adept: "So was it—ever the same! I have aimed at the peeled wand of my God, and I have hit; yea, I have hit" (1: 65) (Crowley, 2015, p. 101).

The second chapter is concerned with the *ruach*, the nature of consciousness and awareness, and the Adept's connection with Tiphareth. It begins with the image of a mountain of lapis lazuli and the image of a green hawk, seated in the throne of the East between two turquoise pillars. Lapis is suggestive of the world of the stars and, therefore, the sense of entering a larger space, while the image of the seated green hawk gives us the sense of the presence of the angel sitting in the midst of the opposites in stillness. This is the beginning of a process of alchemising opposites in which the presence of the angel descends more deeply into the experience of the opposites and the mystery of the One becoming all. We are then presented with the image of a river of blood and a shining steel boat containing a golden image of Isis. Crowley in his commentary (Crowley, 1996, p. 103) tells us that the river is the stream of thought, the boat is consciousness, the purple sails are the passions, and the golden statue the ideal that directs our aspiration. The Adept, through love of the ideal, leaps out of the boat into the river, unifying with the stream of thought. The contemplation of the ideal disturbs the idealised form, which then breaks down as the creative, inspiring idea becomes incorporated within the Adept and their life and, hence, is no longer a shining external image. Nonetheless, the Adept, by persisting in the dialogue with the angel and working with the creative ideal even in its broken and corrupted state, enters an experience of resurrection. This process is shown in the poem by the Adept worshipping the golden statue that blackens, sickens, and decays until it re-emerges as a living goddess—a form of Hathor (Crowley, 1996, p. 104), the goddess of love, beauty, and resurrection. Similarly, the boat, sails, and river transform to be the river of amrit (the elixir of immortality), the chariot of the flesh, and the blood of the heart. This act of resurrection and unification brings us to a place where we discover that our body is contained within consciousness (rather than the reverse); our thoughts are living, immortal ideas; and our passions are unified with our true will.

This expansion of mind and thought is shown in the image of riding through a blue sky on the back of the swan: here, we allow the inspiration of the swan to carry us, abandoning all sense of a goal and ignoring the rational mind, which is described as "A little crazy boy" (2: 20) (Crowley, 2015, p. 104). As a result of the inspiration, the Adept is moved to create an image of beauty that will assist others to experience inspiration. The poem next describes the Adept as a pale, sad boy, weeping and lying upon marble, and Crowley comments (Crowley, 1996, p. 108) that the Adept is seen as Ganymede, the cup bearer of the gods, impacted by the hardness and sadness of the world, having abandoned both lute and music. They are then overshadowed by an eagle from the abyss of glory and their music is revived: "But I heard the lute lively discoursing through the blue still air" (2: 32) (Crowley, 2015, p. 105). The stillness and the blueness is the ground from which the voice of the angel can be heard, and through which the music of the angel can be heard. It is the Adept's submission to the inspiration and the overshadowing of the angel that both rouses up streams of resistant thoughts, as the rational faculties rebel against the primacy of the intuitive mind, and yet begins a process of deep transformation of consciousness.

This process of transformation is imaged initially as an abyss of the great deep, containing a great dolphin lashing from side to side amidst great waves. This gives us a sense both of the depth of the mind and the unsettled and uneasy consciousness symbolised by the restless dolphin. There then follows another process of call and response, the dialogue of the Adept and the angel. The dolphin listens to the tunes of a harper of gold, playing infinite tunes, and becomes a bird. The harper then plays infinite tunes upon the pan pipe and the bird, as a result of the bliss of listening, becomes a faun of the forest. The harper lays down his pipes and, with human voice, sings infinite tunes. The faun is enraptured and follows the sounds. The harper enters into silence and the faun becomes Pan, in the primal forest of eternity. The harper is the angel and the changing forms of the Adept show us a process of stilling disturbance, which travels inwards, becoming more and more pervasive, eventually reaching the deep silence in which the Adept becomes the All and is surrounded by the forest of living, creative ideas, having left behind the dead concepts of the rational mind.

This leads to an immersion in the bliss of creativity and the experience of the heart as the fountain of creativity, wrapped around by the presence of the angel serpent, who embraces us so that no other influences can interfere. The Adept now is passive to the angel, allowing its embrace and serving as its messenger.

The third chapter is concerned with the neschamah and marks the experience of entering the non-dual experience of the supernals, moving from the experience of the Adept to the sense of the Master of the Temple or Geru Maa. This is indicated in its opening verse, in which we are given the image of passing through the deep sea to the land of no desire where we find a white unicorn with a silver collar on which is graven the aphorism: "Linea viridis gyrat universa ['The green line winds around the universe']" (3: 2) (Crowley, 2015, p. 109). The unicorn is the symbol of virginity and the unified will, and the aphorism marks the universal field in which we now work. As we contemplate this, we receive the word of the angel that addresses us as the heart found within "the coils of the old serpent" (3: 3) (Crowley, 2015, p. 109) and bids us ascend the mountain of initiation. The contemplation of the old serpent leads on to meditating on Lilith and on the nature of desire that entraps us. At this stage, many of our patterns have been dealt with, but we are engaging with what is described as "a certain taint" (3: 8) (Crowley, 2015, p. 109) that can draw us back into the nephesch or animal soul to reassert our separateness. It is this taint that can subvert the initiation process and is responsible for the creation of what Crowley elsewhere called "the black brothers" or those who refuse the surrender into the non-dual love, will, and being of the supernals, instead building a false crown in the abyss based on separation, hiding, and resistance. The Adept's struggle with this taint, described as the coils of the old serpent, which is the remnants of an old, resistant, ego-based way of maintaining our life and desire, is aided by calling out for help to the angel. This help is here symbolised by the elephant-headed god Ganesha, who overcomes obstacles, enables us to free ourselves, and to discover that we are enclosed only by an infinite, green circle that also encloses the universe. We find that love and desire are universal, as is our heart, and that the coils of the serpent have an infinite range.

The poem then brings us to the set of verses that we considered in the Introduction and which are pivotal to this whole work and the character of Simon Iff as Master of the Temple (3: 21–26):

> I, and Me, and Mine were sitting with lutes in the market-place
> of the great city, the city of the violets and the roses.
> The night fell, and the music of the lutes was stilled.
> The tempest arose, and the music of the lutes was stilled.
> The hour passed, and the music of the lutes was stilled.
> But Thou art Eternity and Space; Thou art Matter and Motion;
> and Thou art the negation of all these things.
> For there is no symbol of Thee. (Crowley, 2015, p. 111)

This verse, in a certain sense, holds the whole process of the Adept and the angel for, as we move from the sense of I, me, and mine into the communion with Thou we unite the heart and the serpent and speak and act as the unified being who proclaims: "If I say Come up upon the mountains! The celestial waters flow at my word" (3: 27) (Crowley, 2015, p. 111), here acting as the Magus. We remain aware of a further state beyond even this, however, in the line: "But Thou art the Water beyond the waters" (3: 27) (Crowley, 2015, p. 111); this points us to the consummation in Kether, which we cannot yet reach. The remainder of this chapter has the Adept exploring this unified state with the angel in which, more and more, the Adept responds to the prompting of the angel, becoming increasingly fluid and meeting the needs of the moment. This is described as the angel being "the cool still water of the wizard fount" (3: 49) (Crowley, 2015, p. 113), a magical fountain, which the Adept bathes in and looses themselves in the stillness, and finds that on emerging their sex has changed. This is a reference to the mythical fountain of the nymph Salmacis, who loved a man and brought him into her waters, fusing with him, so that they became hermaphrodite. It is used here as a description of the state reached by the Adept and the angel. Finally, the Adept is identified with the Fool of the tarot, who is beyond instruction even by the tarot trumps of the Magician, the High Priestess, the Emperor, the Empress, and the Hierophant, having come to the sense of pure spontaneity (3: 58).

> But I am the Fool that heedeth not the Play of the Magician. Me doth the Woman of the Mysteries instruct in vain; I have burst the bonds of Love and of Power and of Worship. (Crowley, 2015, p. 114)

We then come to the fourth chapter that applies to the part of the soul called the chiah and the work of the Chief Lector Priest, or the Magus. This is a re-engagement with the divine play of the magician and begins with a transformation of the image of the heart and the serpent (4: 1):

> O crystal heart! I the Serpent clasp Thee; I drive home mine head into the central core of Thee, O God my beloved. (Crowley, 2015, p. 116)

There is a deeper union indicated here, as the heart is now of crystal and the head of the serpent is at its core and we see a reversal of tone, in that the serpent addresses the Adept as "O God my beloved". The poem moves on to consider the figure of the Greek poet Sappho, who desired union with the sun and plunged herself into the image of the sun reflected in the sea to attain this union.

> Even as on the resounding wind-swept heights of Mitylene some god-like woman casts aside the lyre, and with her locks aflame as an aureole, plunges into the wet heart of the creation, so I, O Lord, my God! (3: 2) (Crowley, 2015, p. 116)

Here we see the Angel as the Neschamah centred in Binah descending into Tiphareth, the station of the Adept, and deeper yet into Yesod, into the image of the beloved Adept, and through that image working into the roots of matter, "the wet heart of creation".

The sense of the angel's love for the Adept is indicated in its desire to transform the everlasting salt into sweetness, as the mystery of sorrow in Binah becomes the joy and play of the Magus in Chockmah. The angel compares the Adept to "the bezoar-stone that is found in the belly of the cow" (3: 7) (Crowley, 2015, p. 116)—this is a stone formed of closely woven hairs, and conveys the sense of the Adept as formed from a constellation of forces—and invites them to rest in the orchard, laying down this complexity, and enter "the sleep of Shi-loh-am" (3: 9) (Crowley, 2015, p. 117), the infinite lucid sleep of peace.

Within this lucid sleep the angel perceives the universe as a clear crystal without speck and perceives the perfection of union with the Adept. This union is explored in the following verses (3: 15–17):

> Thus spake the Magister V.V.V.V.V. unto Adonai his God, as they played together in the starlight over against the deep black pool that is in the Holy Place of the Holy House beneath the Altar of the Holiest One.
> But Adonai laughed, and played more languidly.
> Then the scribe took note, and was glad. But Adonai had no fear of the Magician and his play. For it was Adonai who had taught all his tricks to the Magician. (Crowley, 2015, p. 117)

There is then a sequence in which the Adept, now operating as the Magister, is tested to see if they can operate within the play of the magician and remain united with the angel. In this entering into the wet heart of creation, and the interplay of angel and Adept, we encounter the nature of distortion and evil, here presented as the evil counterpart of the angel:

> On the threshold stood the fulminant figure of Evil, the Horror of emptiness, with his ghastly eyes like poisonous wells. He stood, and the chamber was corrupt; the air stank. He was an old and gnarled fish more hideous than the shells of Abaddon. (3: 34) (Crowley, 2105, p. 120)

In contrast to the movement, fluidity, and hyperreality of the angel, the evil genius is static, inactive—a toxic ghost generating stagnation. We are next given a picture of the evil figure wrapping its tentacles around the Adept but unable to get a hold as the Adept is anointed with the consecrating oil of the angel. We next witness the descent of the angel, striking the Adept through with the spear of its will, and together they enter into the work of creation which, we are told, has the taint of generation—by which is meant the impermanence and change that is the root of sorrow. We are then presented with a flower in the sunlight, rooted in the dark earth, and the earth is seen as the mother of myriad flowers—phenomena arising out of mystery. This causes a shift of perception in which we, as the conjoined Adept and angel understand and work with the interplay of Hadit, Nuit, and Ra Hoor Khuit as the emergence of the point-instance out of the infinite possibilities that generates the series of magical bodies and constellations. This leads to an understanding in which the angel identifies itself as "the Soul of the desert" (3: 61) (Crowley, 2015, p. 122), causing it to blossom through the transmission of the will of the Magus into Tiphareth and the lower spheres of the tree. This manifestation of the deep will and the work of the Adept/angel is emphasised in the exhortation,

> O my darling, I also wait for the brilliance of the hour ineffable, when the universe shall be like a girdle for the midst of the ray of our love, extending beyond the permitted end of the endless One. (3: 64) (Crowley, 2015, p. 123)

Crowley (Crowley, 1996, pp. 178–180) tells us that describing the universe in this way shows the ray as a limitless line of light and the totality of manifested existence is determined by the will to love of the Adept and angel. This is the formula of love under will in action, which reaches its consummation in the final verse of the chapter:

> Then, O thou heart, will I the serpent eat thee wholly up; yea, I will eat thee wholly up. (3: 65) (Crowley, 2015, p. 123)

The heart that is the locus of the Adept is wholly subsumed in the spiralling life and will of the angel in action.

Chapter V is concerned with the fifth part of the soul, the *yechidah*—the non-dual awareness that is the singularity, the simple point, that generates all and to which all return. Here we touch the root of the letter *yod* (י) of the creative name (יהוה) and this begins with the sense of Adonai, the angel, with the Adept in a treasure house of pearls. Crowley tells us that the pearl is a cloudy nebula representing the *rashith-ha gilgalim* or "the first swirlings", which are the first movement out of the unmanifest in the new universe generated by the union of the angel and the Adept (Crowley, 1996, p. 182). From this union and the first movement there is the generation of a new light, like the moment of *yehi or* (יהי ער), "Let there be Light!", in the Book of Genesis, which transforms the universe.

We are told that the pillar is established in the void; that Asi and Asar (Isis and Osiris) are in union; and that the crowned and conquering child has taken possession of the animal soul—the nephesch. This child appears at midnight and seems like a gnarled, glittering, black stone, for he brings the mystery of the deep to the surface and disturbs all known perceptions because the secret place of silence is revealing a new and deeper mystery. We are shown a new creation in which maidens dance and babies are born. The Adept is shown the path through which they have come to this place and are told that the angel has always dwelt within the Adept as a pure flame in the most intimate place of their being.

The simplicity of the union of the angel and the Adept transforms all that it touches, without effort, for all return into the root of Kether through the mediation of the conjoined angel and Adept. The Adept describes this union with the angel as if being penetrated with four blades: a thunderbolt, a pylon (i.e., a door or gateway), a serpent, and a phallus. These are the four letters of the name *Adonai* (אדני): *aleph* (א) is the swastika, the thunderbolt letter by its shape; *daleth* (ד) is the door or pylon; *nun* (נ) is the serpent; and *yod* (י) is the phallus. The meaning here is that the Adept has been filled and pierced through by the substance of the angel, Adonai. This is followed by the mystery (Crowley, 2015, p. 126) of *Ararita* (אראריתא) "Also he taught me the holy unutterable word *Ararita*, so that I melted the six-fold gold into a single invisible point, whereof naught can be spoken" (5: 15). This word is a letter code for the phrase "One is his beginning, one his individuality, one his permutation", and we are told that the Adept shall live in the world as a precious diamond among cloudy diamonds, crystals, and pieces of glass. Like the diamond, the Adept will reflect the colours of their environment, becoming red like the rose, or green like the leaf, but remaining pristine and unaffected. We are told again that "I am thou, and the Pillar is 'stablished in the void" (5: 23) (Crowley, 2015, p. 127) and that we are beyond the "stabilities of Being and of Consciousness and of Bliss" (5: 24) (Crowley, 2015, p. 127). These are the Advaita categories of *sat*, *chit*, and *ananada*, which are the qualities of awakened awareness. We are being told that this state is beyond even these.

The sense of I and Thou being one, and the pillar's establishment in the void is repeated. We are shown that this pillar is the Middle Pillar of the Tree of Life—"From the Crown to the Abyss, so goeth it single and erect" (5: 26) (Crowley, 2015, p. 127)—that encompasses all manifestation in a single phenomenon. The complexity, through the alchemy of the knowledge and conversation, has been resolved into simplicity. The chapter moves on to show the death of old-aeon god concepts of separation, and the arising of the new aeon symbolised by the crowned and conquering child. We are given an image of parricidal atheists whose souls are "one purple flower-flame of holiness" (Crowley, 2015, p. 128) and who work with the sickle of doubt to reap the flowers of a faith that is not separate from doubt. As a result, fresh springs of life and holiness appear. This is a process Crowley discusses in depth in his essay "The Soldier and the Hunchback" (Crowley, 1909).

We are encouraged to continue deepening the communion of Adept and angel, following the course of the Nile to its source, seeing the priest of Isis perceive the figure of Nuit within the form of Isis, and his becoming in turn the priest of Nuit. Each step of this process is seen as a death followed by a birth.

The work is envisaged as the building of the Great Pyramid of Khefru. A parable is presented of the ibis, the hummingbird, and the uraeus serpent. The hummingbird asks the horned serpent ("the horned cerastes" (5: 52) [Crowley, 2015, p. 130]) for its poison. The uraeus serpent answers ("the great snake of Khem the Holy One, the Royal Uræus" (5: 53) [Crowley, 2015, p. 130]) that it is the inheritance of a million generations and so cannot be given. The hummingbird, depressed by this, flies off into the flowers and is killed by a snake, but the sacred ibis is listening while meditating by the banks of the Nile. He "laid aside his Ibis ways" (5: 55) (Crowley, 2015, p. 131) and becomes a uraeus serpent so that, in many generations, one of his descendants may possess the sacred poison. Such is his devotion and practice that within three moons he has the poison.

This parable is concerned with the attitude of the Adept and the necessity of the process of death and rebirth, and it is connected to the images of the priest of Isis's transformation and the building of the pyramid. The hummingbird is that part of us which is ephemeral, flits from flower to flower, cannot commit, and is easily discouraged.

The uraeus serpent is the angel, who possesses the secret of death and rebirth. A subtlety in this parable is that the hummingbird asks its question of the horned serpent, not the royal or uraeus serpent, and this underlines our capacity to become confused, to look in the wrong place, and to avoid the deep transformations of this way. In contrast, we are shown the figure of the sacred ibis, the avatar of the god Thoth, the god of wisdom, meditating on the banks of the Nile, listening and hearing. He puts aside his ibis ways, becomes a serpent, and works without lust of result, submitting fully to the process, so that in a short time he becomes the royal serpent, possessing the sacred poison that kills and brings alive. It is this attitude that the Adept must continually cultivate and contemplation of the three figures of hummingbird, uraeus serpent, and ibis can assist us as we enter more deeply into the way.

The book ends with the image of Ra gathering together all into a radiant heart that shines like the setting sun, and all being bound together by the uraeus serpent, like a golden girdle, giving all the death-kiss. Here the principles of death and love are united and we are gathered into the process of transformation by death, leading to the birth of the new day and perpetual sacrament of the crowned and conquering child.

The final verse is a statement of continuity:

> So also is the end of the book, and the Lord Adonai is about it on all sides like a Thunderbolt, and a Pylon, and a Snake, and a Phallus, and in the midst thereof He is like the Woman that jetteth out the milk of the stars from her paps; yea, the milk of the stars from her paps. (5: 65) (Crowley, 2015, p. 133)

Here the centrality of the angel, as Adonai, is asserted and we learn that Adonai is also Nuit, the infinite, the endless. She who is none and two, divided for the sake of union and who is the continuous one of Heaven.

Through the contemplation of this book we may gain an insight into the states of awareness that we will touch from time to time, but we must recall that the major task is the communion with our angel through the method that is uniquely our own, which we will consider in the next chapter.

# CHAPTER 10

# Advaita Vedanta and the Holy Guardian Angel

As we have seen, the process of engaging with the angel is very personal and there are many ways to do it. Crowley's starting point for this work was *The Book of the Sacred Magic of Abra-Melin the Mage* and a devotional process of prayer but, if we return to *The Book of the Law*, we will recall that it gives us a set of images that point us in the direction of the mystery of unveiling the star at the centre of our being and letting our light shine. It is summarised by the phrases "Every man and every woman is a star" (I: 3) and "Do what thou wilt shall be the whole of the Law. [...] Love is the law, love under will" (I: 40; I: 57). This is the work that Simon Iff performs in *Moonchild* when he confronts the thing in the garden: he disidentifies with I, me, and mine, and then can hear the music of the deeply interconnected universe and from that place connects with the qliphothic form by affirming the sovereignty of the true will and, through the application of love, draws all into harmony.

The work of disidentifying or unveiling which reveals the simplicity of love and will in action is very powerfully described by the twentieth-century Advaita Master, Ramana Maharshi, who taught the path of *vicara* or "self-enquiry".

Sri Ramana Maharshi

I first came across the picture above in 1972, when I was seventeen. There was something about his expression that conveyed a luminous, still kindness, which, as I look at it today, helps me to soften and relax into the mystery of being.

Ramana Maharshi's method is deceptively simple and involves either focusing on our heart or centre and asking the question "Who am I?" or, alternatively, submitting to the divine self through devotion. He tells us not to make an incantation out of "Who am I?" but to put the question once and then with all our faculties seek the source of the sense of "I" and the thoughts, feelings, and sensations that arise around it. Here we are with the I, me, and mine that Simon Iff contemplates. In Maharshi's work *Self-Enquiry* (included in *The Collected Works* [Maharshi, 1959]) he gives us the following diagram:

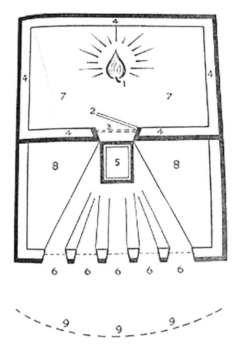

Ramana Maharshi, 1959, p. 23

There are four territories described in this diagram: first, the semi-circle and the 9s represent the body in relationship with the outside world, which we would call Malkuth; second, the lower square designated "8", which he describes as the subtle body in the dream state—the triangle of Hod, Netzach, and Yesod; third, the upper square, designated "7", which he describes as the causal body and we would call Tiphareth, Geburah, and Gedulah; and, fourth, the flame, designated as "1", which he sees as the divine self and we would consider to be the supernal triangle, and specifically the light of Kether.

The diagram describes a dynamic of perception. At its bottom, numbered "6", we see the doorways of the senses which come into connection with our inner experience. Here, they are met by the crystal mirror of the ego, "5" (Yesod on the Tree of Life). Deeper in, and numbered "3", is the doorway that gives access to what Maharshi calls the causal body. This doorway, in the Samkhya philosophy that Maharshi draws on, is called *mahat* and represents the intuitive awareness, or creative aspect of *manas* or "mind" that the Qabalah would call Tiphareth. If the doorway can remain open (as we can see from the diagram) the light of the divine self shines through into the crystal mirror and the senses. But if it remains closed then what emerges is a quality called *ahamkara*, which means "the making of a self" (from *aham*, "I am", and *kara*, "making"). This "making of a self" is a process of reification in which awareness identifies with thoughts, gathering them into connected bundles, which condition both the senses and the interface between the body and the outside world. The crystal mirror acting as the *ahamkara* manifests a vision of self and world that is limited, unstable, and based upon a self-referential dialogue. As we enquire we start to turn the direction of awareness inwards, so that the constructions of *ahamkara* are seen through, and the door to the inner chamber opens. As we enter the inner chamber of the causal body we start to come into direct relationship with the divine self though, even here, there are limitations, for around the flame we see (labelled "4") the walls of *avidya* or "primal veiling ignorance". This is similar to the Qabalistic sephira of Daath, or the prism that bridges duality and non-duality. Maharshi informs us that the process of separation results in what might be called "the reflected consciousness" of the *mahat* translating into the *ahamakara* and then becoming the shaped and known ego. The veiling that is inevitably part of this process increasingly imprisons us in a limited sense of self and world. This created form is called, in Samkhya, the *antahkhara*, which bridges the different aspects of reflected consciousness. Maharshi uses the classic image of red-hot iron as a way of describing the process of manifestation in that the divine self is the fire which infuses the individual iron, making it molten and fluid. If we are present with and participating in the non-dual light and fire of the divine self, the individual, or *jiva*, is said to be *jivanmukta*, "a freed individual", participating in the dance of *maya* ("illusion"), but without the fire we are the inert iron of the separated self and enclosed in our image of self and universe.

Another image he uses is that of the heart, or *hridayam*, by which he means both the heart of the body and the individual self—the place we point at when we say "I" or "me" and the infinite heart of the unity of Nuit and Hadit—the single point that is all. For Maharshi the sense of I is the keystone that holds the whole construction of the separated self in place, and so his principal practice is self-enquiry or *atmavicara*. This simple-seeming practice takes us to the heart of inner work and requires us to reverse the momentum of self and universe, look inwards, and enquire "Who am I?", not as a mantra or cognitive riddle but as a search or quest into that which appears and responds when we continually pose the question. Maintaining our focus here deconstructs all that we know and focuses our awareness on the unfolding, objectless mystery—the longing and desire for freedom and union with the infinite is a version of the knowledge and communion with the angel.

As we pursue this, we may feel tired and resistant to the effort involved in maintaining the direction of our attention because we are reversing the extraversion of our senses, in which meaning and validation is sought externally, and in which we are principally relating to a complex and interwoven image of self and universe that both gives us stability and binds us into a limited form. The major feature of this form is its stability, containing the sense of "this is who I am and this is how the world is" and, however limiting the form, we have long ago made peace with it and can bear to live within it. This is the situation described by Plato in his metaphor of the cave in which we sit in a dark place watching shadows play against the wall whereas, behind us, is the cave mouth and all the light and life of the universe. In Qabalistic terms, Yesod's capacity to create images has overwhelmed and subsumed the direct experience of Malkuth—the crystal mirror acts as a prism, projecting the inner images outwards. As we pursue this enquiry, we come into the room that Maharshi calls "the room of dreaming": this is the place of Yesod, Hod, and Netzach, the world of the psyche and the place where the inner dialogue operates, which generates the sense of self and universe. Here we find ourselves in a more fluid and interrelated world where thought generates feeling, which conjures memory images that in turn summon thoughts, feelings, and so on. If we persist in this enquiry, we start to touch into the place that Maharshi calls the *ahamkara*, the place of the making of the self through identification with the roots of thought— subtle tendencies called *vasanas*, which become the focus for a sense of position and solidity that then collects further thoughts, associated feelings, and images, which are projected out through the crystal mirror of Yesod. It is this place that in Qabalah is called "the Veil of the Temple". If we remain in the enquiry, we pierce this veil, and the self-making of the *ahamkara*, and touch directly the witnessing presence of Tiphareth and what Maharshi calls "the causal body", which he equates with dreamless sleep and unconsciousness. Here, the contemplative barrier is the blanking-out of literal sleep, or the sleep of awareness in which we fall into fantastical reverie or, indeed, back out into the projected extraversion of the senses. If we can maintain our enquiry, here we start to experience ourselves as the witnessing presence working within the sense of space and time and the interplay of opposites. In both the Qabalah and Maharshi's description there is a further step that must be taken, for in this second room we are still walled-in by primal ignorance or *avidya*, "not-knowing". Here, though we have a much expanded sense of ourselves and are operating in a larger and freer universe, we are still separated from the divine presence and see ourselves as a *jiva*, an individual being—we are not yet *jivanmukta*, the fully freed and awakened being. This is the place of the abyss on the Tree of Life and the doorway to this is the place of deep surrender into the mystery of Daath, the knowing of not-knowing, in which we lay down body and mind into the arms of the divine. In this turning around, which can feel like extinction and the blowing out of the flame of life, we become most truly, madly, deeply ourselves. This is the state called Ipsissimus in the traditional Qabalistic grades, and *Asar un nefer* in ancient Egypt, and from here we operate out of what Maharshi called *sahaja samadhi*, a state of spontaneous union where whatever happens just happens without any interference from mind, feelings, or sensations.

In response to a question from a devotee, Samuel Cohen, in which he asked about Jesus's "I am" statements, Maharshi tells us that among all the names of God found in the Bible, the one that captures the essence of the only direct way to realise Him is the name *Ehyeh Asher Ehyeh* (אהיה אשר אהיה), "I am what I am", and those who understand the significance of this name become realised.

As we touch this deeper and more fundamental aspect of our nature we start to experience what Maharshi calls *aham sphurana* or "I–I pulsation", the sense of the activity of the "I am that I am" manifesting. As we become established in this sense, so that it becomes continuous, then we are in *sahaja samadhi*.

If we revisit Simon Iff's utterance about the city of the violets and the roses, we can see the parallels with Maharshi's work: the market place of the city of the violets and roses is the place of desire and memory; the music of the lutes is the *aham sphurana*, the sense of the pulsation of I–I; and the experience of the fall of night, the rising of the tempest, and the weariness, which mean the music cannot be heard, relate to the extraversion of the senses, the dreaming, and the deep sleep that Maharshi speaks of.

The pulsation or music arises from that place of "am-ness" beyond the sense of I, me, and mine. It is not a blankness or absence but a profoundly different way of being and acting. Maharshi's actions and words emerge in direct relationship to his surroundings. When we read his conversations with devotees there is an extraordinary precision in the dialogue; in one moment he is discussing the states of awareness outlined in Advaita Vedanta, in another Heisenberg's contribution of the quantum theory and the measurement paradox of quantum theory and, in yet another moment, he composes hymns and invocations:

> Rejoice eternally! The heart rejoices at the feet of the Lord, who is the Self, shining within as "I-I" eternally, so that there is no [...] night and day. This will result in removal of ignorance of Self. (Maharshi, 1959, p. 127)

> Arunachala! Thou dost root out the ego of those who meditate on Thee in the heart, Oh Arunachala!
>
> Arunachala! Thou dost root out the ego of those who dwell on their [...] identity with Thee, Oh Arunachala!
>
> May Thou and I be one and inseparable like *Alagu* and *Sundara* [Maharshi's father and mother], Oh Arunachala!
>
> Entering (my) home and luring me [...] why didst Thou keep me prisoner in Thy heart's cavern, Oh Arunachala?
>
> Was it for Thy pleasure or for My sake Thou didst win me? If now Thou turn me away, the world will blame Thee, Oh Arunachala!
>
> Escape this blame! Why didst Thou then recall Thyself to me? How can I leave Thee now, Oh Arunachala?
>
> Kinder far art Thou than one's own mother. Is this then thy All-kindness, Oh Arunachala?
>
> Kinder indeed art Thou than one's own mother, such is Thy Love, Oh Arunachala!
>
> Sit firmly in my mind lest it elude Thee, Oh Arunachala!
>
> Change not Thy nature and flee, but hold fast in my mind, Oh Arunachala!
>
> Be watchful in my mind least it change even Thee [...] and rush away, Oh Arunachala!
>
> Display Thy beauty for the fickle mind to see Thee for ever and to rest [...] Oh Arunachala! (Maharshi, 1959, pp. 52–53)

These verses are prayers to the hill of Arunachala that is also Shiva incarnate and the divine self made manifest. In the passion of this and other invocations we find Maharshi fully participating in the mystery of the unfolding universe, just as when he is asked questions he is equally fully present and yet he is not there.. This state of "I am that I am" and pure *sahaja* or spontaneity, which is active, precise, and appropriate to the conditions of the moment brings him into full relationship with whatever arises before him hence the passion of his prayers and hymns, but at the next moment returns into the stillness and zero state that is the essence of the holy hill.

This summoning divine self or magnetic holy hill that calls us home is, for Maharshi, the same being that Crowley gave the name of the Holy Guardian Angel.

What is also interesting, in both Crowley's and Maharshi's approach, is that on achieving union with the reality that is represented by the Holy Guardian Angel or the divine self, the next thing that emerges is a spontaneous activity arising out of *sahaja samadhi*, or the prismatic activity of Daath, as the single point manifests vector and shaping and creates space-time. In both Maharshi's formulation and the Naples arrangement of the Tree of Life there is no obstacle to the unfolding and enfolding of the divine source. The Thou that is present when I and me and mine dissolve manifests in space and time, matter and motion, and the negation of all these.

The living image of the Holy Guardian Angel functions as a connecting point to our deepest self which Maharshi describes as:

> I am that in which the whole universe from *Prakirti* [the divine mother] down to gross matter appears as a mere shadow, that which is the substratum, which illumines all, which is the Self of all, is of all forms, is all pervasive and yet distinct from all, that which is all void, which is distinct without any of the attributes of Maya, that which is scarcely to be known by the gross intellect, which is ether itself, which has neither beginning nor end, which is subtle, motionless, formless, inactive, immutable, that pure Brahman in its natural state, unbroken, eternal, true, aware, endless, self-subsistent Bliss, non-dual Brahman. (Maharshi, 1959, p. 168)

This living image and companion acts as a strange attractor, directing us into circumstances that enable the direct realisation of the divine self, creating methods of communication between the surface self and the Self, which gradually but inexorably enables the apotheosis of the sense of separated selfhood. In Maharshi's case the holy mountain Arunachala, which is the incarnation of Shiva, summons him from his family home while only fifteen and becomes the place where he completes his realisation.

Crowley's Holy Guardian Angel, who reveals *The Book of the Law*, has the name of "Aiwass", and is described as the minister of Hoor Paar Kraat—the silent self—and similarly guides him through his spiritual journey and a process of unveiling the star at the heart of his being. Aiwass points Crowley into the heart of Egyptian tradition, much as Maharshi is pointed into the heart of Vedanta. A Hebrew rendition of "Aiswass" (עיוז) gives us a sense of his symbolic nature: ע (*ayin*), "the eye"; י (*yod*), "the hand and creative will"; ו (*vav*), "the nail", which joins ז (*zain*), "the sword" that splits and divides. The unity of will and perception, creation and destruction, describes a process of dynamic, creative witnessing that is the generative activity of the star at the heart of our being. The three chapters of *The Book of the Law* take us through the details of this process as we move from the Neophyte (man or woman of earth) to being the Adept (lover) before emerging as the Magister (hermit) who embraces all. It brings us also back into the heart of *The Book of Gates* as we take our place in the sun barque as "the meat of Ra" and through working with *heka* (will) and *sia* (perception) bring creative light into dark places, find balance, return to the beginnings of the pool of life, defeat the seven enemies, and bring the new day into being.

For my teacher Tom Oloman, the angel presented itself in the form of a hooded white monk with a face like a shining mirror who taught him the practice of face beholds face and the mediation of the lamp of darkness. It took him through a process of contemplating the mystery of the icon and the idol, as represented by the tarot trumps the Devil and the Lovers, and the unity and the multiplicity as shown in the Fool and the World.

In Tom's, Crowley's and Maharshi's cases, the path of enquiry and prayer creates an inward movement that stills the internal dialogue, which is the mind's making of a self, and brings us into a continuity of awareness that dissolves the walls of primal ignorance so that we enter the union of Hadit and Nuit and become *jivanmukta*.

# CHAPTER 11

# The Way of the Tao and the True Will

Simon Iff describes the deeper practice of magick as "the Way of the Tao" (Crowley, 1929, p. 64), and one of the more interesting innovations that Crowley brings into the Qabalah is the insight and view of Taoism. He made a translation of both the *Tao Te Ching* and the *I Ching*, and he used the *I Ching* as his principal divination method. Tom Oloman also studied the *I Ching* in depth and felt that it gave him a deeper understanding of the flow of life. For me, both the *I Ching* and the *Tao Te Ching* have been important as an adjunct to the practice of Qabalah and have gained in importance as my understanding has deepened. This is true also of the practice of tai chi, which I see as a sacred ritual that holds the whole of the way within it.

The title *Tao Te Ching* can be translated as "the classic of the way of virtue" where *tao* is "way" or "road". *Te* means "the sense of potency" or "emerging energy", and *ching* means a classical work that reveals truth. The title suggests that the book can be trusted to reveal the path of emergent life, which we could also describe as the emergence of the true will. Red Pine, in the introduction to his translation of the *Tao Te Ching* (Pine, 2009) says, "The Tao Te Ching is at heart a simple book. Written at the end of the sixth century BC by a man called Lao Tzu, it is a vision of what our lives would be like if we were more like the dark, new moon"

(Pine, 2009, p. ix). The Chinese word for *tao* is formed from two graphic signs: the sign for "head" and the sign "to go". Pine suggests that the "head" sign relates to the face of the moon, and "to go" suggests watching the face of the moon as it travels its waxing and waning way across the sky. The image of the night sky, moonlight, and waxing and waning perfectly captures the spirit of both the *Tao Te Ching* and the *I Ching* and the sense of the mysterious Way where to go forward is to go back, and to advance is to stay still.

In Crowley's translation, the book begins with the statement:

> The Tao-Path is not the All-Tao. The Name is not the Thing Named.
>     Unmanifested, it is the secret Father of [Heaven and Earth]; manifested, it is their Mother.
>     To understand this Mystery, one must be fulfilling one's will, and if one is not thus free, one will but gain a smattering of it.
>     The Tao is one, and the Te but a phase thereof. The abyss of this Mystery is the Portal of Serpent-Wonder. (Crowley, 1995, pp. 15–16)

This verse is designed to be deeply contemplated and begins by deconstructing the conventional translation of the word "Tao", which is normally translated as "path" or "way". We are presented with the sense of the unmanifest and the manifest, and the secret Father and Mother. We are told that to enter the mystery we must be in alignment with our true will and are then invited to contemplate the unity of the Tao and the quality of *te*, which is normally translated as "virtue" but, perhaps more accurately, can be thought of as "power" or "living energy". As we contemplate the interplay of Tao and *te* we enter into the place he calls "the Portal of Serpent-Wonder", which might remind us of the serpents of *The Book of Gates* and the fiery energy of life.

Crowley's *Tao Te Ching* goes on to tell us:

> The Teh [Te] is the immortal energy of the Tao, its feminine aspect. Heaven and Earth issued from her Gate; this Gate is the Root of their World-Sycamore. Its operation is of pure Joy and Love, and faileth never. (Crowley, 1995, p. 21)

Here we enter into the feminine creative energy that that arises from the gate of the non-dual. This is the energy of Binah on the Tree of Life, the form-building principle, and here we are shown the way in which this energy of creation generates duality. We are invited to trust this energy and to unify with love and joy.

Crowley went on to make explicit links between the Tao, the *I Ching*, and the Tree of Life, as we can see below. The *I Ching* is an oracle system concerned with the emergence of appearance out of mystery as a series of interacting opposites that begin with the principles of *yin* and *yang*. Conventionally these are described as female and male but, if we go back to their root, they represent the bright side of a mountain and the side that is in shade—i.e. they indicate a continuum of relationship and a dynamic of connection. This is indicated in the glyph of the ying–yang symbol:

It has become ubiquitous in spiritual circles but, if we spend a moment or two just looking at this image, we will see that it is always in motion and always in relationship. The *I Ching* is a way of considering this constant movement and the paradox of love and will as a field of union and separation.

In the *I Ching* the bright principle is called *yang* and represented by an unbroken line, while the shady principle is called *yin* and represented by a broken line. Crowley represented the sense of the Tao itself as a simple dot, which is aligned to Kether, the yang principle to Chockmah, and the yin principle to Binah.

The *I Ching* develops its understanding of the process of change by grouping the yang and yin principles in arrangements of three, called "trigrams", and Crowley links these trigrams to the rest of the Tree of Life so that the three unbroken lines of the heaven trigram are found in Daath, while the three broken lines of the earth trigram are in Malkuth. If we consider the diagram below, we will see in the arrangement of the trigrams polarities between the sephiroth indicated. We may notice that the trigram for Tiphareth, which represents fire, is the mirror-image of the trigram for Yesod, which represents the watery abyss, and that thunder trigram of Geburah is the mirror of the wind trigram of Hod, while the lake trigram of Gedulah is the mirror of the mountain of Netzach. If we contemplate the trigrams as particular expressions of yin and yang we will start to understand both the trigrams and the sephiroth more deeply. If, for example, we consider Netzach and the mountain trigram, which is composed of a yang line on top of two yin lines, it gives us the image of brightness or fire arising out of shady earth, and might remind us of a volcano; or, if we consider Hod and the wind trigram, composed of two yang lines above a yin line, we might consider the image of a plant with luxuriant foliage and flowers, and a hidden, invisible root. Similarly, in Geburah, the trigram gives us two yin lines on top of a yang line and may conjure the sense of dark clouds with concealed lightning; while in Gedulah we have two yang lines covered by a yin line, which gives us a sense of the riches of Gedulah manifesting through the irrigation of sweet water. Tiphareth's trigram gives us the sense of the yang lines balanced with a central core of yin, while Yesod's trigram gives us the opposite.

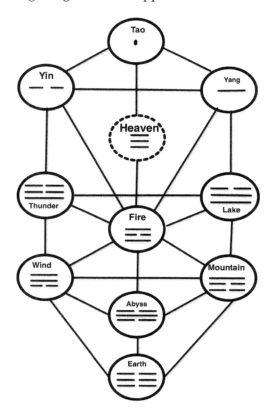

The *I Ching* combines these trigrams into sixty-four "hexagrams", which are generated through an oracular process using yarrow stalks or coin tosses. The hexagram is built up from the bottom. Each yang or yin line can be simply itself or can be a "moving line" that transforms into its opposite. For example, a hexagram of six yang lines, which is the hexagram for Creativity and Heaven:

Then becomes the hexagram for Coming to Meet, if the bottom line is a moving line, thus:

This indicates the shift of one creative cycle as a new yin element emerges at the base of the creative cycle—the possible emergence of a new idea, or just simply the exhaustion of the impulse and the need to turn inwards into the shady stillness.

There are a vast number of possible combinations that emerge through the process of the fixed and moving lines, but each hexagram resolves back first into its component trigrams, then into the principles of yang and yin, and finally into the simplicity of the ying–yang dot of the Tao. The contemplation of the *Tao Te Ching* and the *I Ching* give us access to this unfolding mystery reached through the experience of unknowing and through witnessing and contemplation of that which is not clear. It is a following of a process that waxes and wanes, is shining and dark, which cannot be named, and yet gives birth to all that is named. Both texts give us images and paradoxical suggestions that encourage us to cooperate with what emerges from the mysterious gateway so that we may serve and tend to that which emerges.

We see this process of contemplation in Crowley's translation of Chapter XIV:

> We look at it, and see it not; though it is Omnipresent; and we name it the Root-Balance. [Hadit, the root of ׳ (*yod*).]
>
> We listen for it, and hear it not, though it is Omniscient; and we name it the Silence. [Nuit, the root of ה (*heh*).]
>
> We feel for it, and touch it not, though it is Omnipotent; and we name it the Concealed. [Ra Hoor Khuit, the root of ו (*vav*).]
>
> These three Virtues hath it, yet we cannot describe it as consisting of them; but, mingling them aright, we apprehend the One.
>
> Above, it shineth not; below, it is not dark. It moveth all continuously, without Expression, returning into Naught. It is the Form of That which is beyond Form; it is the Image of the Invisible; it is Change, and Without Limit.
>
> We confront it, and see not its Face; we pursue it, and its Back is hidden from us. Ah! but apply the Tao as in old Time to the work of the present; know it as it was known in the Beginning; follow fervently the Thread of the Tao. (Crowley, 1995, p. 29)

Here we see Crowley making explicit links with the with the principles of *The Book of the Law* and the figures of Hadit, Nuit, and Ra Hoor Khuit, and the letters of the divine name יהוה and we are invited to contemplate:

- Looking, omnipresence, the single point of Hadit, the root-balance, and the letter ׳ (*yod*).
- Listening, omniscience, the infinity of Nuit, silence, and the letter ה (*heh*).
- Touching, omnipotence, the manifestation of Ra Hoor Khuit, concealment, and the letter ו (*vav*).

He tells us that if we unite these ideas or images, as we bring together looking, listening, and touching, we will discover the One in movement, revealing limitlessness and change, and that we will know as it was known in the beginning. As we connect to origins we then follow the unfolding and unspooling thread of the universe, being in this moment the living expression of the interplay of Nuit, Hadit, and Ra Hoor Khuit, and the unity of יהו expressing itself as ה.

To connect with this source we must learn to see, hear, and touch in a particular way, relating to what is normally called dimness, faintness, or subtlety which, if we allow the sense of perception to remain open, unite into a oneness. The process of mingling the senses of touching, hearing, and seeing brings us fully into the present moment, disrupts the internal dialogue, and enables participation with the unfolding way as it waxes and wanes, rises and sets, meeting the new and following the thread. In this way we attend fully to the present, while remaining connected to the origin.

This way of the Tao shows us the true will in action. In Appendix III of *Magick*, Crowley tells us: "Do what thou wilt is to bid Stars to shine, Vines to bear grapes, Water to seek its own level" (Crowley, 1989, p. 352). It is this quality we see in Simon Iff, who is, for most of the book, a background presence, his profound magick imperceptible and subtle. When he deals with the Thing in the Garden it is a consummate example of love under will as he creates connection with it and through it to Douglas and, through affirming the statement, "Do what thou wilt shall be the whole of the Law [...] Love is the law, love under will" (I: 40; I: 57) offers to Douglas the possibility of his own unveiling and alignment with his light, love, and truth. Douglas's rejection of this and affirmation of separation undoes his own plans without any need for action from Simon.

A key aspect of this emergence of the particular will and magick that operates through us is shown by the Taoist sage, Chuang Tzu, in his parable of "the useless tree". He talks of a master carpenter and his apprentice who are walking past the shrine of a village with a vast oak tree growing beside it.

> "Since I first took up my ax and followed you, Master, I have never seen timber as beautiful as this. But you don't even bother to look, and go right on without stopping. Why is that?"
>
> "Forget it—say no more!" said the carpenter. "It's a worthless tree! Make boats out of it and they'd sink; make coffins and they'd rot in no time; make vessels and they'd break at once. Use it for doors and it would sweat sap like pine; use it for posts and the worms would eat them up. It's not a timber tree—there's nothing it can be used for. That's how it got to be that old!" (Watson, 1964, p. 60)

Later the oak appears to him in his dreams:

> What are you comparing me with? Are you comparing me with those useful trees? The cherry apple, the pear, the orange, the citron,

the rest of those fructiferous trees and shrubs—as soon as their fruit is ripe, they are torn apart and subjected to abuse. Their big limbs are broken off, their little limbs are yanked around. Their utility makes life miserable for them, and so they don't get to finish out the years Heaven gave them, but are cut off in mid-journey. They bring it on themselves—the pulling and tearing of the common mob. And it's the same way with all other things.

As for me, I've been trying a long time to be of no use, and though I almost died, I've finally got it. This is of great use to me. If I had been of some use, would I ever have grown this large? [...] (Watson, 1964, pp. 60–61)

As we saw earlier, this is remarkably similar to an image used in the Ancient Egyptian teachings of Amenomope where the Geru Maa is seen as a tree that gives shelter and shade and does not end up in the woodshop with more useful trees. To be useless is to be a subject, not an object. In both the Taoist and Egyptian examples, the tree that we are is simply itself and the shade and fruit it gives comes from its being free to grow according to the needs of its nature. The practice of magick, according to this principle, locates it as an art of deep subjectivity that arises from the star of our being and unfolds the way before us.

Chapter XV in Crowley's translation of the *Tao Te Ching* gives us an understanding of how to work with this unfolding:

The adepts of past ages were subtle and keen to apprehend this Mystery, and their profundity was obscurity unto men. Since then they were not known, let me declare their nature.

To all seeming, they were fearful as men that cross a torrent in winter flood; they were hesitating like a man in apprehension of them that are about him; they were full of awe like a guest in a great house; they were ready to disappear like ice in thaw; they were unassuming like unworked wood; they were empty as a valley; and dull as the waters of a marsh.

Who can clear muddy water? Stillness will accomplish this. Who can obtain rest? Let motion continue equably, and it will itself be peace.

The adepts of the Tao, conserving its way, seek not to be actively self-conscious. By their emptiness of Self they have no need to show their youth and perfection; to appear old and imperfect is their privilege. (Crowley, 1995, p. 30)

The above verses show the way a follower of the way of the Tao would work: at the heart of this is the sense of presence and awareness that is not swept away by the torrents of life; that treats all experiences with the awe and reverence of being a guest in a great house; that dissolves frozenness and continually enters the flow; to be as unworked wood, to allow life to emerge in whatever way it should; to be empty and dull allows space for that emergence and to be old and imperfect is to honour the particular nature of our own form, as Chuan Tzu shows us in the image of the sacred, useless oak.

In Chapter XXII, he shows us the working-out of this unfolding:

> The part becometh the whole. The curve becometh straight; the void becometh full; the old becometh new. He who desireth little accomplisheth his Will with ease; who desireth many things becomes distracted.
>
> Therefore the sage concentrateth upon one Will, and it is as a light to the whole world. Hiding himself he shineth; withdrawing himself, he attracteth notice, humbling himself he is exalted; dissatisfied with himself, he gaineth force to achieve his Will. Because he striveth not, no man may contend against him.
>
> That is no idle saw of the men of old, "The part becometh the whole;" it is the Canon of Perfection. (Crowley, 1995, p. 37)

He shows us here the paradoxical nature of the unfolding of the Tao which is founded on the principle of the part becoming the whole-here we are participating in a profoundly interconnected, fractal universe that is continually in movement so that curves straighten, the old is made new and our task is simply to attend to the unfolding of the true will within us which operates through us as the union of Nuit, Hadit and Ra Hoor Khuit or the interplay of יהו continually manifesting as ה as a field of contemplation which returns us to the beginning even as the manifest brings us back to the concealed.

In Chapter XVIII, which he calls "The Return to Simplicity", he gives as the image of the child.

> Balance thy male strength with thy female weakness and thou shall attract all things, as the ocean absorbeth all rivers; for thou shall formulate the excellence of the Child eternal, simple, and perfect.
>
> Knowing the Light, remain in the Dark. Manifest not thy Glory, but thine obscurity. Clothed in this Child-excellence eternal, thou

hast attained the Return of the First State. Knowing splendour of Fame, cling to Obloquy and Infamy; then thou shalt remain as in the Valley to which flow all waters, the lodestone to fascinate all men. Yea, they shall hail in thee this Excellence, eternal, simple and perfect, of the Child.

The raw material, wrought into form, produceth vessels. So the sage king formulateth his Wholeness in divers Offices; and his Law is without violence or constraint. (Crowley, 1995, p. 43)

Here we are given the image of the crowned and conquering child, conquering not by violence and constraint but through simplicity and the emergence of the manyness from the oneness.

In Chapter LII, "The Withdrawal into the Silence", he brings us back to the interplay of Hadit, Nuit, and Ra Hoor Khuit:

The Tao buddeth forth all things under Heaven; it is the Mother of all.

Knowing the Mother, we may know her offspring. He that knoweth his Mother, and abideth in her nature, remaineth in surety all his days.

With the mouth closed, and the Gates of Breath controlled, he remaineth at ease all his days. With the mouth open, and the Breath directed to outward affairs, he hath no surety all his days.

To perceive that Minute Point is True Vision; to maintain the Soft and Gentle is True Strength.

Employing harmoniously the Light Within so that it returneth to its Origin, one guardeth even one's body from evil, and keepeth Silence before all men. (Crowley, 1995, p. 70)

Crowley identifies the "Minute Point" with Hadit, "the Soft and Gentle" with Nuit, and "the Light Within" with Ra Hoor Khuit (Crowley, 1995, p. 70), much as he links them with the letters of the divine name יהוה earlier, and shows us how to work with all three principles in unity so that we are one with the Tao and one with all that arises from this unfolding way.

# CHAPTER 12

# Moonchild Revisited: The Art of Deep Magick

C rowley's novel *Moonchild* (1929) is (when read closely) a clear and powerful account of the practice of deep magick and of contrasting the way of the Tao with a dualistic magick based on I, me, and mine. It is concerned with the relationship between the sephiroth Yesod and Daath. Yesod is the moon sphere, the gateway into the psyche and the place of the imagination. Daath, by contrast, is the gateway into the non-dual spirit and the creation of duality itself—it is the prism that is the icon of icons through which the united energies of *abba* and *imma*, or will and love, generate space, time, and all that lives within them. Yesod is the reflection of Daath in the universe of I, me, and mine We discover at the end of the book that while we have been closely following the process of Cyril and Lisa there has been another, parallel operation, involving Sister Cybele on Iona under the supervision of a mysterious figure called "Himself" who is the Head of the Order. We hear almost nothing about this operation except that the word for its completion is *Horatii*.

At one level, this book is about the creation of a magical child but, at a deeper level, is concerned with the practice of magick itself in that (from an inner point of view) human beings as the living image of the divine are continually creating life.

115

The book begins in London, takes us next to Paris, to the Profess-House of the magical order carrying out the operation, then to Naples, to the place called "the Butterfly Net" where the operation is carried out, and finally returns us to Paris where we learn the real operation has been happening in Iona. The plot is in some ways a simple one: it concerns the attempt to create a magical child, a "moonchild", that will be an avatar of the inner energies and will improve the lot of humanity. This operation is opposed by a group of magicians who are dedicated to evil and wish to disrupt it. There is a subplot in which the young magician, Cyril Grey, learns the practice of the deep magick of the Tao and is raised to a new level of initiation. The operation appears to end in failure as the mother of the moonchild runs away with a disciple of the Qliphothic Lodge, just before the birth, although, as mentioned above, we learn at the end that the whole operation has been a decoy for the true operation happening in Iona. Much of the book is taken up with the description of the magical dynamics of manifesting the moonchild and the war between the two lodges of light and darkness.

If we analyse the text Qabalistically, we can see that London and Paris are the outer world of Malkuth; the Butterfly Net in Naples is Yesod; the Profess-House is Tiphareth and Iona is Daath.

The book begins with a description of the heart of London, Charing Cross. We are given an image of the city extended in time and space in four directions. What is being hinted at here is the archetypal city that is both an image of the psyche and the universe. What we are next shown is a party given by the dancer Lavinia King for Lisa la Giuffria, a privileged and somewhat pampered world, and a party that has being going on for twenty-three hours. Lisa is the main, obvious protagonist of the novel, and is also symbolically an image of the conditioned aspect of our own soul, that which the Qabalists call *nephesch* or the "animal soul", centred in Yesod. This aspect of the soul is, like Lisa, passionate and reactive, responding to its environment and essentially unstable, but it is the foundation of our expression and must be engaged with by the deeper aspects of the soul if true transformation is to be possible. Into this birthday scene the figure of the magician Cyril Grey appears who is, first of all, fascinating to everyone but, shortly, is entirely forgotten about as he simply sits down on the floor and meditates in silence. Just before he leaves he is noticed and again becomes an object of fascination. What is being shown here is the inability to remain consistently present and the essential instability of the nephesch.

This is something we see in Lisa throughout the plot of the novel. She falls in love with Cyril and then has a meeting with him and Simon Iff in which Simon tells her that the root of her passion is the hunger for the soul. He goes on to teach her about the Holy Guardian Angel and the Taoist doctrine of non-action. Following this we are confronted with the first attack of the dark lodge: one of their disciples turns up with a medium and invites them to a séance with the intent of obtaining some of Lisa's blood.

Simon Iff later explains the principal difference between the magick of light and darkness:

> [L]et me tell you of a paradox in magick. Do you remember a certain chapter in the Bible which tells one, almost in consecutive verses, firstly to answer a fool according to his folly, and secondly, not so to answer him? This is the Scriptural version of a truth which we phrase otherwise. There are two ways of dealing with an opponent; one by beating him on his own ground, the other by withdrawing to a higher plane. You can fight fire with fire, or you can fight fire with water.
>
> It is, roughly speaking, legitimate magick to resolve a difficult situation in either of these two ways. Alter it, or withdraw to higher ground. The black magician, or as I prefer to call him, sorcerer, for the word magick should not be profaned, invariably withdraws to lower planes. Let us seek an analogy in the perfectly concrete case of the bank cashier.
>
> This gentleman, we will assume, finds his salary inadequate to his outgoings. Now he may economize, that is, withdraw himself to a kind of life where money is no longer needed in such quantity, or he may devote himself day and night to his business, and so increase his salary. But there is no third course open to a man of self-respect. The sorcerer type of man appeals to lower planes of money-making. He begins by gambling; beaten there, he resorts to the still viler means of embezzlement; perhaps, finally, he attempts to cover his thefts by murdering his mother for the insurance money.
>
> Notice how, as his plane becomes debased, his fears grow greater. At first, he is merely annoyed about his creditors; in the next stage, he fears being sharped by his fellow-gamblers; then, it is the police who loom terrible in his mind; and lastly the grim form of the executioner threatens him. (Crowley, 1929, pp. 244–245)

This principle of entering into a deeper plane of consciousness, as opposed to the descent into lower planes, we see playing out in the continued assaults of Douglas and his disciples. They all rely on what might be called "sympathetic magic", i.e. creating a physical or energetic connection between the physicality of the persons being worked on, in the first instance by using their blood, or giving them an object such as a coin charged with a particular energy, or sending food charged with toxic energy. There is also the use of intermediaries, as when Gates labels pigeons with the names of the occupants of the Butterfly Net (Crowley, 1929, p. 165), or the literal baptism of Douglas's wife with Lisa's name in the Grand Operation of Bewitchment (Crowley, 1929, p. 269).

This principle, while effective in its own terms, is a degradation of the profound interconnectedness we see in Crowley's Star-Sponge vision and is what Simon Iff means when he talks about the difference between sorcery and the way of the Tao (Crowley, 1929, pp. 247–249). This difference is further underlined when he shows Lisa the way in which higher dimensions penetrate lower dimensions using the analogy of the cone and the water (Crowley, 1929, pp. 60–61) and much more directly when he deals with the Thing in the Garden through the practice of the Tao (Crowley, 1929, p. 64).

Lisa is next taken to the Profess-House of the order in Paris and meets the key brothers and sisters of the Order; it is entered through a modest-looking house set back into the hill in Montmatre and leads to a much larger and secret place, accessed through a group of statues of Mercury guiding Hercules into Hades, just in front of an image of Charon the ferryman in his boat. They assemble in the boat, a coin is placed in the hand of the statue, and the wall slides back. The boat takes them into a great hall with a circular table representing Yesod, Hod, Netzach, Tiphareth, Geburah, and Gedulah, and a triangular table representing Kether, Chockmah, and Binah.

Lisa is then taken into a small chapel with a silver altar at its centre, surrounded by a copper circle with ten iron lamps set in it, where she keeps silent vigil and sees images of horror reflected in the altar top, including images of Cyril making love with Sister Cybele and a bestial orgy that challenges her passion for Cyril. This test of will and dedication is something we all must pass through time and time again as the hopes, fears, and idols of Yesod, arising out of I, me, and mine assault us.

Ironically her jealousy of Sister Cybele has a grounding in truth, for Sister Cybele is the woman at the centre of the operation Lisa is the decoy for.

Having survived the ordeal, she is accepted into the Order and she and Cyril travel to Naples, intending to take a train but, at the very last moment, Cyril takes her off the train and they travel by boat, for the train driver has been given an enchanted coin that causes him to derail.

They arrive at the Butterfly Net, which is to be the place of the apparent operation of the summoning of the moonchild: it is a castle, with terraces that can be reached only by crossing a bridge. On crossing the bridge they come to a square terrace of porphyry with a circular fountain in which stands a statue of Venus Callipyge in black marble. This statue shows the goddess looking behind her and raising her gown so that her buttocks can be seen. This image hints at the true operation in Iona, for the Black Venus is an image of Binah, porphyry is the royal stone, and looking behind the scenes and through the veil points us in the direction of the true operation. We are also shown here the uniting of the circle with the square and connecting to the fountain of life; this is amplified by Cyril telling Lisa that he has two brains and that he is constantly uniting ideas with their opposite, connecting the profound with the mundane (Crowley, 1929, pp. 134–135). He goes on to say that the true work of the imagination clothes being in form, and true images of the unseen function as icons, which enliven, while the conditioned imagination creates idols that dominate us. In this sentence he shows her the whole practice of magick and the moonchild operation.

Lisa then meets Brother Onofrio whose task it is to protect her and the moonchild on inner and outer levels, and Sister Clara who will be her teacher on the inner way. She is then shown to her chamber, which is decorated in blue, silver, and white, each object chosen to reflect the nature of the moon so that her consciousness will attune to it. They then go to the white marble moon terrace, containing a triangular altar of silver and a white basin from which spring water overflows in a series of rivulets. Lisa is renamed "Iliel"—a name of a moon angel—and she and Cyril enact the rite of Artemis and Pan, which begins the active phase of the operation. The next phase of the operation is a period of complete honeymoon in which she and Cyril are idyllically happy, followed by a period in which he withdraws, and in which a series of invocations and banishings ensures that a moon soul implants itself in Iliel. We are told that the soul is "Malkah of the tribe of the Sickles", who was the muse of the poet John Keats (Crowley, 1929, p. 231). As her pregnancy develops, Lisa becomes more and more bored and, to ease her boredom, enters the inner worlds through fantasy. She does this by entering a landscape very like the tarot card the Moon, but we are told that she enters under a waning moon (Crowley, 1929, p. 257), an indication that she is entering the dark side of the moon, which shows the inner worlds in Qliphothic form. She encounters an old woman who, we later learn, is Sister Clara: she has entered the inner worlds to look after Lisa and to teach her the nature of the astral, particularly as Lisa has entered through boredom and fantasy and therefore is experiencing the inner worlds in distorted form. There is an important moment in which Lisa sees how she is creating her own misery.

> [S]he knew, too, that these shapes were born of her own weaknesses; yet, so far from rousing herself to stamp them out in her mind, she gloated upon their monstrosity and misery, took pleasure in their anguish, which was her own, and fed them with the substance of her own personality and will. (Crowley, 1929, p. 262)

It is this commitment to the nature of her own fantasies that pushes her further into the dark side of the moon and that takes her to a distorted experience of the Star-Sponge vision, which she perceives as a Walpurgis Night witches sabbath, in which she at first sees Brother Onofrio and Sister Clara worshipping Cyril, who has taken the form of a Chinese god. She has encountered Sister Clara as an old woman and Brother Onofrio as a chubby clergyman in her visions, and to find them here, with her romantic image of Cyril as a Chinese god, gives her a strong sense of having been manipulated and betrayed. From this place she sees that she is in a web of connections: Cyril and his companions forming one triangle, but there are uncounted numbers of triangles, each with a god and pair of worshippers, all of which lead to a vast spider who devours all within the web (Crowley, 1929, p. 280). This takes her into a predatory sense of the universe and having been deceived by them all.

She then confronts Cyril and he takes her to a statue of Marsyas and Olympas. In mythology Marsyas is a satyr, a master of music, who teaches the youth Olympas the nature of music.

The Faun Marsyas Teaches Olympus to Play the Flute
(Pyotr Basin, 1821)

Crowley uses these figures in his long poem *AHA!* (Crowley, 2014) on the nature of magick, and it is as Marsyas, the teacher of magick, that Cyril shows Lisa how she is perceiving things through her own distortions (Crowley, 1929, p. 283) and tries to show her a different vision of the sabbath, quoting a poem:

> And where Light crosses Light, all loves combine:
>     Behold the God, the worshippers, the shrine,
> Each comprehensive of its single soul
>     Yet each the centre and fountain of the whole;
> Each one made perfect in its passionate part,
>     Each the circumference, and each the heart!
> Always the Three in One are interwoven,
>     Always the One in Three sublimely cloven … (Crowley, 1929,
> p. 285)

And:

> This is the Truth behind the lie called God;
>> This blots the heavens, and indwells the clod.
> This is the centre of all spheres, the flame
>> In men and stars, the Soul behind the name,
> The spring of Life, the axle of the Wheel,
>> All-mover, yet the One Thing immobile.
> Adore It not, for It adoreth thee,
>> The shadow-shape of Its eternity,
> Lift up thyself! be strong to burst thy bars!
>> For lo! thy stature shall surpass the stars. (Crowley, 1929, p. 286)

Here, Cyril presents Lisa with the sense of the true Star-Sponge vision and the theology of Thelema, which does not satisfy her and she continues in a disgruntled state until, with one of her customary shifts of moods, she decides she is fully in love with Cyril again and is the happiest woman in the world. This is just before—with the assistance of a woman called Cremers, a disciple of Douglas—she encounters the handsome young Turk, Abdul Bey, and runs away with him, leaving Cyril and the moonchild operation behind.

This final successful attempt on Lisa by the Black Lodge has been preceded by a series of attacks, beginning with the grimoire-wielding but hapless Arthwait, who initially sends them shellfish charged with the energy of Mars (Crowley, 1929, p. 160), intended to stir up division. In an echo of Simon Iff's absorption of the Thing in the Garden, Brother Onofrio eats them and sends the martial energy back to Arthwait, giving him terrible indigestion. This is followed by a more successful attack from Gates, who is more advanced than Arthwait. He obtains pigeons from inside the Butterfly Net and gives them the names of the occupants. By sympathetic magic he creates division in the group. Brother Onofrio, through tarot divination, discovers the source of the attack and performs a rite of Mars that casts Gates down from the high place he is conducting his operation from (Crowley, 1929, p. 170). A much more significant attack is then made through the involvement of the necromancer Vesquit who, together with Arthwait and Abdul Bey, uses the corpse of Gates and a goat to summon a demon to attack the Butterfly Net (Crowley, 1929, p. 203). Abdul is possessed by the spirit of Gates who tells them to abandon the direct attack and that Hecate shall help them. The operation is defeated by Brother Onofrio who appears in the form of the child god, Hoor Paar Kraat. The encounter with Brother Onofrio as Hoor Paar Kraat causes Vesquit to realise that he has wasted his life and, in an act of self-sacrifice, he invokes the return of the current and dies (Crowley, 1929, p. 209).

The oracle that Abdul receives from the spirit of Gates leads the Black Lodge to their Grand Operation of Bewitchment in which they involve Balloch, a priest of Hecate, and Butcher, a defrocked Catholic priest, and Douglas himself. Here, Douglas's pregnant wife and Abdul are baptised by Butcher in the names of Lisa and her husband, and then married through sympathetic magick. Balloch invokes the goddess Hecate to send a moon demon, called Namah, who is the devourer of children into Douglas's wife's womb to abort the child, so that by sympathetic resonance the same will happen to Lisa. Douglas makes the magical link between his child and Lisa's while pronouncing this curse:

> "Hecate, mother only of death, devourer of all life!" cried Douglas, in his final adjuration; "as I devote to thy chill tooth this secret spring of man, so be it with all that are like unto it! Even as it is with that which I shall cast upon thine altar, so be it with all the offspring of Lisa la Giuffria!" (Crowley, 1929, pp. 274–275)

However, the ritual comes to nothing because just as the child is torn from her womb and she is dying, Douglas's wife tells him that she loves him, and the invocation of love undoes the whole energy of the working. Ironically, the success of the Black Lodge's work comes about through Cremers pretending to be a poor old lady who falls over and needs help, just outside the Butterfly Net, Lisa leaving the premises and being introduced to Abdul Bey and her unstable and passionate nature does the rest (Crowley, 1929, p. 296).

It is at this point that we learn that this whole process has been a decoy for a deeper operation which links to a key subtext of the novel, concerning both the development of Cyril Grey and the creation of a new world.

This subtext is his journey from being the Yesodic magician to mastering the way of the Tao; becoming "Simple Simon" (Crowley, 1929, p. 154) and along the way discovering his identity with Douglas, the black magician, and thus with all living things. We are told that the whole moonchild operation was a blind as the true magical operation was coming into being on the island of Iona under the supervision of

"Himself", the Head of the Order that Cyril and Simon Iff belong to. Cyril learns that the operation has been a success through the code phrase "Horatii" (Crowley, 1929, p. 298), which lets him know that three boys have been born to Sister Cybele. We are also told that Simon Iff has been engaged in "the Quest of the Golden Fleece" and "sowing the Dragon's Teeth" (Crowley, 1929, p. 298)—a work of chaos and destruction that prepares the way for a new aeon to arise. These hints remind us that this story should not be taken literally and that it is something altogether stranger and deeper.

The clue to the deeper operation is given in that it happens on the sacred island of Iona, under the supervision of the Head of the Order who has the grade of Ipsissimus and has completed the Great Work. The mother is Sister Cybele, an Adept of the Order, and her name combined with the code word "Horatii" is a clue to the deeper meaning of the book. The word refers to the legendary beginning of the Roman Republic when the city of Rome was at war with the city of Alba. It was agreed that the war would be settled by a battle between the three sons of the Horatii family, representing Rome, and the three sons of the Curatii family, representing Alba. In the battle, two of the Horatii die and the surviving warrior kills the three Curatii. In Roman history there is another reference to three warriors who defend Rome: they are led by Horatius and defend the bridge against the attacking Etruscans; his companions are killed and Horatius defends the bridge alone, saving the Republic.

There is a famous eighteenth-century painting of the Horatii by Jacques-Louis David, "The Oath of the Horatii", which would also have been in Crowley's mind when he made the reference.

The picture shows the Horatii, on the left, vowing to their father that they will defend Rome with their lives. We can notice that the brothers move as one as they make their vows, and their arms are clasped around each other, and their father holds their swords together, reinforcing the three-in-one motif. On the right, there are sorrowing women who know that whatever happens there will be bloodshed and war.

Cybele is a goddess of Asia Minor whose cult became prominent in Rome and was called *Magna Mater*, "the Great Mother". If we combine all this with Simon Iff's reference to the Quest of the Golden Fleece and sowing the Dragon's teeth, we discover we are amongst the dynamics of the supernal sephiroth and the creation of a new universe through the practice of deep magick. The sense of a new universe is paralleled

by Cyril Grey recognising his identity with Douglas, the black magi-cian, and hence with all beings, and becoming the true magician rather than the ape of Thoth.

Simon Iff comments that the weak point in the operation has always been Lisa's instability (Crowley, 1929, p. 297), and then Cyril reveals the deeper operation involving the Horatii. It is then that we learn that Simon Iff has been involved in a magical operation designed to bring about the new aeon, which he refers to as "sowing the Dragon's teeth".

The scene then changes to Paris and the Great War. Cyril becomes a staff officer and advises the allies on strategy. The moonchild has been born and given to Cremers, who has taken her away. Lisa and Abdul turn up in Paris and have tired of each other. Lisa, having heard that Cyril is in Paris, has a fantasy of reconciliation in which she imagines Cyril wounded and herself as the devoted nurse who brings him back to life (Crowley, 1929, p. 318).

The key encounter in this ending of the novel is between Douglas and Cyril; Douglas has become a French officer and Cyril first encoun-ters him with a young woman who he is corrupting. Cyril reminds

Douglas of the fate of the demonologist Anthony of Prague who was torn apart by wild dogs (Crowley, 1929, p. 312). Later he discovers that Douglas has been executed for espionage and he comes across his body:

> A fatal curiosity drew him to the spot; as he approached, the wild dogs that were fighting around the sinister signal fled in terror from their ghastly meal. A sword had been thrust through the belly of the corpse; the tongue had been torn out. One could recognize at a glance the work of Algerian troops—men who had lost a third of their effectives through the treacheries of the German spies. But, despite all mutilation, he recognized more than that: he recognized the carcass. This carrion had once been Douglas.
>
> Cyril Grey did a strange thing, a thing he had not done for many years: he broke into a strong sobbing.
>
> "I know now," he murmured, "that Simon Iff is right. The Way of the Tao! I must follow that harder path, the Path where he who would advance draws back. (Crowley, 1929, p. 332)

He then encounters Lisa, who confesses all and asks to be taken back, but he tells her that her task is to rescue the moonchild from Cremers and look after her. Cyril returns to the Profess-House of the Order where he encounters Simon Iff, Sister Cybele, and Mahathera Phang. We discover that by realising his identity with the corpse of Douglas he has realised his identity with all living things, and has been raised to high Adeptship and will now go into retreat to stabilise his experiences by undertaking the Buddhist meditation of the corpse torn apart by wild animals.

If we place the main participants on the Tree of Life some interesting features emerge. The safely-delivered moonchild is the end of the operation, so we see her in Malkuth, while Lisa is in Yesod, the sphere of the foundation. Placing Cyril in Hod, the sphere of the mind, might seem an odd choice as he is Lisa's lover but, if we consider his main role in relation to her, he is the magician and teacher. The figure who represents the energy of the lover is Abdul Bey, who is besotted with Lisa and is an ambiguous figure—a disciple of the Black Lodge but, in keeping with the sleight of hand that is continually going on in this working, we learn that he is known to Simon Iff and at the conclusion of the book joins the White Lodge. One of the key qualities of Abdul is to follow his will, wherever it takes him, and this that makes him a candidate for the Lodge of Light.

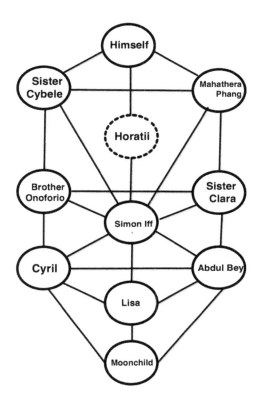

Simon Iff is the centre point of the work. Although not apparently active he is the silent, witnessing presence who intervenes at key points, such as the initial teaching of Lisa, and dealing with the Thing in the Garden by absorbing it, which then gives him a direct connection with Douglas.

The Geburic figure is, of course, Brother Onofrio, who embodies the energy of Mars and is the guardian and protector of the energy sphere of the Butterfly Net. The Gedulah energy of mercy and love is represented by Sister Clara, who looks after Lisa on both outer and inner levels, appearing as the Old Woman who teaches Lisa the nature of the astral plane. The supernal levels of the tree are shown by the operation on Iona, in which the mysterious figure, "Himself", the Head of the Lodge of Light is found in Kether; Sister Cybele, the mother of the true operation is in Binah; and Mahathera Phang, the silent monk, sits in Chockmah. The result of this operation in Daath is the male triplets, the Horatii, of whom we know nothing except that they represent the three-in-one will of the supernals and are connected with collective transformation.

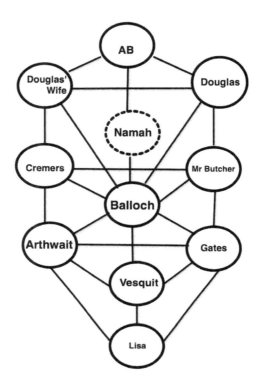

The dynamics of the Black Lodge are all concerned with influencing Lisa and breaking up the operation. At the head of the Lodge is AB who, like Douglas, is said to hold the degree of Thaumiel-Qeteriel: Thaumiel, in the Qabalah, is the distorted image of Kether, represented as two quarrelling heads, the principle of eternal duality rather than the deep connection of the Star-Sponge vision; while Qeteriel is a literal mis-speaking of "Kether". Douglas is the active will and, thus, the Magus in Chockmah, yet, as Simon Iff has pointed out (Crowley, 1929, pp. 155–156), in his refusal of love Douglas's energies are fatally divided, and this we see in the figure of his wife who, through her love, destroys the Operation of Grand Bewitchment (Crowley, 1929, p. 275). This operation is shown in the middle triangle of the tree with Balloch in Tiphareth, Butcher in Gedulah, and Cremers in Geburah. The lesser operations are shown in the lower triangle, with the work of Gates in Netzach, Arthwait in Hod, and Vesquit in Yesod. Malkuth here is Lisa herself as object rather than subject. If we align the two trees we may find some interesting correlations.

Considering this from an inner point of view, some interesting points emerge. The moonchild in Malkuth represents the embodiment of the true will in the outer world, and Lisa the moony qualities of Yesod within us, our imagination and our sense of self and universe as understood by our nephesch or animal soul. This is fluid, responsive, and inherently unstable, and we see in the course of the book Lisa at times passionately involved with Cyril and the work, but at other times very bored. Boredom is the experience that undermines her will and commitment to the operation and the art of magick for it is from boredom that ultimately she abandons the operation and runs off with Abdul. This is an aspect of our nature that we continually have to work with in order for our magical operations and, indeed, our lives to be successful.

If we consider Lisa's journey on the Tree of Life we will see this more clearly:

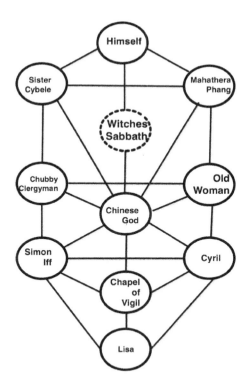

Initially, we see Lisa intrigued by the teachings of Simon Iff and in love with Cyril and the romance of the operation, but one of the key problems here is that she is not relating to the deeper aspects of her own soul; rather, she is relating to the image Cyril as "My Chinese God" (Crowley, 1929, p. 19) who ravishes and excites, and so she is vulnerable to the pushes and pulls of her desires. There is a crucial moment (Crowley, 1929, pp. 142–143) in which Cyril tells her that the key to the operation is in maintaining her oath, no matter what the circumstances, and it is this that she abandons when she leaves the Butterfly Net and runs off with Abdul, and which leads to her inner experiences being distorted, so that in place of the direct experience of the Holy Guardian Angel, and the qualities of love and will, she experiences the "Chinese God", chubby clergyman, and the old woman and the witches sabbath. This also obscures her perception of the Star-Sponge vision, which would have led to her sense of herself as one with Sister Cybele, partaking of the silence of the Mahathera Phang and, in the end, knowing herself as herself. What is being described here is a Yesodic version of the ascent of the tree where we are increasingly exposed to fantasy and disturbance, leading to the vision of a predatory universe. At this point, we either fall into the abyss or (like Abdul Bey and Lisa at the end of the book) we must begin again.

If, however, the oath is kept then what happens is this:

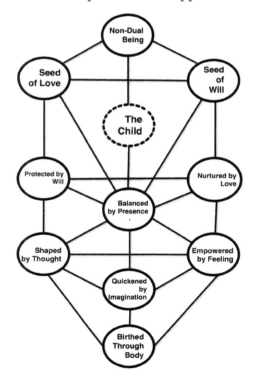

We might notice that this is very similar to Crowley's Naples arrange-ment, in the sense of the single point of non-dual being manifesting the line or the seed of will, and the shaping seed of love manifesting the surface, then space, time, and reflective presence, etc. for it is this pattern that underlies the moonchild operation and, if we consider the novel with this in mind, we will understand much.

# PRACTISING THE WAY—THE WORK OF THE ADEPT

Having established our awareness in Tiphareth we next proceed to the practice of magick and mastering the processes of banishing and invoking. From there we work with uniting love and will and through the central practice of the Mass of the Holy Ghost enable the full expression of that creative will which Crowley demonstrates in the Moonchild operation.

# CHAPTER 13

# Quantum Creativity

As we approach the practice of deep magick, let us return again to this key verse from *The Book of the Heart Girt with the Serpent*:

> I, and Me, and Mine were sitting with lutes in the market-place
> of the great city, the city of the violets and the roses.
> The night fell, and the music of the lutes was stilled.
> The tempest arose, and the music of the lutes was stilled.
> The hour passed, and the music of the lutes was stilled.
> But Thou art Eternity and Space; Thou art Matter and Motion;
> and Thou art the negation of all these things.
> For there is no symbol of Thee. (3: 21–26) (Crowley, 2015, p. 111)

And this from *The Book of the Law*:

> Every man and every woman is a star. (I: 3)
> Do what thou wilt shall be the whole of the Law. (I: 40)
> Love is the law, love under will. (I: 57)

These three quotations are at the centre of the practice of this way, because as we recall that it is our nature to be a generative star and allow the expression of the union of love and will in each moment, all complexity falls away and, like Simon Iff, we are still until we are moved, centred in the singularity at our heart that opens us to the infinite field of stars. Increasingly, as we free ourselves from bondage, we enter into communion with that presence that cannot be symbolised but is indicated as "Thou", which emerges into time and space and event as an unified field of presence. The three-in-one focused will of the Horatii, which both destroys a world and brings a new world into being, now manifests as we perceive a new and moving universe opening to us. This opening of the way that cannot be named, but can be hinted at, takes us into the position that Maharshi holds as being the divine Self that expresses all and, also, the worshipper of Arunachala. It is here that the single point of Hadit becomes the vehicle of the infinity that is Nuit and, through the unity of will and love, or vector and shaping, enables space and time to come into being. What appears in this moment within space is a sense of growth and expansion as the infinite points of view are expressed through the singularity at the heart of our being. This is the seed point of the beginning, which brings about the new world that we met in the phrases *botsina d'qardinuta* and *alma d'ah-tay*.

As we embody this potential, we enter into solidity, taking up space and being in space, moving from the non-duality of the three-in-one of the supernals to the dualistic four-square extension of Chesed. At its most straightforward, we experience embodiment having not just position but extension in the sense of our body and the world around us. In this moment the single point that has acquired vector and relationship enters into duality and actuality, becoming extended in space as well as existing in space. The infinite sense of possibility is now expressing itself through one of its points, building on the sense of vector and will and relating or love.

The four-squareness of the solid form, having left and right, in front and behind, and above and below, is topological at this stage, a matrix of possibility rather than a concrete form, and, as yet, there is no movement because time and motion have not yet emerged, but what has appeared is the sense of the opposites, of the one and the many, and the sovereignty of the one that expresses through its particular nature the infinity of Nuit. Hence, in *The Book of the Law*, we find these verses:

> Then saith the prophet and slave of the beauteous one: Who am I,
> and what shall be the sign? So she answered him, bending down, a
> lambent flame of blue, all-touching, all penetrant, her lovely hands
> upon the black earth, & her lithe body arched for love, and her soft

feet not hurting the little flowers: Thou knowest! And the sign shall be my ecstasy, the consciousness of the continuity of existence, the omnipresence of my body [...]

    None, breathed the light, faint & faery, of the stars, and two. For I am divided for love's sake, for the chance of union. (I: 26–29)

There are four gates to one palace; the floor of that palace is of silver and gold; lapis lazuli & jasper are there; and all rare scents; jasmine & rose, and the emblems of death. Let him enter in turn or at once the four gates; let him stand on the floor of the palace. Will he not sink? Amn. Ho! Warrior, if thy servant sink? But there are means and means. Be goodly therefore: dress ye all in fine apparel; eat rich foods and drink sweet wines and wines that foam! Also, take your fill and will of love as ye will, when, where and with whom ye will! But always unto me. If this not be aright; if ye confound the space-marks, saying: They are one; or saying, They are many; if the ritual be not ever unto me; then expect the direful judgements of Ra Hoor Khuit. (I: 51–52)

In the embrace of the prophet and Nuit, and the proclamation of none and two, division and union, and the appearance of the palace with the four gates, we are shown the emergence of dualistic space and are encouraged to take shape and form within it and participate in the dance of one and many.

    This appearance of space is complemented by the second chapter of the book and the manifestation of Hadit, the single point, expressing itself through the principle of will and motion, so that the dance of Nuit and Hadit produces the interplay of space and time and aspects of consciousness. We see Hadit described as "not extended" (II: 2), and the house of Hadit as the "Khabs", Furthermore, Hadit declares itself to be "the flame that burns in every heart of man" and "in the core of every star" (II: 6) and as the Magician, the Exorcist, and as the Snake that gives knowledge and delight (II: 22).

    This might remind us that the *ankh* cross carried by all Egyptian gods is also seen as a sandal strap and represents movement and going. The activity of Hadit as magician, exorcist, and as the snake takes us back into *The Book of Gates* where the journey through the night involves the enchantment and exorcism of Apep before the new day is magically recreated, and snake energies are fundamental to the successful journey of the sun barque. The final scene of the book in a sense shows us this activity in a nutshell.

Birth of the new sun and new day

Here we see the personification of the Nun, the waters of the beginning, lifting up the boat of Ra, who appears here as Khephera, the self-
generating one, and implying the constant motion of Hadit. On either
side of Khephera are the sisters Isis and Nephthys. In the barque is Heka
(will), Sia (perception), Hu (utterance), Shu (the god of space), and Geb
(the earth god). On the left is a door with Isis and Nephthys depicted as
uraeus serpents, who open the door of ascent.

At the top of the image is the figure of Osiris, his body wrapped
around the *duat* and representing the whole of the process of the
gates. Arising from his body is the goddess Nut, who receives the
sun disc. Here, Osiris is the green barley god, the energy of life and
movement, the activity of Hadit, and we see how this activity and
motion energises space and substance, bringing time into being. The
principles of Heka or will, Sia or perception, come together in Hu,
or utterance, as the horizon is crossed, the new day dawns, and all is
recreated.

We see this beautifully described in Pharaoh Akhenaten's hymn to the sun:

> Thy rising is beautiful in the horizon of heaven,
> O thou Åten, who hadst thine existence in primeval time.
> When thou risest in the eastern horizon thou fillest every land with thy beauties,
> Thou art beautiful to see, and art great, and art like crystal, and art high above the earth.
> Thy beams of light embrace the lands, even every land which thou hast made.
> Thou art as Rā, and thou bringest [thyself] unto each of them, and thou bindest them with thy love.
> Thou art remote, but thy beams are upon the earth.
> So long as thou art in the heavens day shall follow in thy footsteps.
> When thou settest in the western horizon the earth is in darkness, and is like a being that is dead.
> They lie down and sleep in their habitations,
> Their heads are covered up, and their nostrils are stopped, and no man can see his neighbour,
> and all their goods and possessions may be carried away from under their heads without their knowing it.
> Every lion cometh forth from his den,
> and serpents of every kind bite;
> The night becometh blacker and blacker,
> And the earth is silent because he who hath made them hath sunk to rest in his horizon. When thou risest in the horizon the earth lightens, and when thy beams shine forth it is day. Darkness taketh to flight as soon as thy light bursteth out, and the Two Lands keep festival daily.
> Then [men] wake up and stand upon their feet because thou hast raised them up,
> They wash themselves, and they array themselves in their apparel,
> And they lift up to thee their hands with hymns of praise because thou hast risen.
> [Over] all the earth they perform their work.
> All beasts and cattle repose in their pastures,

and the trees and the green herb put forth their leaves and flowers.
The birds fly out of their nests, and their wings praise thy Soul
as they fly forth.
The sheep and goats of every kind skip about on their legs,
and feathered fowl and the birds of the air also live [because]
thou hast risen for them.
The boats float down and sail up the river likewise,
For thy path is opened when thou risest.
The fish in the stream leap up towards thy face,
and thy beams shine through the waters of the great sea.
Thou makest male seed to enter into women, and thou causest
the liquid seed to become a human being.
Thou makest the man child to live in the body of his mother.
Thou makest him to keep silent so that he cry not,
And thou art a nurse to him in the womb.
Thou givest breath that it may vivify every part of his being.
When he goeth forth from the belly, on the day wherein he is born,
Thou openest his mouth that he may speak,
And thou providest for him whatsoever is necessary.
When the chick is in the egg, and is making a sound within the
shell,
Thou givest it air inside it so that it may keep alive.
Thou bringest it to perfection so that it may split the eggshell,
And it cometh forth from the egg to proclaim that it is a perfect
chick,
And as soon as it hath come forth therefrom it runneth about
on its feet.
How many are the things which thou hast created! […]
Thou didst create the earth at thy will when thou didst exist by
thyself […] (Wallis Budge, 1969 [1904], pp. 75–77)

From this background of space, time, and reflective awareness, the
many forms of appearance of the universe take shape, as we see in the
hymn. The Ancient Egyptian image of Ra and the unity of will and
perception, which continually opens the way through the underworld,
now expresses itself in the utterance that brings the new day into being.

This emergence of appearance, or the *khu* or magical body, is shown
in *The Book of the Law* as Ra Hoor Khuit—more accurately in Egypto-
logical terms called Ra Harakhty (or "Ra of the *akhet*" or "horizon").

This appearance of the khu is the manifestation of self and world, which is shown in the Stele of Revealing as the dynamic of Ra Hoor Khuit and Ankh af na Khonsu and the offering formula, in which the fruit of the world is offered back to its creator. It is this that we see described in the third chapter of *The Book of the Law*, in which Ra Hoor Khuit, twinned with the silent child, manifests as a destructive presence breaking down all that obstructs the simplicity of the emerging Aeon. This is what is meant in *Moonchild* (1929) by the emergence of the Horatii, and "the sowing of the Dragon's teeth".

The interplay of Nuit, Hadit, and Ra Hoor Khuit shows us the emergence of actuality from essentiality, followed by motion and direction, and from this charged dynamic the appearance of all the thousand things, all of which are two-fold in that their visible form, Ra Hoor Khuit, is backed by the silent child, Hoor Paar Kraat. This dynamic is completed by the experience of the perceiver, who is Ankh af na Khonsu, the living dead man whose life is given to the moonchild, Khonsu, and who offers back the fruits of the magical work to Ra Hoor Khuit, Hadit, and Nuit.

This is the magick of working with the play of appearances, which Ramana Maharshi shows us, as he becomes the devotee of Shiva in Arunachala and which Crowley's barebones Qabalah, the Naples arrangement, describes. It is also the practice of the divine faces of *Yehshuah* (יהשוה), practised by Tom Oloman, as he unites the inner and outer worlds in the mystery of face beholds face. The divine play, or *lila*, is the Star-Sponge vision in practice, in which every generative point is joined to each other, creating continuous colloquy and conversation. This quivering web of creation is what Crowley called the "mystic Sabbath of the Saints of God" (Crowley, 1929, p. 284) in contrast to the distorted, predatory web that Lisa perceived. The difference is in how each point is at the centre of the whole, and free to express its own nature as a particular formulation of love and will as opposed to each point being subservient to the presence at the web's centre. Working with this web is the work of magick, in contrast to mysticism, in which we simply return to the stillness from which all arises. When Simon Iff encounters "the Thing in the garden" and Cyril Grey recognises his identity with Douglas, they are working with the mystery of particularity and infinity. Their own freedom from "I, me, and mine" gives them the fluidity necessary to embody the deep will that was surging forward. This, in both cases, was a love that embraces all possibilities and wishes for all the complete expression of their deepest natures as expression of the "Sabbath of the Saints of God".

# CHAPTER 14

# Being the Magician

In order to take our place within this "Sabbath" we step into the role and aspect of being the magician in the midst of the magick. In Crowley's *Book Four* (Crowley, 1972a) we find him taking the image of the traditional magician, with his robes and weapons, circle, and triangle of art, and interpreting these forms in a new way.

He tells us that the temple is the universe, the circle the magician's delineation of the sphere of their work, which is both a replica of and aligned with the universal will. The central altar represents the fixed will and dedication to the Great Work. Of the magical implements, the wand is the will of the magician, the cup their understanding, the sword their reason, and the pentacle their body. We can place this formulation on the Tree of Life in which Kether is the lamp of the uncreated light, Chockmah the wand of will, Binah the cup of understanding, Daath the altar in which the will and understanding of the magician unite, Gedulah and Geburah the principles of invocation and banishing, which come together in Tiphareth, the sword of focus and awareness. This constitutes the magical circle from which the magical current arises, whereas the triangle of manifestation gives us the current in operation. We see in the sephira of Hod the mind, and the particular oath of the operation; Netzach, the place of being enflamed by the invocation; Yesod, the place of the appearance of the spirit image; Malkuth, the pentacle and earthing of the operation.

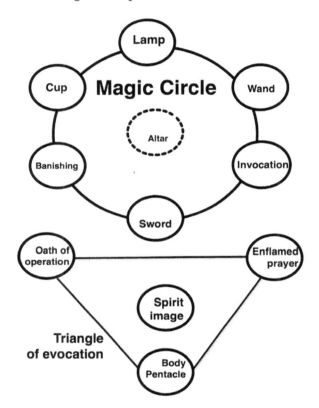

Magick, therefore, is an art of incarnation that creates a new world and begins with banishing, so that the field of operation is clear and as the universe described in Genesis: *Tohu ve Bohu*, empty and possessing all potential (Genesis 1: 2). The banishing is normally accomplished through the use of the symbolism of the pentagram, the star that is the house of Hadit and the vehicle of will. We met this symbol in the work of the Neophyte, but are now taking it to a new level by contemplating its geometry and its relationship to the proportions of the Golden Ratio.

If we connect the vertices of a pentagon by straight lines we obtain a pentagram, which then encloses an upside-down pentagon, which in

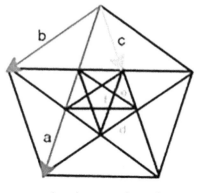

a:b = b:c = c:d = e:f

turn generates a reversed pentagram, which encloses an upright pentagon, and so on, infinitely extending outwards and inwards. Furthermore,
the ratio of the larger to the smaller lines in the shape (line a to line b, line
b to line c, line c to line d, and line e to line f, etc.) gives us the value of phi
1.6180339887 … an infinitely extending irrational number. The proportions of the Golden Ratio are aesthetically pleasing and as such are linked
to the Venusian sphere on the Tree of Life, Netzach. Oddly, the orbits of
Earth and Venus around the sun, relative to each other over eight years
in Earth time and thirteen years in Venusian time, trace out the form of
a pentagram. The five-fold shape of the pentagram is also attributed to
the sphere of Geburah and the principle of will, so the form gives us an
expression of the fusion of love and will. The Golden Ratio is found in
nature as the Fibonacci series of expansion in which, in a series of numbers, such as 0, 1, 2, 3, 4, 5, etc., if the latest number is divided by preceding numbers, it increasingly approximates the Golden Ratio. One divided
by one is one. Two divided by one is two. Three divided by two is 1.5.
As the sequence increases something interesting begins to happen. Five
divided by three is 1.666. Eight divided by five is 1.6. Thirteen divided
by eight is 1.625. Twenty-one divided by thirteen is 1.615. As the series
goes on, the ratio of the latest number to the previous number converges
on 1.618, getting increasingly accurate, but never quite reaching the
Golden Ratio.

This series is found frequently in nature, particularly in plants. Many
plants that branch outwards towards the sun do so in numbers of
branches equal to Fibonacci numbers. The original stem comes up from

the earth and, at first, just sprouts upwards before developing develops meristem points—points from which new branches can form—and those sprout into two separate branches. Those branches push upwards for another period of time, and then develop two points of their own. The overall number of sprouting points develops in a Fibonacci series, often in a spiralling pattern, such as we see in the way a sunflower arranges its seeds.

The same sequence can be seen in the development of the shell of a nautilus.

If we superimpose the diagram of the golden rectangle, i.e. a rectangle created according to the Golden Ratio, and subdivide the rectangle according to the golden proportions and inscribe a curve linking one corner of nested square to another, this produces the spiral form that is found in plants and in the nautilus shell.

Sunflower Fibonacci sequence

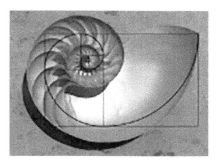

Nautilus shell and Fibonacci

The pattern can be found also in weather systems, as in this picture of Hurricane Katrina.

And in the shaping of a spiral galaxy.

This fractal principle of the Golden Ratio (also known as the Golden Section) shows the deeper aspects of the pentagram and its use. This is shown also in the medieval poem *Sir Gawain and the Green Knight*:

> Then they brought him his shield that was of brilliant red
> with the pentangle depicted in pure golden color.
> [...]
> It is a symbol that Solomon once upon a time set
> as a token of Virtue, as it properly is;
> for it is a figure that has five points,
> and each line overlaps and is linked with another,
> and in every direction it is endless; and the English, I hear,
> everywhere call it by the name the Endless Knot.
> So it suits well this knight and his pristine arms;
> forever faithful in five points, and five times in each point,
> Gawain was acknowledged as good as gold refined,
> devoid of every vice and with virtues adorned.
>                    So there
>           the pentangle painted new
>           his shield and armor wear,
>           as one of word most true,
>           this knight of bearing fair.
>
> First he was found faultless in his five senses,
> and next in the five fingers he never failed with,
> and firmly he held faith in the Five Wounds

that Christ received on the cross, as the Creed tells us;
and wherever the brave man went into battle,
he sincerely reflected on this beyond all other things:
that he always gained his courage from the Five Joys
that Heaven's courteous Queen received from her Child.
[...]
The fifth five that was used, I find, by this knight
was generosity and fellowship first before all,
and chastity and courtesy ever changeless and straight,
and piety surpassing all points: these perfect five
he held to harder than any other man.
Now this series of fives, in truth, were stuck on this knight,
and each was knit with the others and had no ending,
but was fixed at five points that never failed,
colliding at no point nor breaking apart,
not ending in any corner anywhere, as I comprehend it;
nowhere does it start and nowhere does it end.
Therefore, on his shiny shield, there was this shape of the knot,
royally colored with red upon gold:
this is the pure pentangle as educated people
have taught. (Mantyk, 2021, pp. 35–37)

Here the pentagram is linked with King Solomon, the archetypal magician; imaged in gold on a red background and described as "the endless knot" that brings together the five senses, the five fingers, the five wounds of Christ, the five joys of Mary (the Annunciation, the Nativity, the Resurrection, the Ascension, and the Assumption), and the five chivalric qualities. Here, in a Medieval dialect, we see the same fractal qualities: beginning with the five senses and fingers. The poem then contemplates the wounds of Christ, the journey of both Christ and the Virgin, culminating in the Assumption, which represents the fusion of matter and spirit, before returning to the chivalric qualities of friendship, generosity, chastity, courtesy, and piety. We are told that each of the fives is bound to each of the others without end, much in the way that fractals work, and we are given an image of Gawain's shield with the image of the Virgin on the inside and the pentagram on the outside, in an echo of Nuit and Hadit.

The use of the pentagram therefore brings together the principles of will, love, and generation, and so, shaped as the endless knot, the intention that informs its generative fractal activity is brought into being through its topology.

Plotinus in his *Enneads* (5, Tract 8, Section 9) summarises the process of banishing and invoking thus:

> Bring this vision actually before your sight, so that there shall be in your mind the gleaming representation of a sphere, a picture holding all the things of the universe moving or in repose or (as in reality) some at rest, some in motion. Keep this sphere before you, and from it imagine another, a sphere stripped of magnitude and of spatial differences; cast out your inborn sense of Matter, taking care not merely to attenuate it: call on God the maker of the sphere whose image you now hold and pray Him to enter. And may He come bringing his own universe with all the gods that dwell in it—He who is the one God and all the gods where each is all, blending into an unity, distinct in powers but all one god in virtue of that one divine power of many facets. More truly this is the one God who is all the gods, for in the coming to be of all those this, the one, has suffered no diminishing. (Cited in Critchlow, 1980, p. 35)

The ritual most commonly used for banishing in the Qabalistic tradition is the Banishing Ritual of the Pentagram we have already worked with but, in keeping with the theme of the deeper magical practice of this phase, we will consider Crowley's ritual of the Star Ruby.

This is a more advanced ritual, found in Crowley's *The Book of Lies* (1981) (a series of instructions for Babes of the Abyss) and is based upon Greek Chaldean theurgic tradition rather than Hebrew. The Star Ruby has a deeper intention than the Banishing Ritual of the Pentagram. In the latter, we begin in Malkuth and banish the elements of Malkuth and then invite the archangels to sanctify us in Malkuth. With the Star Ruby, we begin in Tiphareth, purify the sephiroth Netzach, Hod, Yesod, and Malkuth, step up to Binah, and from Binah reconfigure the universe. It relies on our capacity to stabilise ourselves in Tiphareth and to at least touch the deeper spheres of the tree. At the heart of the ritual are the gestures called the NOX signs, which invite the state of consciousness Crowley calls "the Night of Pan". This "night" is the supernal non-dual consciousness that is so far beyond the illumination of Tiphareth that it appears as darkness.

The NOX signs are based upon this image:

This circled cross, which is in itself a symbol of the conjunction of many opposites, contains the opposites of light and darkness, as the Latin translations for these words are, respectively, LVX and NOX, and the letters of both words are contained within its shape. This ritual is designed to enable us to access this night, which is brighter than light and, in Crowley's philosophy, the process of entering this new awareness is preceded by a surrender of all our achievements and our entire identity into the non-dual presence of Binah. Here, this is envisaged as Babalon the Mother, who receives all and generates all and who holds the chalice into which every drop of our blood must be poured. Crowley derives this from the Book of Revelation in which the Great Whore, the Whore of Babylon, is drunk with the blood of the saints (Revelation 17: 6) and this is part of his repurposing the Christian myth of his childhood. As part of the act of surrender, we become a Babe of the Abyss, adopting the form of the silent child Hoor Paar Kraat, until the process concludes with us dwelling in Binah in the City of the Pyramids. We then arise in the form of the generative and creative mother, the servant of the star and the snake, stepping forward as Ra Hoor Khuit, the manifester of will.

The ritual begins by adopting the sign of silence and becoming Hoor Paar Kraat, with our forefinger against our lip, and then, with an outward sweeping gesture, becoming Ra Hoor Khuit and clearing our sphere. The ritual is performed widdershins, against the flow of the sun, and the elements of the four directions follow the pattern of *YHVH* (יהוה): hence, East is fire, North is water, West is air, and South is earth.

Standing in the centre of the ritual space, facing East, draw a deep breath, close your mouth with your right forefinger pressed against your lower lip. Then, sweep down your hand back and out, expelling your breath forcibly, and cry: ΑΠΟ ΠΑΝΤΟΣ ΚΑΚΟΔΑΙΜΟΝΟΣ (*Apo Pantos Kakodaimonos*, "Away, every evil spirit").

Perform the Qabalistic Cross. With the same forefinger, touch your forehead, and say: ΣΟΙ (*Soi*, "Thine"). Place your hand on your pelvis and say: Ω ΦΑΛΛΕ (Ô Phalle, "O Phallus"). Touch your right shoulder, and say: ΙΣΧΥΡΟΣ (Ischuros, "the mighty"). Touch your left shoulder, and say: ΕΥΧΑΡΙΣΤΟΣ (Eucharistos, "the beneficient"). Then clasp your hands, locking the fingers, and cry: ΙΑΩ (Iaô).

Advance to the East. Imagine strongly a pentagram in your forehead in brilliant red light. Drawing your hands to the eyes, fling the pentagram forth, making the sign of Horus (stepping forward with the left foot and thrusting out your hands) and vibrate ΧΑΟΣ ("Chaos"). Step back and draw back your hand in the sign of Hoor-paar-Kraat (forefinger placed against the lips in the sign of silence). Go round to the North and repeat, but say ΒΑΒΑΛΟΝ ("Babalon"). Go round to the West and repeat, but chant ΕΡΟΣ ("Eros"). Go round to the South and repeat, but vibrate ΨΥΧΗ ("Psyche").

Completing the circle widdershins, retire to the centre and chant: ΙΩ ΠΑΝ (Iô Pan, "Hail Pan"), making the signs of NOX (shown below). Then extend the arms in the form of a Tau and say low but clear:

ΠΡΟ ΜΟΥ ΙΥΓΓΕΣ (Pro mou iunges, "Before me the Iunges").

ΟΠΙΣΘΩ ΜΟΥ ΤΕΛΕΤΑΡΧΑΙ (Opisô mou teletarchai, "Behind me the Teletarches").

ΕΠΙ ΔΕΞΙΑ ΣΥΝΩΧΕΙΣ (Epi dexia sunocheis, "on my right hand the Synoches").

ΕΠΑΡΙΣΤΕΡΑ ΔΑΙΜΟΝΕΣ (Eparistera daimones, "on my left hand the Daemones").

ΦΛΕΓΕΙ ΓΑΡ ΠΕΡΙ ΜΟΥ Ο ΑΣΤΗΡ ΤΩΝ ΠΕΝΤΕ (Phlegei gar peri mou ho astêr tôn pente, "For about me flames the Star of Five"). ΚΑΙ ΕΝ ΤΗΙ ΣΤΗΛΗΙ Ω ΑΣΤΕΡ ΤΩΝ ΕΞ ΕΣΤΗΚΕ (Kai en têi stêlêi ho astêr tôn hex hestêke, "And in the Pillar stands the Star of Six").

Repeat the Qabalistic Cross, return to standing in stillness and finish.

The very first gesture alone, if completely embraced, is the whole work of banishing and makes use of the forms of Hoor Paar Kraat and Ra Hoor Khuit to clear our world of all opposition.

It is followed by a very particular version of the Qabalistic Cross. Placing our hand on our forehead and saying ΣΟΙ (Soi) we invite the Kether presence, which is our deepest nature—Asar un nefer ("the Osiris made beautiful"), our immortal nature. Placing our hand on our pelvis we say Ω ΦΑΛΛΕ (O phalle). This phrase is easily misunderstood as representing a literal phallus, whereas it represents the union of the vagina (Ω) with the phallus (ΦΑΛΛΕ) and hence the profound creativity of the divine, while we visualise the pillar of light connecting us to the centre of the earth.

As in the pentagram ritual, we next invite horizontal polarity, using the names *Ischuros* and *Eucharistos*—respectively, the strong almighty (Geburah), and the beneficent blessing (Gedulah)—and then bring the energy back to the centre, clasping our hands and chanting *IAO* (Tiphareth).

Unlike the pentagram ritual, where the pentagrams are traced, these are visualised in bright red and projected forwards in the gesture of Ra Hoor Khuit and given the intention of invoking each presence.

Here, as the operator, we extend the inner light as יהוה; hence, in the East, "Chaos" (here a God-name of Chockmah), the letter י (*yod*), and the expression of will and fire. Here we step from Tiphareth into Netzach. As we step back into the sign of Hoor Paar Kraat, and make the sign for stillness, we enter the mystery of the zero.

Turning to the North, we step forwards again into Hod and here the direction is of water, we bring in the letter ה (*heh*), Binah, and the name of "Babalon", which is linked to Binah. Going to the West, we step into Yesod and the element of air, bringing in the letter ו (*vav*), and the name "Eros", which is linked to Tiphareth. Next, turning to the South and stepping into Malkuth, we bring in the final letter ה (*heh*), the name "Psyche", and the element of earth.

The principles of the name יהוה are brought into Netzach, Hod, Yesod, and Malkuth, so that the deep will of Chockmah and *yod* (י) is extended into Netzach, the profound love of Binah and *heh* (ה) embraces Hod, the awareness of Tiphareth and *vav* (ו) descends into the spinning wheel of Yesod, and the solidity and ground of Malkuth and the *heh* final (ה) infuses the psyche and sphere of sensation.

Having purified and aligned the lower spheres of the tree, we return to the centre point of Tiphareth and, through the use of the chant IΩ ΠAN (*Io Pan*) bring in the qualities of the higher reaches of the tree. Pan, here, is the divinity that includes all. We may recall the invocation of Pan at the beginning of *Liber Liberi Vel Lapidis Lazuli*, and the images of swimming in the heart of God as a trout, or of being a priestess of the druids contemplating the oak, or the *vesica piscis*, or the contemplation of the white cat on a wall with sparks coming off its fur. The whole of this holy book is relevant to this invocation. IΩ (*Io*), as well as being an exclamation of praise, represents the union of the phallus and *kteis* and, by extension, the union of all opposites and a reiteration of the creative energy invited via the Qabalistic Cross.

The signs of NOX are a series of bodily gestures that invoke the qualities of Geburah, Gedulah, entering the abyss, and Binah. They are *puer*, the boy; *vir*, the man; *puella*, the girl; *mulier*, the woman, culminating in *Mater Triumphans*; and they bring us into the Night of Pan, the surrender of I, me, and mine into Thou, and our absorption into the womb of Babalon.

They begin with the sign *puer*, the boy, linked to Geburah:

The right arm forms an "L", with closed hand, thumb pointing towards the head. The closed left hand rests at the base of the torso, thumb pointing away from the body.

Then *vir*, the man, connected to Gedulah:

Place closed hands at the temples with thumbs facing outwards, resembling horns.

Next, *puella,* the girl, the first gesture of the Babe of the Abyss:

Standing upright, place the open right hand over the breast, and the open left hand over the groin.

*Mulier*, the woman, is the second gesture of the Babe of the Abyss:

In *mulier* the arms form a ninety-degree angle above the head, elbows bent slightly, with hands open. The feet are a little over shoulder width apart, facing forward. The head looks upwards.

Finally, *Mater Triumphans*, the Triumphant Mother, linked to Binah:

The head is looking downwards, the right hand pinches the left nipple, while the left hand cradles just below the solar plexus, as if holding a baby.

As we adopt these postures, in *puer* we attune to the fiery energy of Geburah, adopting the fighting form of the war god Montu; in *vir*, to the creative power of Gedulah as the horned Pan; in the abyss, as *puella*, we become the enclosed feminine; and in *mulier* the feminine that receives all before arising as the Triumphant Mother of Binah.

From this place, as the Triumphant Mother, we extend our arms in the Tau gesture, which links to the path between Yesod and Malkuth and the principle of manifestation, and to the direct awareness of Binah, which is indicated in the NOX sign of the Triumphant Mother. We then invite the creative energies of the universe: the *iunges* who generate; the *sunoches* who maintain; the *teletarchai* who transform; and the daemones who embody. The iunges can be envisaged as fiery swirls or wheels; the sunoches as thrones with shadowy beings sitting on them; the teletarchai as spiralling, lion-headed serpents; and the daemones as winged androgynes. These angelic forms are potent creative figures who transmit the power of creation, much as we find in Rilke's second of the *Duino Elegies*:

> Every angel is terrifying. And yet, alas,
> I invoke you, almost deadly birds of the soul,
> knowing about you. Where are the days of Tobias,

when one of you, veiling his radiance, stood at the front
    door,
slightly disguised for the journey, no longer appalling;
(a young man like the one who curiously peeked through the
    window).
But if the archangel now, perilous, from behind the stars
took even one step down toward us: our own heart, beating
higher and higher, would beat us to death. Who *are* you?

Early successes, Creation's pampered favorites,
mountain-ranges, peaks growing red in the dawn
of all Beginning,—pollen of the flowering godhead,
joints of pure light, corridors, stairways, thrones,
space formed from essence, shields made of ecstasy, storms
of emotion whirled into rapture, and suddenly, alone,
*mirrors*: which scoop up the beauty that has streamed from
    their face
and gather it back, into themselves, entire. (Rilke, 2009, p. 11)

This is what is being invoked into our circle and, in this moment, we contemplate the union of the hexagram and pentagram, and bring a new world into being. Finally, we repeat the Qabalistic Cross, affirming our sovereignty and centrality within this new world. It is from the state of mind that we find ourselves in, having performed this ritual, that we practice the Mass of the Holy Ghost and the continual incarnation of love under will.

# CHAPTER 15

# Magick and the Mass of the Holy Ghost

This capacity to work creatively with the web of creation was called by Crowley "The Mass of the Holy Ghost" and was the prime secret of his organisation the OTO (or "Order of Oriental Templars"). This quasi-masonic body was gifted to Crowley by its then Head, Theodor Reuss, and was recreated by Crowley as a vehicle for the transmission of the principles of *The Book of the Law* and the practice of sexual magick. Crowley uses the archaic spelling "magick" for differentiation from stage magic but, also, we are told by Symonds and Grant (the editors of *Magick*), that the addition of the letter K for him symbolised the word *kteis* (or "vagina") (Crowley, 1989, p. xvi) to indicate the sexual basis of magick. This is perhaps the most controversial aspect of his teaching, and the aspect that draws most interest. In its simplest and most literal form his sexual magick involves sexual arousal as invocation and, at the point of orgasm, focusing our will on the subject of the ritual. The resulting fluids of the sexual act are seen as potent talismans that carry the consecrated energy of will and imagination and can be applied to external objects to earth the energy, painted onto the body, or absorbed either orally or through the mucosa of the genital organs themselves. We find it described (appropriately enough) in Chapter 69 of *The Book of Lies* (Crowley, 1974):

THE WAY TO SUCCEED—AND THE WAY TO SUCK EGGS!
This is the Holy Hexagram.
Plunge from the height, O God, and interlock with Man!
Plunge from the height, O Man, and interlock with Beast!
The Red Triangle is the descending tongue of grace; the Blue Triangle is the ascending tongue of prayer.
This Interchange, the Double Gift of Tongues, the Word of Double Power—ABRAHADABRA!—is the sign of the GREAT WORK, for the GREAT WORK is accomplished in Silence. And behold, is not that Word equal to Cheth, that is Cancer, whose Sigil is a ♋ ?
This Work also eats up itself, accomplishes its own end, nourishes the worker, leaves no seed, is perfect in itself.
Little children, love one another! (Crowley, 1913, pp. 148–149)

The chapter begins with the sense of separation between God and Man, and Man and Beast, and then comes to the interpenetration and interlocking of the red and blue triangles—the experience of union. Interestingly, he reverses the normal order of the triangles in which the red triangle ascends, and the blue triangle descends following the general activity of fire flaring up and water flowing down. Here the fiery will of the angel descends while the water rises up as a fountain in the act of prayer and longing because this is an act of love and will that interrupts and supercedes the normal order of the world.

Crowley shows us this process in the ritual of the Star Sapphire, also found in *The Book of Lies* (Crowley, 1981, Chapter 36). At one level, this is Crowley's replacement for the Hexagram Ritual and is based upon the formula יהוה here shown as the Father, Mother, Son, and Daughter. It is sometimes thought of as a sexual ritual, and can be carried out in that way, but that would be a particular application of the form rather than its essential nature. The other refinement Crowley brings is his use of the unicursal hexagram, which enables the figure to be traced in a continuous line.

He went on to place a five-petalled rose at its centre to symbolise the union of the pentagram and the hexagram.

This ritual involves the interlocking of the three triangles of the Tree of Life—the supernal triangle of God (Kether, Binah, Chockmah), the middle triangle of the illuminated human being (Gedulah, Geburah, and Tiphareth), and the lower triangle of the beast (Netzach, Hod, and Yesod). It is an act of incarnation, thus the downwards-pointing triangle is the red flame of descending Grace, linked to the Hebrew letter *shin* ש and the fiery dove, while the upwards-pointing triangle is the ascending tongue of prayer, linked to the letter *teth* (ט), the fluid creative serpent. The union of the triangles thus gives us *ShT* (שט) which Crowley uses as indicating the Egyptian god Set, who appears at the end of the ritual. We will return to this question later, but this ritual is linked to the formula *LAShTAL* that Crowley describes in depth in his commentary to the Ritual of the Mark of the Beast in *Magick* (Crowley, 1989, p. 411). This formula, linked to *AL*, the title of *The Book of the Law* (*Liber AL vel Legis*) describes the components of the Star Sapphire and indeed the process of the Mass of the Holy Ghost that manifests in every moment. *LA* (לא) means "not" and refers to the unmanifest union of Hadit and Nuit, whereas *AL* (אל) shows us Nuit and Hadit working through the balanced contraries of the tarot trumps, the Fool and Justice. The middle letters of *ShT* (שט) show us the magical dynamic of transformation, symbolised by the fusion of the dove and serpent and the unity of the woman and the beast. The Thelemic writer James Eshelman, on the basis of seeing some of Crowley's private correspondence, maintains that Crowley only once in his life performed this ritual (Eshelman, 2013, p. 136) and its importance perhaps is less as something to do, but rather as a text which shows us important aspects of the moment-by-moment practice of the Mass of the Holy Ghost.

At its centre is the formula of *ARARITA*, a word formed by the process called *notariqon*, in which the Qabalist takes the initial letter of each word of a sentence to represent the formula of that sentence. The sentence is אחד ראש אחדותו ראש יחודו תמורתו אחד (*AChD RASh: AChDVThV RASh YYChVDVThV: ThMVRThV AChD*, "one is His beginning; one is His individuality; His permutations are one"). We first find this name in the writings of the thirteenth-century Iyyun Circle (or "Circle of Contemplation"). In *The Book of Contemplation*, we are told:

> [...] I asked Rabbi Nehuniah b. ha-Kanah, saying to him, Rabbi, show me the Glory of the King of the universe, in order that the knowledge of Him, like his other actions, will be clarified in my heart. He said to me, Son of the proud, come let us delve into the great ring on which is engraved the name and *aR'aRYet'a* is His name, as well as the ring of the earth, which is *'aHV*. I will show you everything.
>
> I entered inside, into the Outer Holy Palace, and removed from there R. Nehuniah b ha-Kanah's book, entitled *Book of the*

*Celestial Palaces,* and discovered the following, written at the start of the book.

Mighty within the rooms of grandeur is He who sits on the wheels of His chariot, with the seal *'ehyeh 'asher 'ehyeh* (I will be who I will be), and with a great ring on it which is engraved the name *'aR'aRYeT'a,* which is His name. It denotes: One, the Start of his Unification, the Start of His Unity, His Permutation is One, Individual and Unique; Individual, Unique, One. Also, with the ring of earth that is *'aHV,* which is His name, denoting: One who Was And will be. The intermediary between both of them is He who is. "A word spoken appropriately" (Prov. 25: 1). He was prior to when He created the world; He is in the world and He will be in the world to come. This is symbolized by: He did, He does, He will do. (Verman, 1992, pp. 102–103)

And, again, in a commentary on *The Book of Contemplation* by Rabbi Meir, we find:

The knowledge and insight into why He is called *'aR'aRYeT'a,* that is to say, that which the sages, of blessed memory, stated, "a lion (*'arya'*) was crouched on top of the altar [attached] by a red cord." Its name was *'aR'aRYeT'a.* This [alludes to] "for the Lord created something new in the land: a woman shall encircle a man" (Jeremiah 31: 22). This is the Primal Ether (*'avir ha-kadmon*). She is ascribed by the ancient sages to be the final point—sometimes she is emanated and sometimes she emanates; sometimes she is influenced and sometimes she influences. She is two-faced: the tree of life and the tree of knowledge. From her are created spiritual entities and sensual beings, as well as the roots of the fundamental elements that are emanated and arranged and drawn out and proceed in every direction. This is alluded to in the Torah, "And upon the earth He showed you His great fire" (Deuteronomy 4: 36). (Verman, 1992, p. 203)

This is a formula, therefore, of unity; of bringing opposites together into a higher and deeper unity. The image of the lion and the red cord and the woman encircling a man reminds us of the union of the woman and the beast in the tarot trump Strength, or Lust, which unites the principles of Geburah and Gedulah or will and love.

In his notes on the twenty-second aethyr in *The Vision and the Voice* (1972), Crowley comments:

> The use of this Name and Formula [*ARARITA*] is to equate and identify every idea with its opposite; thus being released from the obsession of thinking any one of them as "true" (and therefore binding); one can withdraw oneself from the whole sphere of the Ruach. (Crowley, 1972, p. 74)

And, again, in *The Book of the Heart Girt with the Serpent*:

> Also he taught me the holy unutterable word Ararita, so that I melted the sixfold gold into a single invisible point, whereof naught may be spoken. (5: 15) (Crowley, 2015, p. 126)

One of Crowley's Holy Books is called *Liber Ararita* (Crowley, 2015, pp. 169–182) a book of seven chapters, each identified by a letter of the name. In the first chapter he describes the magical images of the ten sephiroth of the Tree of Life; in the second, the magical images of the Qliphoth; in the third, the root idea of each sephira; in the fourth, he contemplates them from the place of deeper unity, seeing both their imperfection and their use; in the fifth, he is the contemplator, one with Maharshi's Self; in the sixth, he proclaims his vision of the universe; and in the seventh dissolves all in the holy fire of awareness.

The Star Sapphire ritual is, in a way, quite simple, using the word *ARARITA*, the symbol of the hexagram, and the uniting of the letters of the divine name יהוה.

Crowley describes it thus:

Let the Adept be armed with his Magick Rood [and provided with his Mystic Rose]. In the centre, let him give the L.V.X. signs; or if he know them, if he will and dare do them, and can keep silent about them, the signs of N.O.X. being the signs of Puer, Vir, Puella, Mulier. Omit the sign I.R.

Then let him advance to the East, and make the Holy Hexagram, saying: PATER ET MATER UNIS DEUS ARARITA ["Father and Mother are the one God ARARITA"].

Let him go round to the South, make the Holy Hexagram, and say: MATER ET FILIUS UNUS DEUS ARARITA ["Mother and Son are the one God ARARITA"].

Let him go round to the West, make the Holy Hexagram, and say: FILIUS ET FILIA UNUS DEUS ARARITA ["Son and Daughter are the one God ARARITA"].

Let him go round to the North, make the Holy Hexagram, and then say: FILIA ET PATER UNUS DEUS ARARITA ["Daughter and Father are the one God ARARITA"].

Let him then return to the Centre, and so to The Centre of All [making the ROSY CROSS as he may know how] saying: ARARITA ARARITA ARARITA. [In this the Signs shall be those of Set Triumphant and of Baphomet. Also shall Set appear in the Circle. Let him drink of the Sacrament and let him communicate the same.]

Then let him say: OMNIA IN DUOS: DUO IN UNUM: UNUS IN NIHIL: HAE NEC QUATUOR NEC OMNIA NEC DUO NEC UNUS NEC NIHIL SUNT ["All in Two; Two in One; One in None; These are neither Four nor All nor Two nor One nor None"].

GLORIA PATRI ET MATRI ET FILIO ET FILIAE ET SPIRITUI SANCTO EXTERNO ET SPIRITUI SANCTO INTERNO UT ERAT EST ERIT IN SAECULA SAECULORUM SEX IN UNO PER NOMEN SEPTEM IN UNO ARARITA ["Glory be to the Father and the Mother and the Son and the Daughter and the Holy Spirit without and the Holy Spirit within as it was, is, will be for ages and ages six in one through the name seven in one ARARITA"].

Let him then repeat the signs of L.V.X. but not the signs of N.O.X.; for it is not he that shall arise in the Sign of Isis Rejoicing. (Crowley, 1974, pp. 82–83)

The rose and cross are the principles of love and will; the signs of NOX are the series of bodily gestures we discussed in the chapter on the ritual of the Star Ruby which here invoke the qualities of Geburah, Gedulah, and entering the abyss. In this ritual the sign of the Triumphant Mother is not used and is replaced by the signs of Set Triumphant and of Baphomet.

We begin in the East, tracing the hexagram uniting the Father and the Mother (י and ה); move to the South, uniting the Mother and the Son (ה and ו); next, the West, the Son and the Daughter (ו and ה); then the North, the daughter and the father (ה and י). We then return to the centre and chant *ARARITA*, making the signs of Set and Baphomet.

Sign of Set. Raise arms above the head at an angle of sixty degrees to each other, and throw the head back, as if looking upwards. Stand up on the balls of both feet

The sign of Baphomet is identical in posture to that of the sign of *Mulier*:

Sign of Baphomet. Arms form a ninety degrees angle above head, elbows bent slightly, with hands open. Feet are a little over shoulder width apart, facing forward. Head looks upwards

The combination of the signs of Set (which is the union of the dove and serpent) and Baphomet is the precursor to the practice of the Mass of the Holy Ghost, for we have thoroughly united the opposites and, in the Baphomet sign, which is a repetition of the *Mulier* sign for woman, we are receptive and awaiting the manifesting will.

Having established ourselves within the unity and aligned with the name יהוה and thus with the interplay of Hadit, Nuit, and Ra Hoor Khuit, and the workings of the Tao, we then proceed to working with the Mass of the Holy Ghost. This Mass is the primary process of the incarnation of the embodiment of will and of our own and the universe's eroticism, and this fundamental sexuality of life is indicated in the Star Sapphire Ritual through the union of the Father, Mother, Son, and Daughter to generate the potency of the united name יהוה.

What is being addressed here is the eroticism of life, which includes expressive genital sexuality but much is more than that: it includes the opposites of maleness and femaleness, night and day, and all other opposites. Tom Oloman regarded this work as concerned with union with the beloved other, surrender, and absorption into the fruits of that union and embodying the results of the union. The beloved other appears in Tom's practice of "face beholds face" through which we unite ourselves with all that appears to us. This, of course, takes us beyond genital sexuality and beyond gender itself into something much more dynamic and fluid. It is this dynamic sexuality of each moment and each encounter that takes us into the art of alchemical love that Simon Iff demonstrates in *Moonchild*.

The interlocking of God and Man, and Man and Beast, which Crowley describes as "the Holy Hexagram" (Crowley, 1974, p. 148), with its descending red triangle and ascending blue triangle, is his way of describing this art. It involves the manifestation of the three-in-one will of the supernal sephiroth, the Horatii, and its successive incorporation through the triangles of Geburah, Gedulah, and Tiphareth, and Netzach, Hod, and Yesod, before its absorption in Malkuth.

Crowley's *Liber Aleph* (2005), "The Book of Wisdom and Folly", a series of letters to Frater Achad, who, at that time he considered to be his magical son, is entirely concerned with the development and practice of this central secret. In chapter 86 of that book (in some editions this chapter is indicated by the Greek letters Γη), we are told:

> DE FORMULA TOTA. ["On the Complete Formula"]
> Here then is the Schedule for all the Operations of Magick.
>
> First, thou shalt discover thy true Will, as I have already aught thee, and that Bud thereof which is the Purpose of this Operation.
>
> Next, formulate this Bud-Will as a Person, seeking or constructing it, and naming it according to thine Holy Qabalah, and its infallible Rule of Truth.
>
> Third, purify and consecrate this Person, concentrating upon him and against all else.
>
> This Preparation shall continue in all thy daily Life. Mark well, make ready a new Child immediately after every Birth.
>
> Fourth, make an especial and direct Invocation at thy Mass, before the Introit, formulating a visible Image of this Child, and offering the Right of Incarnation.
>
> Fifth, perform the Mass, not omitting the Epiklesis, and let there be a Golden Wedding Ring at the Marriage of thy Lion with thine Eagle.
>
> Sixth, at the Consumption of the Eucharist accept this Child, losing thy Consciousness in him, until he be well assimilated with thee.
>
> Now then do this continuously, for by Repetition cometh forth both Strength and Skill, and the Effect is cumulative, if thou allow no Time to dissipate itself. (Crowley, 2005, p. 86)

In this chapter we find the whole of the Moonchild operation sum-marised, both in its successes and failures, but, to truly understand it, we must more deeply consider the nature of sexuality and desire. The formula that Crowley uses here is "Love under Will" which links desire back to the true will that is the unfolding vector of our life and what Ramana Maharshi would call the *aham sphurana*, the I–I current of the Atman, or deep self. In Crowley's account of the operation he brings us firmly back to the true will and asks us to consider any such operation as a bud of that will, hence "bud-will": a new growth from the stem of our own Tree of Life. The next step is the personification of that will, its emergence as a new expression of that will; for example, say I wish to have more energy in my life in order to accomplish my will, then the bud-will or child I am seeking to incarnate is of myself endowed with more physical energy and life force. Or, let us say I wish to heal somebody or something: the bud-will is the image of that person whole and hale. I connect this bud-will with the Tree of Life, visualising its connection with the deeper divine schema, and then focus my attention upon it to the exclusion of all else, building an awareness of this until I am ready to perform the act of incarnation. The Mass of incarnation begins with an expression of intention and a vivid visualisation of the child who is seeking to be born through this rite. Crowley uses the term "Introit" here, which is the part of the Christian Mass in which the inten-tion of the mass is stated and is the entrance to the rite proper. The per-formance of the Mass, which is the place of the fusion of the opposites described in *The Book of Lies* (Crowley, 1974), relies upon the principle of inflaming through prayer and the consecration of desire, which enables what he calls the "Epiklesis", or descent of the Holy Ghost, or incarna-tion of the child of the operation. This activation of love under will is in relationship with the sense of self, if working alone, or with the sense of another person, if this work is performed by a couple, or with what-ever represents the sense of the beloved other. Crowley's image of the golden ring and the alchemical images of the eagle and lion represent the moment of orgasm or fusion and the incarnation of the child, and may be a literal sexual orgasm, or can be the arousal of desire through the passion of prayer in which we reach out to the divine and attain a moment of surrender and union in which subject and object vanish.

In the post-orgasmic moment of release and surrender comes the absorption, which, in the case of sexual magick, may involve the lit-eral consumption or absorption of the fluids, or may again happen at other levels. The key stance here is one of surrender and the embodiment of the living presence now evoked into being. The sense of losing your consciousness in the child, until it is well assimilated in you, underlines this.

Crowley's six points, if contemplated deeply, describe not simply a magical operation but the whole nature of our expression of our true will in each and every moment. If we place this process on the Tree of Life we find this:

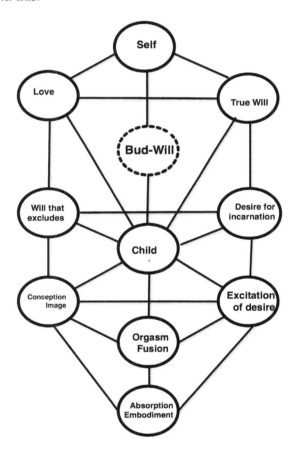

We may notice similarities between this tree and the tree at the end of Chapter 12, which shows the completed moonchild operation.

This whole process of the tree can be summarised in the practice of the divine name יהוה in which the point above the *yod* is Kether and Self; *yod* (י) is Chockmah and true will; *heh* (ה) is Binah and love; *vav* (ו) is the bud-will that becomes the incarnating child, and includes the spheres Daath to Yesod; and *heh* final (ה) is Malkuth, the process of embodiment and absorption. Another way of thinking about this is to see the Kether point as the unity of Nuit and Hadit, Chockmah and will as Hadit, Binah and love as Nuit, the emergence of the child as Hoor Paar Kraat in Da'at, becoming Ra Hoor Khuit in Tiphareth and Ankh af na Khonsu as manifestation of the child in Malkuth.

*Moonchild*, and the chapters from *The Book of Lies* and *Liber Aleph* that we have been looking at, present the magical work as distinct ritual operations but we are all the time formulating bud-wills and uniting with aspects of whatever is perceived as the beloved other in order to incarnate desire. The question is whether we are operating from a connection to true will and being or to a separated and enclosed sense of self. The characters of Douglas and Simon Iff in *Moonchild* show this difference in action. Simon Iff's stepping away from I, me, and mine, and his embrace of the mystery of Thou brings him into a position and capacity in which, through love, he can assimilate all contradictions in a deeper unity. Douglas, on the other hand, in his commitment to separation, creates more and more division and destruction, which ultimately destroys him.

Because we are continually practising the Mass of the Holy Ghost, formulating the Introit, bringing the child into being, and performing the fusion or orgasm that brings about embodiment, what we align with and whether we act as Simon Iff or as Douglas becomes an urgent question.

# CHAPTER 16

# The Qabalah of the Fountain, the Mountain, and the Moon

As we enter into this more fluid practice of magick, working with invocation and banishing to enable the manifestation of the child, so too does our practice of the Qabalah become more fluid. We may recall Crowley's images of the oak tree, the vesica and the Naples arrangement, as well as the traditions of the divine name יהוה. The Iyyun tradition shows us this more fluid work with the tree and the name as the contemplation of a fountain:

> [Continue] until you investigate, consider, seek out, reconcile, and establish the four Names dependent upon the yod. This constitutes the explanation of the four Names dependent upon the *yod*. These are the four letters that are like a coal connected to a flame, and the flame divides into four heads. All refer to one subject. Accordingly, this *yod* is a gushing fountain and its waters spread out into twenty-four parts. Each part has four roots. Each of the roots has four branches. Each branch has four vocalizations. The vocalizations split into an indeterminate [number], until they return again to the fountain from whence they ushered forth. (Verman, 1992, p. 52)

And again:

> Know, understand, investigate, consider, comprehend, and juxta-
> pose one thing against another and consider the analogies, until you
> fathom the explanation of these matters. For all wisdom and under-
> standing, all comprehension and thought, inquiry, knowledge,
> vocalization, rejection, speech, whispering, voice, action, guarding,
> and undertaking—all are found in this Name. (Verman, 1992, p. 52)

And:

> The *yod* is the fountain. Its roots are rooted and its streams are connected
> and the droplets are based in the *tikkun* of the circle. The circle sur-
> rounds that which encompasses, thereby encircling that which stands,
> causing it to stand, thence to inquire, to be still, and finally to shout.
> As the shout issues forth, it gives birth, springs forth, and expands.
> This expansion strengthens and radiates. This is the Primal Ether. In it
> all the general principles return to details and the details to principles.
> All are included within the grid. They all ring out and return and shout.
> In their return they become a circle. In their circle they are heated and
> flow like molten silver that is heated by fire—until all are joined, one
> with the other, like a piece of silver that is refined and soldered, this to
> that, through being heated by fire. The pieces are joined, piece to piece,
> until they return as one. (Verman, 1992, pp. 53–54)

What is being described in these excerpts is the process of creation,
the manifestation of will, which Crowley describes as the Mass of the
Holy Ghost. We may recall, in *Moonchild*, Cyril Grey teaching Lisa La
Giuffria the art of uniting opposites on a square, porphyry terrace with
a circular fountain, within which stands a statue of the Black Venus; and
the teaching given before the statue of Marsyas the satyr, the teacher of
music and mystery. Cyril quotes this verse:

> And where Light crosses Light, all loves combine:
>     Behold the God, the worshippers, the shrine,
> Each comprehensive of its single soul
>     Yet each the centre and fountain of the whole;
> Each one made perfect in its passionate part,
>     Each the circumference, and each the heart! (Crowley, 1929,
> p. 285)

This sense of being centre and circumference is found in the writings of the Iyyun circle (quoted above); in the cosmology of *The Book of the Law* and in the essentialised Qabalah of the Naples arrangement. What is being described is a dynamic of manifesting and returning as the *yod*— that is, the source of the fountain becomes the circle before returning to the single point. The Iyyun text the Fountain of Wisdom (Verman, 1992, pp. 50–64) tells us that the primal fountain manifests an infinite series of fountains, all of which are the centre point and circumference of the whole. However, it goes on to explain how this flowing process can become frozen and disrupted:

> Each wellspring divides into seven aspects. Each aspect becomes a source; each source becomes a structure. The structure freezes and the congealing becomes a coal. Within this coal all the well-springs grasp. Concerning this, it is stated, "flames attached to a coal. (Verman, 1992, p. 55)

In this situation we see structure and form replacing flow as a process of freezing and congealing takes place. The image of flames attaching to a coal is used in place of the fountain that flows in a circle and returns to the centre. This is the process that Maharshi would call the manifestation of the *ahamkara* and the appearance of self and world as separated forms. It is the moment where the icons of Yesod become idols and manifest in Malkuth as solid, frozen, and congealed forms with will and love tied into a knot through the process of attachment. It is this experience of solidity and substance that must be inquired into. The Fountain of Wisdom tells us:

> This is the root-principle that everything turns backwards and proceeds to dissolve until it returns to ether, as it once was. The Ether is the root-principle. (Verman, 1992, p. 56)

The turning backwards and dissolution returns us to the world of the living tree and the fountain and into the world of simplicity and spontaneous activity that the Tao speaks of. In this process of reversal we release the attachment to form and return into the unknowing instant— the return to simplicity, which involves the letting-go of belief, knowing, and past desire, is the natural movement of the Tao. It is the knotted loop of will, love, and belief, turning inwards on itself, that maintains the attached form and keeps us rooted in the congealed and frozen universe of substantial self and substantial world. A key aspect of this process of reversal is our capacity to soften the edges of our experience, so that our relationship to the world is less polarised. The *Tao Te Ching* advises us:

> The Tao is empty; in application, it does not overflow.
> Fathomless! As though the ancestor of the myriad beings.
> Blunt the sharpness
> Untie the knots;
> Harmonise the brightness;
> Unite with the dust.
> Deep! As though it exists.
> I do not know whose offspring it is; it is an appearance that preceded Di [i.e. the primordial ancestor of the Shang dynasty.] (Komjathy, 2023, p. 151)

### The Practice of the Tree and the Fountain

The practice of the tree and the fountain is an essentialised Qabalah practice working with the primordial tree in the garden and the fountain of life and light that is found at the centre of the tree, and which flows through the worlds to irrigate and renew them.

It is based on Crowley's images of the priestess of the oak, and of the universe as a vulva of stones in *Liber Liberi vel Lapidus Lazuli* (Crowley, 2015, p. 159) and begins by being the oak.

The practice begins by simply standing with unlocked knees, embracing your sense of being extended in space and time, noticing your senses and through them reaching out into your life and the universe that sustains you, allowing contact and colloquy and letting the universe touch you even as you touch and impact the universe. Then, enter into stillness and, following Maharshi's enquiry, enter into relationship with the centre point of origin within your form, the place of the union of Nuit and Hadit, feeling the infinite love of Nuit and the fiery will of Hadit in potential but not expressed. Next, contemplate the *yod* (ᵞ) arising as a flame out of the pregnant void, being both void and flame, and allow the expression of the love and will of the primal point to pour through you, being the green fool of the tarot. As we contemplate the letter ה (*heh*) become aware of space around you, the sense of universe shaping and reflecting the fountain of life and fire, arising from the single point and manifesting as Nuit. Notice the interplay of the *yod* and the *heh*, the axis of fire and the containing shape of the universe, entering into the play of Hadit and Nuit and the mystery of the Star-Sponge vision. From that interplay, feel the arising current of will and love manifesting through awareness as you contemplate the ו (*vav*), and take shape as the living human in the living tree. Finally, relax into the presence of embodiment, contemplating ה, the final *heh*. In this moment you are the priestess of the oak contemplating the universe as the temple of the vulva of stones that is also the Star-Sponge vision. Within us is the fountain of the name, continually returning to and manifesting the primal point so, with root and branch, we reach out and embrace all that manifests, seeing in the arising, dynamic mystery the activity of the single point and its constant reflections and iterations. As Crowley does, we see each phenomenon that appears as an expression of this interplay; just as he contemplates the white cat for each singular appearance is embedded in and arises out of the whole.

We can also use Crowley's Naples arrangement in this practice, thus: raising our hands upwards above our head, like a chalice, in a gesture of prayer, we contemplate the one point and, as we bring our hands downwards, we speak: י (*yod*), ה (*heh*), and experience the point passing through the gate of Chockmah and Binah, acquiring the principles of will and extension and love and relating. We speak ו (*vav*), and experience the singularity acquiring solidity, motion, reflective balance, the bliss of its being, the concept of its being and the image of its being. Bringing our hands into contact with our body we embrace our form, speak ה, *heh* final, and allow the point to embody in us. Opening our hands, we allow the living form to pass through us into the wider world in a gesture of release and blessing. We might visualise this as a fiery dove, descending from the supernals into our body and through our body into the universe. Having released the point-impulse or dove we then return into the stillness of the beginning.

## The Mystery of the Moon and the Mountain

Another important early tradition of the Qabalah, which has some relevance here, is found hidden within the Korahite psalms. The Korahites were an early Israelite priesthood concerned with the practice of descending into the underworld, the freeing of lost souls, and the exorcism of demonic forces. As far as can be understood, they were a northern priesthood associated with the sanctuary of Tel Dan, a sacred hill connected to the source of the Jordan, which, in the earliest days, was said to contain the cult statue of the Golden Calf. In the Exodus story at Mount Sinai the calf is referred to as an idolatrous idol that corrupts the Israelites and is the cause of the destruction of the first version of Tablets of the Law and Moses's withdrawal back up the mountain (Exodus 32). The Korahite priesthood appears to have come into conflict with the Levitical priesthood and we are told in the Bible (Numbers 16: 1–34) that Korah, the archetypal ancestor of the cult, is swallowed up whole into the underworld and his followers consumed by fire. The children of Korah are spared, then appointed as singers and doorkeepers in the first Temple of Jerusalem. This is a process that looks like the absorption of one priestly order by another, and contains within it one of the enduring tensions within the Abrahamic religions: ambivalence concerning images, which can act either as icons or idols. The image of the Golden Calf is believed to be an image of the ancient moon god, Sin (Key, 1965, pp. 20–26), father of Inanna (goddess of Venus) and Shamash (god of the Sun). The fact that the mountain where the Tablets of the Law are received is called Mount Sinai gives us a clue that the mountain was holy to Sin. When Moses descends from the cloud at the mountain's summit he is seen as having horns of light, which also hints at a connection to Sin, whose cult image was a gold bull-calf with crescent horns and a beard of lapis lazuli. His main cult centres were the cities of Ur and Harran, both sites associated with Abraham. The cultic bull is found all over the Middle East, notably in Babylon as the winged human-headed, bearded bull doorkeeper who guards the holy city and temple and who, in combination with the winged lion, eagle, and human being appears in the vision of Ezekiel (1: 5–14).

It is notable, therefore, that as well as being singers and dancers in the temple, the Korahites are the doorkeepers who preserve the ancient lunar teachings of the moon and mountain. They hold also the mystery of the Kerubim, who constitute the throne and place of manifestation of divine presence and the principle of polarity and divine sexuality that refreshes and renews the world. Psalm 87 shows the principles of this ancient practice.

> By the Sons of Korah, a psalm, a song,
> His Foundation is in the Holy Mountain,
> YHVH loves the gates of Zion
> More than all the dwelling places of Jacob
> Glorious things are said of you
> City of God Selah.
> "I mention Rehab and Babylon to those who know me
> Behold, Philistilia. Tyre with Cush,
> This one was born there."
> But of Zion it was said, "A man and a man was born in her
> And he, Elyon, established her."
> YHVH takes account when he writes down peoples:
> "This one was born there." Selah.
> "And singers as well as dancers
> All my springs are in you." (Rautenbach, 2010, p. 22)

Within this psalm is an advanced Qabalistic contemplation of the path we have been considering in this book. We are given a symbolic landscape of the holy mountain that contains the holy city, holy temple, and Holy of Holies. Surrounding this holy place are the cities of the plain, which represent the disturbed and demonic forms that are not connected to the roots of life.

This path begins, like Crowley's moonchild operation, in the contemplation of the lunar sphere of Yesod, which is the foundation of the sense of self and universe. To enter this place requires us to enter the moonlit dream of Yesod that underlies the apparent solidity and clear edges of outer life.

Psalm 87 uses the word יסדתו (*yesodtow*), which has the meaning of inscribing a decree or making a mark that cannot be erased. To align our foundation with the foundation of the holy mountain is to begin the process of *tikkun*, as described in the writings of the Iyyun circle. It is the turning of attention inwards, as Maharshi suggests in the act of self-enquiry and, in this act, erasing the *samskaras* or "foundation marks" that uphold our sense of constricted self. It is this process that is being described in *The Fountain of Wisdom* as "the melting of silver" and the return to oneness.

The next step is the contemplation of יהוה, identifying with this through visualising the letters of the name within us and around us.

Here, the *yod* is in our head; the *heh* embraces our shoulders and chest; the *vav* begins at our heart and extends into our pelvis; and the *heh* final, our hips and legs. Here we identify with the pattern of the name, the point above the *yod* being our spiritual root, the *yod* being will, the *heh* being love, the *vav* our mediating presence, and the *heh* final our capacity to embody. Being one with the name, we turn more deeply inwards, surrendering into this presence, and we encounter the door-keeper of the gates, who opens and closes the way into the innerness of the holy mountain. This figure can be envisaged as the golden, winged bull-calf that opens or closes the way into the presence of the mystery of the moon-mountain. Here, we wait in silence before the gates and in the presence of the doorkeeper until there is an opening. This is the sitting before what the *Tao Te Ching* calls "the mysterious pass" in which, we are told:

> The five colours cause one's eyes to become blind,
> The five sounds cause one's eyes to become deaf,
> The five flavours cause one's mouth to become dull,
> Galloping and hunting cause one's heart-mind to become mad,
> Difficult to get goods cause one's activities to be disrupted.
> Therefore the sages,
> Focus on the belly, not the eyes.
> Thus leave that and adopt this. (Komjathy, 2023, p. 167)

As we sit in this place we recall the transformation of יקוב, "Jacob", into ישראל, "Israel": the name "Jacob" means "follower" or "heel grabber" and refers to the aspect of Jacob and ourselves that is the trickster and manipulates the world to obtain the "difficult to get goods". Israel is a name that can mean "one who struggles with God", or a being, a "prince or princess of power". This transformation comes about through the struggle through the night with a figure who is called simply איש, "a man" (Genesis 32: 24). This name is formed from the insertion of the letter י yod within the word אש, the word for "fire", and indicates that the man is a soul of fire who bears within him the will of the divine. This struggle through the night, like the journey of Ra's boat, culminates at daybreak in the man wounding Jacob in the thigh and blessing him with the new name of "Israel". The place within which this struggle has happened is then called "Peniel", the place where God is seen face-to-face. This act of seeing face-to-face is hinted at in the phrase איש ו איש, "a man and a man" in Psalm 87, which points us to the communion with the Angel of Tiphareth and the mirroring that happens between this deeper aspect of ourselves and the known self that emerges. This aligns Yesod and Tiphareth, Hod and Netzach, and Geburah and Gedulah, so that the image of ourselves and universe becomes illuminated, our mind aligns with will and our feelings open into the deeper sense of love and compassion. The act of surrender and the blessing of the new name opens the gate and, just as we are transformed, so is our environment, which is now עיר ה אלהים, "the city of God". If we consider the Hebrew word עיר, it is formed from ע, "the eye", י, "the hand", and connected to ר, "the head", or source of life. This indicates the fusion of hand and eye, or will and perception. ה אלהים is the name of God applied to Binah, the sphere of non-dual love. As the dweller in the city in continual communion with the divine presence we notice the presence of the Qliphoth, those forms within us and within the world that generate the energies of separation. The images of Rehab (or Egypt), Babylon, Philistia, Tyre, and Kush are used are images of the places that generate the energies of separation and disruption, and we are asked to consider both the existence of these forms and the energies that enable them to arise.

The psalm moves on to another step, moving from the city of God into the temple, locating us within the sphere of Daath. This step is shown by the word יְכוֹנְנֶהָ, which has the meaning of being set upright and given a firm base; the image is of a plant that grows upwards into the sky while deeply rooting into the earth. Daath is the higher analogue of Yesod, and here we are asked to root ourselves in mystery and between the opposites. As we manifest here, we are seen and recognised by the divine, the word for "recognition" being יספר, a deeper aspect of face beholds face, in which we are known and know our interdependence with the divine; in effect, we become one who dwells within the temple.

There is one deeper transition that the psalm gives us as it concludes for it speaks of another birth in saying, "This one is born there. Selah." Selah is a musical pause and interruption; it is a radical stop and entrance into silence. We are now presented with two images: first singers שרים. The image here is of a travelling singer who transmits a decree or spell from one in authority. Then dancers כחללים: here the root image is of a flute or something pierced and hollowed, which, anciently, would be a hollow bone that is blown through, and suggests the image of the *ruach ha qodesh*, the divine spirit blowing through us and directing the dance. Of both these figures it is said, "כל מעיני בך" "All my springs are in you." The word מעיני means spring and fountain and the combination of these images tells us of the union of the supernals and of the mystery of the enfolding of the All within the singularity of awareness. This is the union of Nuit and Hadit and the place at the ending of Moonchild where Cyril Grey realizes his unity with Douglas. Here we are within the Holy of Holies.

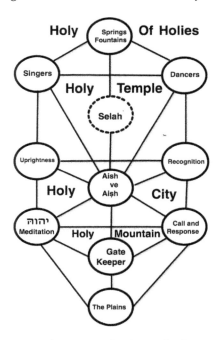

Psalm 87 on the Tree of Life

This practice can be carried out as a visualisation. We find ourselves in a desert area at the foot of the mountain of Sinai, which towers above us and is topped with a great cloud within which there is a sense of a great presence. We ascend the mountain until we find ourselves just at the level of the cloud.

We become aware of a great doorway of stone in the mountain, engraved with the form of a winged bull, and we become aware of the sense of the moon mountain of revelation and of our identity as a dweller on the holy mountain.

As we contemplate this engraving, the form becomes three-dimensional and living, taking the shape of the Golden Calf with a beard of lapis lazuli, and we enter into dialogue with this figure. We hold the intention of moving inwards, into the mysterious mountain, so that our Yesod aligns with the Divine Yesod, following the advice of the *Tao Te Ching* to soften the edges and untie knots (Komjathy, 2023, p. 151). The doorkeeper may change shape and present us with images of the past and present that have to be softened and untied. At a certain point there will be a sense of rapport and permission and the door will open, and then we find ourselves within the holy city within the holy mountain. The shape of the city will be different for each of us and may, indeed, differ from occasion to occasion. However it presents, we will find a pathway that leads inwards to the temple that is at the centre of the city, and we may notice a sense of active stillness and presence focusing upon us, which creates a dialogue of wills and a sense of call and response. As this arises, we contemplate the name יהוה and the phrase איש ו איש, following the process of call and response, until we find ourselves drawn to the temple at the centre of the city. Just as with the city, the temple will present itself in a different form to each of us, and differently at different times. We embrace our identity as a server of the temple, exploring our priestly identity as the embodiment of the name and as איש ו איש.

The sense of peace, communion, and growth deepens until there is a sense of the further step that presents itself as a pause and stopping point. We contemplate "Selah!" and at this point surrender into the unknown, releasing all, becoming the wandering singer, the hollowed-out bone, and discovering כל מעיני בך, that all the springs, all the fountains of the divine are within us. It is from this place that the divine fountain flows through us without hinderance and the Mass of the Holy Ghost is instantaneously accomplished. Here we are the one who dwells within the Holy of Holies, from whom the rivers of Paradise flow.

This practice is deepened through the continual contemplation of Psalm 87 and the four steps of being (1) the dweller in the mountain, contemplating the divine letter ה; (2) dweller in the city, contemplating the letter ו; (3) dweller in the temple, contemplating the letter ה; and (4) dweller in the Holy of Holies, contemplating the letter י.

# MASTERING THE WAY

This final section is concerned with the crossing into the non-dual roots of the tree and the different modes of operating from these roots. The differences are tonal only, as the three supernal sephiroth are constantly in union but, broadly, the Magister Templi's focus is on the expression of non-dual love and being the living tree who irrigates the garden; the Magus's focus is on will and the generation of life and change; and the Ipsissimus's focus is on singularity and multiplicity.

# CHAPTER 17

# Crossing the Abyss

This process is concerned, as *Liber Liberi vel Lapidis Lazuli* says, with "the Birth-Words of a Master of the Temple" (Crowley, 1989, p. 313) and the emergence into the non-dual roots of the Tree of Life. In Crowley's Enochian workings, described in *The Vision and the Voice* (Crowley, 1972b, pp. 133–176), this particular transition is described as the Adept giving all their individual life into the divine presence of Binah, seen as Babalon, the divine whore, who unites with all. The Adept is then described as a pyramidal pile of ash sitting in the City of the Pyramids, contemplating the mystery of the Trance of Sorrow, which arises from the experience of impermanence. This mystery of sorrow is later balanced by the experience of the Magus, who is change personified, and who experiences the same mystery as perpetual joy. Above and beyond these perspectives is that of the Ipsissimus, whose comprehension of the mystery is beyond all description and hint.

The crossing is summarised in the holy book *Liber Cheth vel Vallum Abiegni* (Crowley, 2015, pp. 207–209). This book is concerned with the secret of the Holy Graal, seen as the sacred vessel of Babalon, the scarlet woman, the divine presence in Binah who loves all and receives all and is the bride of chaos, the divine beast of Chockmah. The crossing of the abyss into her presence is envisaged as the pouring of all our blood into her chalice, mingling our life with the universal life, not keeping back a single drop for ourselves. This sense of surrender and deconstruction results in us being reduced to a pile of ashes, which is gathered up by the angel and placed in a pyramidal form within the City of the Pyramids. In *The Vision and the Voice* we are told that our name is no more and that now we are *Nemo* or "no-one" (Crowley, 1972, pp. 139–144). Surrendering all into the presence of the angel who presents herself as Babalon takes us through the interruption of the abyss, for it is our longing and will to abandon our prior skill and mastery that enables us to navigate this enormous transition. This pouring out of our blood and our surrender takes us into the state of being a babe in the womb of Babalon who is impregnated by Chaos or Pan. Here, we encounter the dark mother as well as Pan in his Panphage form (the "All-devourer"), before being born of the bright mother and Pan in his Pangenitor ("All-begetter") phase. Meanwhile, all the forms and shapes of our existence are a pyramidal pile of ashes in the City of Pyramids within the great NOX that is the Night of Pan. The ashes are resurrected as the Master of the Temple, who brings his or her non-dual love and understanding to life within a particular aspect of the manifest universe. This is sometimes described as the Master being "cast out" into a particular sephira that defines their work so that for example one whose work is concerned with healing and balancing would be concerned with the work of Tiphareth or somebody concerned with the issue of truth and justice would be aligned with the work of Geburah.

The Holy Book *Liber Liberi vel Lapidis Lazuli* begins with these lines (Prologue: 1–16):

> Into my loneliness comes—
> The sound of a flute in dim groves that haunt the uttermost hills.
> Even from the brave river they reach to the edge of the wilderness.
> And I behold Pan.
> The snows are eternal above, above—
> And their perfume smokes upward into the nostrils of the stars.
> But what have I to do with these?
> To me only the distant flute, the abiding vision of Pan.
> On all sides Pan to the eye, to the ear;
> The perfume of Pan pervading, the taste of him utterly filling my mouth, so that the tongue breaks forth into a weird and monstrous speech.

The embrace of him intense on every centre of pain and pleasure.
The sixth interior sense aflame with the inmost self of Him,
Myself flung down the precipice of being
Even to the abyss, annihilation.
An end to loneliness, as to all.
Pan! Pan! Io Pan! Io Pan! (Crowley, 2015, p. 135)

The text goes on to describe a search for union with the divine, with Pan considered to be "the All" and successively imaged as a reclining nymph, as a centaur, and as a little white rabbit in the burrow of night, as well as goat-hoofed, horned, and a pillar of lightning from which pearls and black specks of nothingness fall. This is a direct and intimate encounter with the living universe so that each event of life is experienced as a particular meeting between the infinite and our soul.

Crowley gives us many images in this text, which describes the process of surrendering our sense of self and life and the emergence of a new world. Underneath the profusion of images is a process of extinction in which we are surrounded on all sides, all senses (including the sixth sense of gnosis) filled with Pan, the All, and are cast down into the NOX or night of being whose darkness is brighter than light. This sense of the dazzling darkness brings us to the new sense of self and universe.

The sense of night or NOX and the giving of ourselves into the mysterious presence is underlined in the verses,

I woo thee with a dagger drawn across my throat.
Let the spout of blood quench Thy blood-thirst, O, my God.
(*Liberi Liber Lapidus vel Lazuli* 1: 12–13) (Crowley, 2015, p. 136)

*Liber Cheth* underlines this,

1   This is the secret of the Holy Graal, that is the sacred vessel of our Lady the Scarlet Woman, Babalon the Mother of Abominations, the bride of Chaos, that rideth upon our Lord the Beast.
2   Thou shall drain out thy blood that is thy life into the golden cup of her fornication.
3   Thou shalt mingle thy life with the universal life

Thou shalt not keep back one drop. (Verses 1–3) (Crowley, 2015, p. 207)

*Liberi Liber Lapidus vel Lazuli* also gives us the symbol of the trident, which is the implement of the worshipper of Shiva, the yogic god who dissolves all opposites and who is often envisaged as a phallic pillar of light and flame. The trident is also associated with Neptune, the god of the sea, who is the earth shaker. This image is combined with that of the phoenix wand, and we are told that the trident or phoenix wand spears the wicked. All this underscores the profound transition and the sense of conscious dying into a new life. The divine is then addressed as the goat-hoofed horned one who is also the pillar of lightning, from which fall pearls and from the pearls fall black specks of nothing. The Pearls are like nebulae the first swirlings of Kether whilst the black specks of nothing indicate the unmanifest. We are then reminded of the 0 = 2 equation and the Naples arrangement and enter the experience of interconnection and emergence from mystery described in the verse "I based all on one, one on naught" (1: 25) (Crowley, 2015, p. 137). This breakthrough is described as being afloat in the aether, in the Divine presence; as being filled with light and entering into the experience of the open eye that dissolves duality. This leads to the experience of the Trance of Sorrow, described here as "the ever weeping one" (1: 29) (Crowley, 2015, p. 137). The fusion of dualities here is not simply the embrace of complementaries but also the fusion of contraries, here imaged as Horus and Typhon. We are told also that thought is evil, for it disturbs the pristine stillness, and are shown the experience of Daath as the diffraction of the parallel light arising out of infinity. Our devotion to the angel causes us to rise up through the diffraction and the ascent is also part of this dissolution and compared to a funeral pyre. We are told what when the God shall know us our flame will expire in the great empty night that is the divine presence.

In the second chapter, the sense of fusion of dualities is taken up again in the witnessing of two galaxies colliding, which turn upon us so that we are crushed by the collision. We are, however, sustained by the angel as the tortoise who sustains the worlds, and we experience entering into its carapace, sitting in the heart of the angel. We then contemplate the angel under the form of a black Nubian slave, an image of the Black Isis and Binah, and find ourselves in the House of Pertinax, a slave who became a Roman Emperor. We contemplate the sense of Pan as the goat, going beyond rationality into the divine madness, and experience the union of beauty and ugliness through the experience of the kisses of Pan that are bloody and stinking and like sunlight shining on a blue sea and the scent of roses.

The third chapter brings us into the god form of Amun Ra in his temple in Thebes where also, in the inmost shrine, we find Bacchus as the priest showing us the principle of intoxication and ecstatic long-ing at the heart of the temple. In this longing we are given an image of ascending through terraces to an oyster shell containing a pearl, having at its centre a glitter too bright to look on. This is an indication of the ascent of the tree into the single point of Kether.

In the fourth chapter we are given the image of the Magister Templi as a maiden bathing in a clear pool of fresh water who calls out to the angel: "I see Thee who is dark and desirable rising through the water as golden smoke"(4: 1–2) (Crowley, 2015, p. 149). The angel is experienced as radiant, golden, and seen face-to-face. The symbol of a sword passing through and beyond the body of the golden angel is used as an image of the mind aligning with the universal mind, and then we are given a sense of falling into the arms of the infinite, moving out of time into eter-nity, where we find rest in the City of Pyramids under the Night of Pan. In this place we call out to Iacchus the daimon, initiator of the mysteries of Eleusi and we may recall that at the heart of the Eleusian mystery is the presentation of an ear of grain cut in silence—the experience of death and resurrection. We are then asked to remember the father son dialogue of the Greek Gods Uranus and Eros and the conversation of Marsyas the satyr and Olympas his pupil, which are versions of the col-loquy of the Adept and the angel. As we enter into the new awareness that arises in us, each thing that we experience becomes an access point to and representation of the All. This is shown in the contemplation of a white cat sitting on a trellis, which we see as the stillness of the divine, around which the worlds turn and from whose fur sparks fly and create the worlds. We are told that the Adept has seen more of the divine in the encounter with the cat than in contemplating the mysteries of time and space for this is not an abstract mystery but the meeting of the infinite and the finite, the personal and the universal.

In the fifth chapter, we swim in the heart of God as a trout in a moun-tain stream, leaping from pool to pool with joy, experiencing our mind as a crystal cave of thought. We contemplate the tarot card The Star and enter into the river of space and time as the shining, silver, generative star, experiencing every act of breath, word, thought, and deed as an act of love under will. We see the deep interconnection between all acts, seeing them as hyberbolic curves arising from the intersection of the vortex or cone of manifestation with an infinite ray of light. We are told:

> Nor by memory, nor by imagination, nor by prayer, nor by fasting, nor by scourging, nor by drugs, nor by ritual, nor by meditation; only by passive love shall he avail.
>
> He shall await the sword of the Beloved and bare his throat for the stroke.
>
> Then shall his blood leap out and write me runes in the sky; yea, write me runes in the sky. (5: 46) (Crowley, 2015, p. 158)

The connection between the hyperbolas and the cone and ray, and the leaping forth of the Adept's blood into the sky, is again the mingling of the personal and universal that is enabled through the practice of passive love.

This sense of the interconnectedness of the All and the small is further deepened by the understanding given in the sixth chapter of the universe as a temple of stones in the shape of the *vesica piscis*, the vulva of the deep mother formed from the intersection of the circles of the opposites in union, while the divine is imaged as a priestess of the Druids, knowing the powers of the oak. The vesica and the oak as the world tree take us more deeply into the organic interchange of love and will that is the basis of the universe. Participating in this mystery we come into the Chapel of the Graal of Babalon, in which we secretly drink of the sacrament of the union of the personal and universal. This is the wine of Iacchus, the fruit of the mysteries, that magnifies all events like an alchemical tincture. We are told: "our red powder of projection is beyond all possibilities" (6: 39) (Crowley, 2015, p. 161). This transforming power affects all our senses so that the old world is split apart and a new one is born.

The seventh and final chapter begins with the unbinding of the feet of the mummified Osiris and the appearance of forward movement, which brings us to the contemplation of the Black Isis as a black marble statue, and then the shaking of the statue by the appearance of the crowned and conquering Horus child. The mystery of this resurrection is given in the word "Abrahadabra", the eleven-fold word that we have already contemplated, and which represents the union of the personal and the universal, the pentagram and the hexagram. There is then a reference to the seven-fold word that refers to both the seven chapters of *Liber Liberi vel Lapdis Lazuli* and the word *ARARITA*, the word of unity that we worked with in the ritual of the Star Sapphire.

This seven-foldness is resolved into the image of the camel striding over the desert to the crown of Kether, and the sense of the vast Night of Pan that swallows up all into the nothingness that is not I, not Thou, and the achievement of the union of the one with the many. Going into the deeper silence of the unmanifest, we concentrate a centre that is the smooth point and, from here, the expression of love under will is poured out upon the manifest world as wine for those who do not know, wine that creates inspiration in the dull, life in the lifeless, love in the loveless. From here the word that is our own particular formulation of love and will arises and, in our incarnation of this word, we discover the true faith—the faith of experience.

# CHAPTER 18

# Sitting on Cold Mountain

A s we work with the contemplation of the one and the many, as we speak our word and enter into the holy mountain, holy city temple, and Holy of Holies, we come into a state of mind described by Ch'an adept and poet Han Shan, who tells us:

> I reached Cold Mountain and all cares stopped
> no idle thoughts remained in my head
> nothing to do I write poems on rocks
> and trust the current like an unmoored boat (Pine, 2000, p. 159)

Cold Mountain is Han Shan's version of the holy mountain of Psalm 87 and he uses the image of sitting on Cold Mountain as entering into the presence of what Maharshi would call the Self and the ancient Egyptians the Geru Maa, and shows us the activity of non-dual love as writing poems on rocks, trusting the current, finding the whole unfolding universe just here and now in this form, in the midst of these conditions.

There was an old Taoist tradition of retreat into simplicity, into places such as Cold Mountain, but, in keeping with their tradition of paradox, this apparent retreat is in actuality a deeper engagement with the universe, working with the deep tides and activities of that universe.

Central to this is the concept of *wu wei*, or the action of non-action, in which *chi*, or energy, follows the principle of intention and will.

In this practice we come to the simplicity that underlies all and to be on Cold Mountain, just as to be in the moon mountain of Sinai, requires us to be untethered and trusting of the currents of life that rise and fall. Writing poems on rocks refers to the practice of embodying these rising and falling currents. Poems, in the way Han Shan understands them, are focused living images that are a particular expression of love and will, which embodies the moment, and which, when contemplated, awaken us to a deeper life and service. In the following poem, he shows us the state of mind that is necessary for us to work in this way:

> My mind is like the autumn moon
> clear and bright in a pool of jade
> nothing can compare
> what more can I say (Pine, 2000, p. 39)

In this short poem he asks us to be like the harvest moon reflected in a jade-green pool and to be beyond comparison and speech. The harvest moon festival is an important one in China and is seem as a time of rest and the enjoyment of the fruits of the harvest while also appreciating the cycles of the moon linked to the agricultural cycle. To be aligned with the moon, and to reflect in a pool of green jade, is to be a vehicle for the manifesting energy of life and, like the singers and dancers of Psalm 87, we allow the passage of the spirit through us and bring the moonchild into manifestation. The poem shows us the true alignment of Daath and Yesod on the Tree of Life, and it is notable that in this process there is no comparison; the verse ends with there being nothing else to be said. Here, the complexity of mental activity is not needed and the act of reflection and embodiment silently proceeds. This might remind us of the true operation of the manifestation of the child in *Moonchild*, in which the Horatii are triplets, born without drama or complication and watched over by the silent sage, Mahathera Phang.

Han Shan goes on to tell us more about this state of mind and heart:

> Before the cliffs I sat alone
> the moon shone in the sky
> but where a thousand shapes appeared
> its lantern cast no light
> the unobstructed spirit is clear

> the empty cave is a mystery
> a finger showed me the moon
> the moon is the hub of the mind (Pine, 2000, p. 43)

Here he shows us an image of sitting on Cold Mountain witnessing the thousand shapes appearing, but remaining in touch with the clear and unobstructed spirit and the empty cave. The reference to the finger and the moon may remind us of a Ch'an Buddhist injunction to look towards the moon, not the finger that points towards that moon, and is a reminder to not become emeshed in the thoughts, beliefs, and ideas about the path. What we must simply be with is the experience of the moon itself, which here is described as "the hub of the mind"—a reference to verse 11 of the *Tao Te Ching* "Thirty spokes converge on a hub / but it's the emptiness / that makes a wheel work" (Pine, 2009, p. 22). It also shows us the true work of the mind, which is to simply, silently, reflect; to allow the appearances to pass through us so that the concept of the being of the moonchild can combine with its desire to be and become the living image of its being and be born.

He then gives us some advice about what happens when we make our home in this state of awareness:

> From the start, my home has been
> Here on cold mountain.
> Where I roost atop the stony cliff,
> Cut off from karmic pains.
> All phenomena, when submerged,
> leave no trace behind them;
> Unspooled, they'll then flow everywhere
> through the endless universe.
> A flashing image of shadow and light
> glows against the ground of Mind;
> Yet not a single dharma comes
> to face me in the Now.
> At last I know that solitary
> single mani gem
> Is boundless in its usefulness,
> perfect in every way. (Rouzer, 2016, p. 128)

In this poem we are shown that from this place we can touch all other places of the universe for we are within the cloud of Mount Sinai, within the Holy of Holies, the centre point on which all converges and from which all things diverge. We are told that this has been our home from the beginning and are taken into the contemplation of the supernal sephiroth as representing the true root of our being, will, and love. We are given the images of submerging and unspooling as the indication of how each act of love and will is everywhere present in the universe and simultaneously self-destructs to leave no enduring mark. This is further enhanced in the experience of the appearance of images, of shadows and light, which flash in and out of being. The "mani gem", like the Philosopher's Stone is that quality within the heart and mind that returns everything to its original nature. It is an ancient Buddhist symbol, found in the ancient mantra *om mani padme hum*, which, broadly, means "homage to the mani gem in the heart of the lotus, blessings!" The gem is said to be perfectly circular, to have no corners or edges and, therefore, able to move in all directions, to be unbound and therefore boundless, perfect, therefore, even in imperfection.

If we place some of Han Shan's images on the Tree of Life we may get some sense that what is being described here is the way of the empty hand, returning to essence, witnessing the movement of shady and bright, allowing unspooling and submerging and being the mani stone without corners or edge. Here we allow the moon to be the hub of the heart and mind and simply allow the movement of the Tao in all its modes.

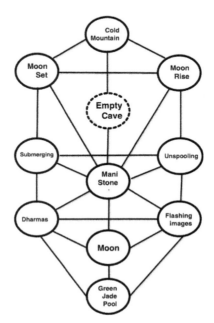

Han Shan gives also the image of an ancient tree:

> There's a tree, older than the forest;
> Twice as old, by the count of it.
> Roots shifted with the hills and valleys,
> Leaves have changed in the wind and frost.
> All will laugh at the outside withering;
> None admires the grain within.
> But when its bark will peel away,
> Only the Real and True remain. (Rouzer, 2016, p. 122)

The great Zen master Hakuin tells us (Rouzer, 2016, p. 123) that Han Shan is speaking of himself here, and describes him as a shadowless tree in the mountain of his own residence, and that the tree has passed through wind and frost and an alchemical process of refinement and suffering. As a result of these processes, it finds its original appearance, which Hakuin describes as being like a Zen abbot's staff. The Zen staff is a seven-foot-long, untrimmed stick that every Zen master cuts for himself in the mountains as a symbol of authority, and a reference to true nature as being the uncarved wood of the *Tao Te Ching*. The image of the withered tree whose real and true nature is at last visible, because the bark has peeled away, points back at Chuang Tzu's sacred and useless oak (Burton Watson, 2013, pp. 30–31), as well as Amenope's tree (Karenga, 2012, pp. 98–99) that will never go to the carpentry shop. This is an image that takes us right into the heart of our subject, of being unified with true will, the processes of life having rid us of our concealing bark. The bark here represents what the Qabalah would call "the Qliphoth" (Rees, 2022, pp. ix–xvi) the shells that obscure light, and what *The Book of the Law* would describe as the veil of the modest woman that must be torn (II: 52). The uncarved staff is then the magical staff of the true will, which, like the wish-fulfilling gem of the mani stone, enables all it touches to align with its own deepest will.

Han Shan contrasts this with the tree that is made use of:

> Heaven gave rise to a lofty tree
> Men trimmed it to form long beams
> A pity—this wood for rafters
> Got thrown into some hidden gulch
> Core still strong after all these years,

> Though bark peeled off as the days passed.
> But if a knowing one will bear them off—
> They can still prop up a stable. (Rouzer, 2016, p. 119)

Here we are shown the way in which our manipulative sense of mind seeks to make use of this deep quality of will and life that springs out of the depths of the Tao. We are shown both how that distorted aspect of our being is unstable and chaotic: the tree, having been formed into rafters, is forgotten and thrown into a hidden gulch and, even when found, is only used to prop up a stable. Nonetheless, we are told that the core of the wood remains strong despite its hard usage.

It is this manipulative and reactive aspect of ourselves that distorts our experience and generates the sense of I, me, and mine, and is a particular feature of when the spheres of Hod, Netzach, and Yesod organise themselves around this separated sense of self and our relationship to inner and outer worlds becomes obscured. Han Shan shows this in (first of all) the sense of the tree of our deep nature being trimmed to make rafter beams, and then forgotten about and dumped in a gulch, and then being remembered only dimly so and used to prop up a stable.

This is in contrast to the Cold Mountain tree, in which each of the sephiroth instantaneously mirror each other. In Buddhist tradition there is a particular quality of the heart and mind called *papanca*, which is similar to both the term in Advaita *ahamkara*, and the internal dialogue of Hod, Netzach, and Yesod. *Papanca*, which could be translated as "proliferation", has the sense of being like a clinging vine, or an overgrown jungle that fills all space and entangles ourselves and everything we touch. It is said to have a sticky quality, in that, whatever it comes into contact with, it seizes hold of and sorts it into something to be kept close, something to be sent away, or something to be ignored. The great Zen Master Hakuin comments on Han Shan's uncarved staff:

> I found a stake on Mount T'ien-t'ai smothered with clinging vines.
> I dragged it with all its coils and convolutions up here to Hōrin-ji.
> I will choke monks intent on pulling the weeds from their minds,
> Or insert nails and wedges from the stinking softness of my heart. (Waddell, 2017, p. 152)

Here he shows us how this quality of being the uncarved wood and the simplicity of true will becomes obscured by *papanca*, and the work of the teacher involves choking off the tendency to proliferate and using teachings that penetrate the apparent solidity of conditioned consciousness like nails and wedges to break up its structure. Mount T'ien-t'ai is Cold Mountain and Hakuin uses the poems as ways of inserting nails and wedges to choke off the tendency for *papanca*.

In the Anguttara Nikaya, one of the very early sutras of the Buddha, we are given a sense of the simplicity of the mind without papanca,

> One perception arose in me: "Cessation of becoming is Nibbana." Another perception faded out in me "Cessation of becoming is Nibbana," just as, your reverence, from a fire of splinters, one flame arises and another flame fades out, even so in me one perception arose; "Cessation of becoming is Nibbana" and another perception faded out, "Cessation of becoming is Nibbana." Yet at the same time, your reverence I consciously perceived. (Nanananda, 1986, pp. 60–61)

The commentator, Bhikkhu Nanananda, comments that, here, in the consciousness of the awakened one, the sense of I (which Nanananda describes as *papanca* par excellence) has been burned away by the fire of awareness. What remains is a moment-by-moment simplicity of being, perception, and action, in which we witness the arising and ceasing of experience and participate in the same without becoming involved in the manipulation of our own or others' experience. While, conventionally, *Nibbana* is thought of as "enlightenment", its root meaning is "to be blown out", for what is blown out is the sense of I, me, and mine, which is the generative root of *papanca*, the entangling vine of the heart and mind.

It is for this reason that Simon Iff is referred to as "Simple Simon" for his thoughts, words, and deeds come from this immediate sense of spontaneity and connectedness. The freshness and immediacy of such a presence can be very disturbing to those of us who are not only entangled in our own vine but actively growing and protecting it. This is why the radical teacher Hakuin talks of choking and hammering nails and wedges into his monks and nuns.

Han Shan brings us back to the simplicity that underlies all this:

> Honour your own nature—
> alone, it has no companion.
> If you look for it, you can't see it.
>
> It goes in and out without a gate.
> If you shrink it, it exists in one square inch.
> If you stretch it, it is everywhere.
> If you don't trust and treasure it,
> You cannot encounter it. (Tanahashi & Levitt, 2018, p. 161)

Here, we are asked simply to honour the simplicity of our nature, which is just here and now and everywhere; if we look for it, we have forgotten that it is just our own true nature. It is infinitely small: "one square inch"; this phrase in Chinese also means "the centre of the heart mind"—the place Maharshi points to when he asks us to ask, "Who am I?" It is infinitely large and everywhere. It goes in and out without gates or boundaries and, if we do not trust and treasure it, we will not meet it. What we meet here, as we trust and treasure it, is: "Thou art Eternity and Space; Thou art Matter and Motion; and Thou art the negation of all these things. For there is no Symbol of Thee" (2: 21–26) (Crowley, 2015, p. 111).

It is from this place and to this place we continually return finding, as Han Shan tells us, that at times we are in the compressed, inward space, and at other times infinitely large and ushering in a new aeon. At all times we remain the uncarved staff of will, whose deepest grain is now fully revealed, and from this centre point all acts of love under will revolve.

# CHAPTER 19

# Simon Iff at Prayer—The Work of the Magister Templi

The place that is reached as we sit on Cold Mountain is the surrender of all knowing into that aspect of the soul that is the *neschamah*, who manifests in the deep understanding of non-dual love and receives all being and conditions without reservation. Crowley refers to this aspect of the angel as Babalon, the holy whore, who receives all into her body and to whom all sense of independent identity must be given. He gives us the image of being a pyramidal pile of ashes in the City of the Pyramids, sealed up to mature our understanding (Crowley, 1972b, pp. 171–173). The other image he gives us is of being the gardener whose task it is to tend the garden that is our particular field of attention (Crowley, 1972b, pp. 139–144). This, for him, meant the teaching of the Knowledge and Conversation of the Holy Guardian Angel and the proclamation of the Law of Thelema but each of us who access this level, are given a particular task and a particular prayer allotted.

Prayer, in this sense, is nothing other than the performance of the Mass of the Holy Ghost, enabling the single point to acquire substantial being and appear as the crowned and conquering child. These acts of love under will are expressions of the momentum of the true will as it meets the unfolding conditions of life, and are the activity of the what the ancient Egyptians call the Geru Maa (the silent wise one) within manifestation. This tending of the garden of life draws on the image of the Geru Maa as the living tree that provides shade and irrigation to the world and whose prayers ensure the continuance of both shelter and nourishment.

This art of Gnostic prayer has its antecedents in the Neo-Platonic tradition. There we find Proclus, the last of the great Neo-Platonists, telling us that the masters of the hieratic art are concerned with contemplating the appearance of things and noticing the sympathy or resonance between those appearances and the causal roots of those appearances. It is this contemplation of appearance and the roots of causality that constitutes the tending of the garden.

Proclus in his work "On the Hieratic Art" quoted by Henry Corbin uses the heliotrope or sunflower as an image of prayer, asking us to contemplate the movement of the sunflower as it follows the motion of the sun across the sky, invisibly and insolubly connected to it through a sympathetic passion. He tells us:

> What other reason can we give for the fact that the heliotrope follows in its movement the movement of the sun and the selenetrope the movement of the moon, forming a procession within the limits of their power, behind the torches of the universe? For, in truth, each thing prays according to the rank it occupies in nature, and sings the praise of the divine series to which it belongs, a spiritual or rational or physical or sensuous praise; for the heliotrope moves to the extent to which it is free to move, and its rotation, if we could hear the sound of the air buffeted by its movement, we should be aware that it is a hymn to its king, such as is within the power of a plant to sing. (Corbin, 1969, p. 105)

He goes on to speak of the sympathy between the flower and the sun as representative of the connection between the visible and the invisible, and this tropism or movement being the action or attraction of the angel whose name it bears. Its heliotropism he describes as a "heliopathy" (Corbin, 1969, p. 107), the passion or pathos that is generated by the attractive power of that angel, and this pathos becomes the act of prayer that reveals the sympathy between the angel and the flower. It is this capacity for sympathy which enables the descent of the angel into manifestation and the union of the sun and the sunflower.

There is a hidden meaning to this image of the heliotrope flower, as, for the Neo-Platonists, the development of inner work creates within us what, following the Chaldean Oracles, is described as the flowering of the mind or intellect, meaning by this not the cognitive intellect but what the Ch'an masters would call the heart-mind and, in the Qabalah, we would name the meeting of the *neschamah* and the *ruach* in Daath. The key text in *The Chaldean Oracles* which applies to this process is:

> For there exists a certain Intelligible which you must perceive by the flower of mind for if you should incline your mind towards it and perceive it as perceiving a specific thing, you would not perceive it. For it is the power of strength, visible all around flashing with intellectual divisions. Therefore you must not perceive that Intelligible violently but with the flame of mind completely extended which measures all things, except that intelligible. You must not perceive it intently, but keeping the pure eye of your soul turned away, you should extend an empty mind towards the Intelligible since it exists outside of your mind.
>
> Arrayed from head to toe with a clamorous light, armed in mind and soul, you must cast into your imagination the entire token of the triads and not go toward the empyrean channels in a scattered way, but with concentration. (Majercik, 2013, p. 49)

The "Intelligible" relates to the supernal triangle of the Tree of Life and represents the divine root of our being, which we meet as our awareness both blossoms and catches fire. The image of the sun and the sunflower describes this process of our awareness deepening into alignment with this root of our being. This process is subtle and we are told it cannot happen with violence or vehemence. This may recall Crowley's thoughts on this in *Liber Liberi vel Lapidis Lazuli* in which neither meditation, memory, prayer, or any active method will work; only the practice of passive love enables the communion.

This reaching out of the fiery flower of our awareness locates us in a dynamic stillness, in Han Shan's empty cave; and here we wait, extending our awareness, but not to a thing: being open like a blossoming flower, and energised and lucent like a flame, we are open to receive the touch of that Intelligible that is the self-generating source of life.

There are many forms and ways to do this, depending on our particular relationship with the angel. We may contemplate the name, the tree, an image, a song, etc., for at this stage of the work the *sunthemata* are integrated into us and our conversation with the angel. The response is the descent of the will of the angel into the pool of awareness in Yesod and its birth through our bodies, which constitutes the birth of the moonchild and the completion of the Mass of the Holy Ghost.

Proclus regards the person who prays in this way as possessing Σωφροσύνη, *sophrosyne*, a word that is often linked with the idea of a balanced, grounded, and prudent attitude towards life. In Homer's *Odyssey*, for example, Odysseus avoids being turned into an animal by the enchantress Circe by consuming the magical herb *moly*, which has been given him by Athena and Hermes and which is believed to symbolise *sophrosyne*. Proclus takes the definition of the word more deeply, however (Layne, 2013, p. 349), believing in a cosmos that is interpenetrated or underwritten by the signatures or *sunthemata* of the divine and which represent the gods continuing Φιλία or love for creation. To be of good sense in a world thus constituted is therefore to be one who relates to and works with that signature within themselves, and thus establishes themselves within the goodness of the gods, understanding that within all things lie the divine traces of kindness, awareness, and love of the divine will.

He goes on to tell us (Layne, 2013, p. 350) that because human beings are the living bridge between the intelligible or divine world and the sensible or material world, if we are to be like a god we must (like a god) develop the capacity to act freely, to be self-generative. Otherwise, like all other sensible beings, we are under the rule of *moira*, or fate, and have no free will. The whole work of discovering and unveiling and aligning with the star at the heart of our being is entirely concerned with this experience of "being of good sense", in Proclean terms, and then working with the expression and will that arises as a result of that unveiling. Proclus's prayer of the sunflower, which continually tracks the deep root of the sun or star at the heart of our being, shows us the way in which the person of Σωφροσύνη, *sophrosyne*, conducts their days. Each act of thought, heart, and body arises in the moment from the star at the heart of our being, manifests, comes to a conclusion, and then is released, returning us into the communion with this deep root of being. Proclus goes on to insist (Layne, 2013, p. 354) that the essence of prayer is to join together that which is secondary or contingent with that which is its prior cause, working with the divine signatures within us and everything to return to the true heart and home. This is the return to the holy mountain, whether that be Sinai, Arunachala, Cold Mountain, or anywhere else that represents the beginning point that ultimately is our deep centre, the khabs, which manifests the magical child.

Proclus then says (Layne, 2013, p. 359) that this ongoing art of prayer is aided by a process of becoming familiar with the gods and their traces or *sunthemata*. He uses this word οικείωσις ("familiarisation") in quite a literal sense, in that, in this process, we become part of the divine family, learning their arts and ways, much as you would if you are adopted into a family. The ancient Greek word οικοις (*oikois*) means "hearth", "house", and "family", so, as we become more expert in prayer, so do we increasingly enter into the divine household and become one of the family. He describes this skill of prayer as having four active stages (Layne, 2013, pp. 358–359). First, there is the knowing of the gods and the recognition of the divine traces. This represents the capacity to still the interior dialogue and start recognising what is underneath the whirl of thought, emotion, and memory images. Second is this process of "familiarisation", which increasingly relies upon being able to access the reflective stillness of Tiphareth and receive the influx from the deeper spheres. Third, there is the experience of touching the divine, which he calls συναφή (*sunaphe*), which means to directly connect with the edge of the divine. This is the process of the fiery flower of the deep mind presenting itself before the deepest aspect of the angel, open, concentrated, still, and waiting. Fourth, there is the approaching, described as illumination or the entering into the divine light, which vivifies and directs all our actions. This is the experience of being the Magister Templi who is at the service of the non-dual will and love that now manifests from the supernal triangle and moves outwards in response to the prayer to bring the divine will and love into operation through us. This continual practice of theophanic prayer deepens our understanding of all four steps, but it is important to remember at each moment we must begin at the beginning with the sense of simple presence and aligning our fractured and distracted will with the true will that, like the unfolding of the Tao, can be experienced as a hidden, subterranean river that carries us forward.

Simon Iff in *Moonchild* talks about this task of unifying with the true will thus:

> Look! [...] why does a man die when he is struck by lightning? Because he has a gate open to lightning; he insists on being an electrical substance by possessing the quality of resistance to the passage of the electric current. If we could diminish that resistance to zero, lightning would no longer take notice of him.
>
> There are two ways of preventing a rise of temperature from the sun's heat. One is to oppose a shield of non-conducting and opaque material: that is Cyril's way, and at the best it is imperfect; some heat always gets through. The other way is to remove every particle of matter from the space which you wish to be cold; then there is nothing there to become hot; and that is the Way of the Tao. (Crowley, 1929, p. 69)

It is this process of reducing our resistance and allowing the acts of will and love to manifest as easily and simply through us that is the aim of this art. Simon Iff again holds up to us the ideal that we are seeking to emulate:

> To have assimilated all things so perfectly that there is no longer any possibility of struggle. To have destroyed the idea of duality. To have achieved Love and Will so that there is no longer any object to Love, or any aim for Will. To have killed desire at the root; to be one with every thing and with Nothing. (Crowley, 1929, p. 69)

The absence of resistance and struggle is the crucial point and enables us to be simple, responding fully in each moment to the demands of that moment, and exercising that Proculean "good sense" in the service of one and all as we tend to the garden.

# CHAPTER 20

# Embodying Chiah—The Practice of the Star and the Serpent

The step beyond the Geru Maa or Master of the Temple, as the vehicle of the non-dual love of Binah is, in Egyptian terms, to be the Chief Lector Priest, or the Magus, who embodies the deep will of Chockmah and who generates creative change and activity. To be the servant of the star and the snake we become magick personified, embodying that part of the soul the Qabalists call חיה (*chiah*). This aspect, which is focused in Chockmah, generates the root of duality— the word חיה itself shows us the nature of the function: it begins with the letter *cheth* (ח) whose root meaning is "a fence or boundary", thus demonstrating the sense of division that is intrinsic to duality. The letter is seen as being formed from the preceding letters *vav* (ו) and *zain* (ז) thus:

This shape is said to indicate a marriage, with the *vav* being the groom and *zain* the bride, the link between them being the wedding canopy. The hieroglyphical roots of *vav* and *zain* are also "the nail" and "the sword", representing joining together and division as aspects of will. The other two letters in *chiah* are י and ה, the beginning letters of the divine name יהוה, again amplifying the meaning of generation. The word *chiah* also arises out of the two-letter root חי (*Yod Cheth*) which means "life" and so, in this place, we come into direct relationship with the roots of life and will. All of the supernal sephiroth are deeply connected and so the shifts at this level are of emphasis rather than kind, but the shifts are significant. In the place of the *neschamah* the emphasis is on love and understanding; here, the emphasis is on the generation of change, of the power of life flowing through us so that our presence is a ferment. In *Moonchild* (1929) this is the place where Simon Iff talks about sowing dragons' teeth to bring about a new age. In the New Testament it is the place where Christ says:

> Think not that I am come to send peace on earth: I came not to send peace but a sword. For I am come to set a man at variance against his father, and the daughter against her mother, and the daughter in law against her mother in law. And a man's foes shall be they of his own household. (Matthew 10: 34–36)

Crowley gives us the image of the ashes of the Master of the Temple being seared by fire to perfect glowing whiteness, and gives as examples of Magi the founders of the great religions. This may be the task for some but, fundamentally, as we touch on this level of the soul we become incandescent generators of life and this will manifest through us in whatever way is appropriate for our conditions of life and to whatever extent we can maintain our awareness here. If, just for a moment, there will be a flash of fiery inspiration that will enable the manifestation of a new idea, new way of being, new job, new life; if we are able to maintain our awareness here, in a more stable way, then the sense of being a continual centre of growth and new possibilities will become present. It is as if we become silently turbocharged. If we recall Allan Bennett's image of the heart-mind as a great steam engine (Chapter 1, above) then this is the place where that engine is unified and working effortlessly to its ultimate extent.

Here we return to the practice of the star, the khabs that is the house of Hadit, the point that extends itself and, if we return to these verses from Chapter II of *The Book of the Law* we see:

> I am the flame that burns in every heart of man, and in the core of every star. I am Life, and the giver of Life, yet therefore is the knowledge of me the knowledge of death.
>
> I am the Magician and the Exorcist. I am the axle of the wheel, and the cube in the circle. "Come unto me" is a foolish word: for it is I that go. (II: 6–7)

And:

> I am the Snake that giveth Knowledge & Delight and bright glory, and stir the hearts of men with drunkenness. (II: 22)

In this phase, the will that generates duality and newness passes through us with ease and clear purpose, just as a steam engine's parts work harmoniously together to enable whatever movement is required. In some ways there is nothing to do but to participate in this, but there are two practices that can assist us to engage with the use of will and imagination at this level. They are adapted from Crowley's *Liber Thisarb* (Crowley, 1912, pp. 107–116), normally thought of as connected with the development of the magical memory, but this has a deeper application in working with the *chiah*. The Hebrew title of Thisarb is תישרב which is the reversal of the first word of Genesis BRIShT which represents the energy of creation. The deeper meaning of Thisarb is the return to the beginning, the realignment and refreshment of will.

## The Practice of the Star

The first practice, which we may call "the practice of the star", is to sit in silence and to be aware of all of the universal forces that are in action enabling us to sit here, from gravity, the motion of the moon around the earth, the earth around the sun, the movement of the Milky Way around the galactic core, then the internal forces, our skeleton, our bodily systems, which enable us to sit here, our psychology and our history, which have interested us in this subject and led to us reading this book and trying out the practice. Having gained a sense of the conjunction of inner and outer elements responsible for us just sitting here, we then isolate a key element and contemplate it. For example, we consider our will to sit here silently and motionless and investigate the immediate cause of this will. Having discovered this, we may pursue the matter more deeply—what enables this cause to come into being?—until we enter into a contemplation of our whole relationship with will at all its levels. Here we focus on verses II: 6–7 from *The Book of the Law* (quoted above) and contemplate the place of being the Magician and the Exorcist, axle of the wheel, the cube in the circle, and being the flame in the heart of each and all. This is a work of extension in space.

## The Practice of the Serpent

The second practice, the practice of the serpent, is hinted at in verse II: 22 and asks us to work with the power of our imagination and awareness through time, contemplating the activity of will and imagination and causation within the dimension of time.

This requires us to follow our memory backwards, initially for just a few moments, reversing the flow of time, but, with practice, travelling backwards through our life, assimilating the causes and conditions that have brought us to this present moment.

Allan Bennett, Crowley's teacher, describes this method:

> You sit down in your place of meditation, and you think of yourself seated there. Then you begin to think backwards. You think the act of coming into the room. You think the act of walking towards the room, and so you go on, thinking backwards on all the acts that you have done that day. You then come to yourself, waking up in the morning, and perhaps you remember a few dreams, and then there is a blank, and you remember your last thoughts as you went to sleep the night before, what you did before retiring, and so on, back to the time of your last meditation. (Bennett, 1911)

Crowley goes on to examine the alchemical formula *solve et coagula*, "to dissolve and reform", in the light of this practice, interpreting it as the dissolving of the self in the infinite (*solve*) and the presentation of the infinite in concrete form (*coagula*). This apparently simple practice of moving backwards through our life does just this in dissolving the fixed forms of self and enabling the free energy released by that to emerge in a new way. It is not an easy practice, however, and we should begin by taking a small period of time—say, five minutes—and move backwards through it. Initially, the mind will just jump to the beginning of the five minutes, and so we must focus, step by step, on the events of those five minutes using our magical imagination and will to gain an embodied experience of reversing time. When that felt sense is definite and perceptible then we may work with longer and longer periods of time. One of the major effects of this work is the freeing of the magical imagination to work with time, space, and event as aspects of awareness, because, as we increasingly learn to work with *solve et coagula*, we experience time and memory as fluid and alive rather than fixed and determined. What appears here is the sense of "Knowledge & Delight and bright glory" that the *Book of the Law* verse speaks of (II: 22) as the past is both dissolved and resurrected; the "drunkenness" is the freeing of the heart-mind from linearity.

If we bring these practices together we find that we come into direct awareness with will and are upheld by the magical imagination, like the goddesses we find in *The Book of Gates* who are seated on the serpent and hold the star in their hands. This opens us to the third and deepest phase of this practice, in which we unify our will and imagination, letting the serpent seat uphold us and feeling the power of the star in our hands.

From here we contemplate our place in the universe and the work that presents itself to us, sensing our place within the Star-Sponge vision and the capacity of our imagination to work with time, space, and events. It is the place that Han Shan speaks of when he talks about sitting on Cold Mountain and unspooling through the universe as he contemplates the mani stone. It is from here that the magical body (or *khu*) appears and we can work with the Body of Light as the vehicle of true will and magical imagination.

This activation of the magical imagination and the Body of Light can be aided by contemplating the image of the Magician in the Waite–Smith tarot pack.

THE MAGICIAN.

This figure stands in a garden surrounded by red roses and white lilies, is clothed in red and white, is of indeterminate sex, wears a serpent as a belt, is crowned with a lemniscate, and holds a double wand of power, and points above and below. Before them is a table with a wand, sword, pentacle, and cup. Like Han Shan, the stance of the magician is one of stillness although, around them, activity is constantly manifesting. This stance is that of being the axis of the universe, encircled by the horizontal snake; holding the double wand of power and perceiving the table, which is the field of manifestation. Within the manifesting field we work with the will to create of the wand, the will to destroy of the sword, the manifesting love of the chalice, and the embodiment and solidity of the pentacle. The roses and the lilies remind us of the fusion of the five and the six, because the cross-section of the rose is the pentacle and the cross-section of the lily is the hexagram and we recall the formula of *ARARITA*.

If we adopt the stance of the magician and simply stand, extending our arms in the way the magician does, the sense of being the axis and the still centre of the moving world becomes very clear. We may feel what Han Shan does, as he sits on the stony cliff, witnessing the moon rise and set, or as the ancient tree that is the uncarved staff. The experience of being clothed with the opposites and of being a nexus point through which the infinite energies indicated by the lemniscate pass in and out of manifestation becomes very vivid, just as Han Shan's moon shines into the jade-green pool. We might indicate this activity of shining and reflection by contemplating some additional tarot trumps thus:

The Fool gives us the sense of the unmanifest energies passing into form through the stance and intention of the magician.

It is this sense of youth and beginnings that we might also describe as the manifestation of the Tao, or the appearance of the child or bud-will that initiates the magical process. This then works with the energies of the cards the Lovers and the Devil: respectively, that which permits flow and colloquy, and that which denies it. In the Lovers we see the communion of the man and the woman and the angel; in the Devil there is no communion and, instead, a sense of binding and oppression. These cards show us the activity of Gedulah and Geburah, the expansion and contraction, allowing and disallowing, banishing and invoking, as the child takes shape within the form of the Magician, manifesting into the universe as a tangible and living form. This is shown in the tarot card the World in which we see the androgynous dancer holding the double wands within a wreath that is a *vesica piscis* formed from the overlapping of the two circles in the act of fusion. This is will expressing itself in the world or, to put it another way, י and ה appearing as ו and embodying as ה. The four forms of the lion, eagle, man, and bull that hold the wreath or vesica underline the sense that this emergent form is being held in the process of creation.

The sense of axis and stillness, which enables the manifestation of the living light and love and the communion with the divine artist, enables the unspooling of the unfolding line that is our own particular connection to our deep roots. Each of our actions, then, are predicated on the unfolding of that line in each and every moment.

The stance of the magician is the practice of uniting all the opposites in an act of creative unfolding as the Fool steps into time, space, and motion, invokes and banishes and appears as the child, the will made flesh. This is the posture found in many Egyptian statues, in which the left leg steps forward and, in one hand, the *was* wand of will is held, and in the other the *ankh* of life, love, and motion. When we take this stance we embrace our capacity to hold the meeting of opposites that results in the appearance and embodiment of the child. We literally are then the embodiment of the $0 = 2$ equation, allowing the moment by moment emergence of the opposites out of the void. As we embody this stance at all levels of our being we become simpler and simpler as our true will emerges and as the alchemical fusion of love under that will transforms our environment.

In the holy book *Liber B vel Magi* (Crowley, 2015, pp. 203–205) Crowley tells us that the grade of the Master of the Temple teaches the mystery of sorrow, the Magus the mystery of change, the Ipsissimus the mystery of selflessness (also called the mystery of Pan). The particular task of the Magus is to raise each of these qualities to infinity so that their nature reverses and sorrow becomes joy, change is stability, and selflessness is self. Completing this opens the grade of Ipsissimus (of which more later), but transforming qualities into their opposites is fundamental to the Magus who works with the principle of *maya* (or "illusion") or *lila* ("the divine play"). The nature of the Magus is linked to the receiving of a word, which is a formula of change and transformation that constitutes the being in action of the Magus. The divine name that is applied to Chockmah is *YHVH* (יהוה)—the name of both being and creating, and that contains within it a continual conversation between the four letters of the name which, as we have seen earlier, relates to the faces of the divine: the father, the mother, the son, and the daughter. We may recall also that Crowley related this name to the work of the Tao and the senses, seeing the first movement of the Tao as the letter *yod*, connected to looking, omnipresence, and the generative point, which is then balanced by the sense of listening to the unfolding way as the letter *heh* (ה), before emerging into activity and action as the letter *vav* (ו) and the sense of touch, and coming together as *heh* final (ה), in the unified movement described as *wu wei*, the work of the empty hand.

The word or name that a Magus receives is not a literal word, as such, but a formula of creation and alchemical change that moves through us as an expression of our life force. It is actually our unification with our true will or the activity of the Tao without hesitation, reservation, or repetition. While the work of the Master of the Temple is suffused with the sense of that understanding love which embraces sorrow, the Magus radiates a generative joy that turns the world. The work of the star and the serpent, described earlier in this chapter, sets up the conditions for this receiving and speaking of the word or, rather, the entering into the conversation of change.

This emergence of and unification of the will creates, as we have seen, a new sense of self and activity, one in which selflessness is self, sorrow is joy, and stability is change. Our awareness therefore expands and our sense of body and senses similarly changes. Our body is not just an anchor and earthing point in this case, for it becomes the literal Philosopher's Stone, which reacts to and with all that it touches, reorienting the inner and outer worlds so that the fusion of the eye and hand, perception and action, brings into being a fluidity and luminosity in self and other.

This emergence is sometimes referred to as "the Body of Light" or "the Diamond Body", which is not simply a replica of the physical body but is the deep love or imagination made flesh. It is here that we discover that our body is the universe and that our work consists of manifesting that body and returning to the source. The qualities of the Body of Light are luminosity and density, a combination of particle and wave in which our particle nature forms a singularity of diamond-like density. This expresses itself in a radiating wave of light that embraces all.

In order for this body to manifest we must align with our will to remain at the centre of body, world, and experience as we enter into the mystery of the beginning of duality—the appearance of $0 = 2$. From this we maintain an openness to the creative will that arises and reshapes both us and the universe. Then we must develop the capacity to bear the intimacy of awareness as the gravity well of the new form draws all towards itself in its ignition into a wave of solid presence. From this place we discover that we can (like this description from *The Hermetica*):

> Become higher than all heights and lower than all depths. Sense as one within yourself the entire creation: fire, water, the dry and the moist. Conceive yourself to be in all places at the same time: in earth, in the sea, in heaven; that you are not yet born, that you are within the womb, that you are young, old, dead; that you are beyond death. Conceive all things at once: times, places, actions, qualities and quantities; then you can understand God. (Salaman, 2000, p. 57)

One way of practising with the Body of Light is to make use of Ernest Butler's contemplation phrase,

> Now do I descend into the inner sea whose waters rise and fall within my soul. Let the inner waters be subdued and still as I immerse myself within the living waters and emerging therefrom unfold from latent stress to potent image the Body of Light, Prayer and Blessing. (Rees, 1973)

We allow our sense of self and universe to dissolve as descending into the inner sea come into alignment with the deep will letting the imaginal form of the Body of Light take shape around us, feeling its qualities of being both particle and wave upholding us, making us a true image and vehicle of the presence of the angel. The form that emerges arises out of the will that is being expressed, but the form that I learned from my teacher Tom Oloman and I which I have mostly used as a beginning point, is a white-hooded monk-like form with a face that is a mirror.

We then simply settle into this form, letting it be our vehicle of perception and action. Initial exercises consist in making the body of light do certain things, moving about the room, perceiving the room through inner senses. Having become confident in moving around the room then extend its reach, moving beyond the room, exploring the inner environment so that you gain a sense of confidence in operating from the Body of Light. Trust the promptings of the *chiah* and experiment as *The Hermetica* suggests—expand the body so that you are as large as the universe, become smaller than an atom, project the body through space and time. Let the body flow into different forms, entering into communion with other beings, organic and inorganic. This whole process is pendant to the key work of communion with will of the *chiah*, because the Body of Light is used at its direction, the *khu* appearing from the *khabs*. At the end of the process we draw the Body of Light back into the physical form. It is a specialised application of the deep imagination and is a vehicle through which our will can reach places, situations, and people to complete our work. It is the practice that is sometimes called "astral projection", though it is often described in overly dramatic ways. It is rare to completely lose a sense of the physical body in this practice—it remains as a background sensation while our main attention is operating in the Body of Light and its environment. The sense is of being extended and able to reach and relate to situations that would otherwise be unreachable.

This was the practice in which Ernest Butler excelled. Having experienced the Body of Light early in his life, through the help of Robert King, he developed it through the use of the contemplative phrase, "The flyer must descend into the sea". This descent of awareness into the fluidity of the inner world of Yesod, and the communion with his angel, whom he experienced as the Christ within, took him into immersion into the great sea of Binah, from which he would arise in the transfigured form of the Body of Light. This was linked with his contemplation of the Gospel of John and the sense of being a Christomorph or living form of the Christ. He was a priest of the Liberal Catholic Church and this inner practice was linked with his saying of his daily office and his communion with the divine. Increasingly, however, his practice became one of silence, simplicity, and generating radiance and, while entirely different in form, was very like that of Han Shan: *wu wei*, the action of non-action, the simultaneous sitting on Cold Mountain while unspooling through the universe.

# CHAPTER 21

# The Apotheosis of Cyril and the Silence of Mahathera Phang

There is a final step in the novel *Moonchild* that is very easy to miss. It is right at the end of the book and follows the scene of Cyril having encountered the body of his nemesis, Douglas, lying on a gun carriage and being devoured by wild dogs. He is deeply affected by this; it takes him into a deep contemplation of the nature of the sorrow within all human experience. As he wanders, contemplating, he finds himself in the Place de la Concorde, which has at its centre an obelisk which reveals to him in an instant the deep structure of Egyptian magick (Crowley, 1929, p. 334). The obelisk represents the unifying pillar of the Tree of Life, topped with the pyramidal Benben stone that represents creation and resurrection and shows the infinite extension of the divine will and the uniting of all into the single point of Kether. Following this experience, Cyril meets with Simon Iff and is instructed to go into retreat to find his new way:

> "There is a meditation," said Cyril firmly, "given by the Buddha, a meditation upon a corpse torn by wild beasts. I will take that."
>
> Simon Iff acquiesced without comprehending. He did not know that Cyril Grey had understood that the corpse of Douglas was

his own; that the perception of the identity of himself with all other
living things had come to him, and raised him to a great Adeptship.

But there was one to comprehend the nature of that initiation.
As Cyril walked, leaning on the arm of Sister Cybele, to the room
appointed for his prescribed solitude, he beheld a great light.
It shone serenely from the eyes of the Mahathera Phang. (Crowley,
1929, p. 335)

This is the place in which Cyril surpasses even his master Simon Iff, for
Simon does not seem to grasp what has happened to Cyril, who is stepping into the crown of the tree. We are given a hint of this in that the two
people who accompany him to his retreat room are Sister Cybele and
Mahathera Phang, two of the three connected with the true moonchild
operation on Iona. The third is called simply "Himself"—the final grade
of the Hermetic degree system is called "Ipsissimus", which means "to
be my very own self", so what we see here is the place where Cyril
becomes Himself. Crowley describes this stage as the beatific vision and
as the direct and perpetual experience of the "Love is the Law, Love
under Will". He goes on to say that, "its nature is the perpetual sacrament
of energy in action and that the arising of this awareness depends upon
the perfect mastery of the mysteries of sorrow and change, with thor-
ough identification with that of Individuality" (Crowley, 1985, p. 29).

Crowley further discusses this question of energy, describing it as
"the Sacramental Motive of Event" (Crowley, 1985, p. 55). This curious
phrase highlights the sacred nature of any event, which is a meeting
of the infinite points of view of Nuit with the single point-instance of
Hadit and the emergence of the duality of Hoor Paar Kraat and Ra Hoor
Khuit. The use of the word "motive" indicates the vector of the emergent event, which is then experienced as an interruption of the already-
existing continuum of the universe, or a compensation for the existing
momentum of the universe, or the withdrawal of both interruption and
compensation. Later, he quotes from *The Chaldean Oracles*:

For the King of all previously placed before the polymorphous
World a Type, intellectual, incorruptible, the imprint of whose form
is sent through the World, by which the Universe shone forth with
Ideas all various of which the foundation is One, One and alone.
From this the others rush forth, distributed and separated through
the various bodies of the universe and are born in swarms through
its vast abysses, ever whirling forth in illimitable radiation.

> They are intellectual conceptions from the paternal fountain partaking abundantly of the brilliance of fire in the culmination of unresting Time.
>
> But the primary self-perfect Fountain of the Father poured forth these primogenial ideas. (Cited in Crowley, 1985, pp. 85–86)

And again, Crowley himself writes:

> True Will should spring, a fountain of Light from within, and flow unchecked, seething with Love into the Ocean of Life [...] it is our Will that issues, perfectly elastic, sublimely Protean, to fill every interstice of the Universe of Manifestation which it meets in its course. (Crowley, 1985, p. 77)

It is this stage, which Proclus describes (Layne, 2013, p. 367) as the fifth step in prayer, being beyond prayer as an action, calling it simply unification and the place where we truly enter into that part of the soul called the One. The Qabalah calls it *yechidah* (יחידה), which means "oneness expressed through the particular and singular"—this is the mystery of individuality, the selflessness that is Self. This is the awareness that Maharshi would call *sahaja samadhi*—the spontaneous and uncontrived union. It is this simplicity of awareness and practise that we return to now and in regard to Crowley's work this simplicity is found in the teaching he received from Eckenstein and Allan Bennett which remained at the core of his inner life. If we combine Eckenstein's teachings on the control of the mind, which ask us to contemplate static images, then moving images, which then become multi-sensory inner worlds, with Allan Bennett's image of the mind as a steam engine which, through the right application of awareness, becomes unified, we will discover the practical application of the principle: "For pure will, unassuaged of purpose, delivered from the lust of result, is every way perfect" (I: 44).

The bringing together of their methods give us a sense of the profound unification of our mind and senses, all our parts working together seamlessly as the energy of the fountain of life moves through us into the All, experienced as a field of unity—one phenomenon. This is the sense of the one white cat as the entire universe—the All enfolded within the particular—the mystery of individuality. The experience of Cyril Grey that Crowley related in *Moonchild*, in which Cyril realises his identity with his arch-enemy Douglas, is a particularly potent example of this mystery. It is the direct experience of the one will in its purity;

the emergence of an entire universe from singularity without resistance—pure spontaneity. Crowley's phrases "the Perpetual Sacrament of Energy" and "the Sacramental Motive of Event" point us at this sense of continual spontaneous emergence in which the unmanifest infinity concentrates into a single point, which then becomes the fountain of wisdom and its thousand reflections and yet remains singular and particular. This is the experience that Crowley termed "the Star-Sponge vision" and beyond this is, literally, no place to go, for it combines not just the one and the many but existence and non-existence so that our locus of awareness is everywhere and nowhere.

It is this capacity to unite the vast and the particular that I most saw in the presence of Tom Oloman—a solidity within a fluid and vulnerable presence that adapted to his surroundings, bringing with him a sense of coherence and confluent dialogue which silently transfigured all that he came into contact with. He was curious about his limitations, for all that he noticed was for him an aspect of face beholding face, and so was to be embraced and not defended against. The simplicity of his practice, which, by the end of his life had no outward forms at all, gave his work a concentrated, alchemical power. The unity of the spark of darkness and the mirror womb, which continually manifested through him as what I can only describe as an instantaneous, tangible blessing, meant that whatever and whoever came into touch with him experienced this silent transfiguration. I don't mean by this that he was in the habit of consciously blessing; rather, he had become the presence of blessing and therefore all his thoughts, words, and actions carried that presence. The sense of unification in everything he did created what might be called a sanctifying field of grace, not in any pious way for, in some ways, there was very little trace of spiritual practice visible in him. It was rather that he was unified with whatever he was involved in, whether that was driving too fast in his beloved Mini along in country lanes (he learned to drive when he was seventy), cooking a complicated recipe, or talking about life. The simplicity and concentration of this unification of the All with the small, or the universal with the particular; this experience of unification as it would be described in the Qabalah, is what I continually remember when I think of him.

# CHAPTER 22

# Iff!?

So, at the end we return to Simon Iff, the silent fulcrum of the novel *Moonchild* whose function it is to show us the dynamics of magick in all its forms, from superstition and self-delusion to the unveiling of the depths of the soul and the universe and the constant colloquy of call and response that generates our life and the lives of all.

The question that was posed at the beginning of the book "What is the point of this?" has been addressed through the experience of Aleister Crowley, Ernest Butler, and Tom Oloman; through Ancient Egyptian tradition; through the Advaita tradition of Ramana Maharshi; through the mysterious poetry of Lao Tzu and Chuang Tzu; the Cold Mountain meditations of Han Shan; and the fluid contemplations of the Iyyun Circle. Here, at the end, we return to ourselves and the particular way this question hangs in the air before us.

As correlates of this question we must consider the fruit of our life and practice, and notice what is it that comes to birth through us: in what way does the trinity of awareness, will, and love appear (or not) in our sphere of influence. The truth is that all human beings are magicians, applying and exercising their capacity to create and make manifest deep will, love, and awareness to the limit of their understanding. The novel *Moonchild* gives us many examples of this: we see Lisa la Giuffria's powerful, passionate, but unstable combination of love and will continually manifesting new worlds; the kindness of Sister Clara, creating a womb of nourishment; the clear will of brother Onofrio, a fortress of protection; while Cyril Grey manifests a complex and fascinating field of magick, excitement, and power. In the Black Lodge, Douglas shows us the image of the Magus committed to separation, and in the end destroyed by it, while the other members of the Black Lodge, to varying degrees, are reflections of this devotion to the separate nature of self and the rejection of love. The most effective of them is the decidedly non-magical Cremers, whose will is subtle and focused so that, in the end, it is she who sabotages Cyril Grey's operation through her understanding of Lisa's passionate instability.

Alongside this we have the non-charismatic Simon Iff, who barely acts, but when he does the acts are memorable and long-lasting. His teaching on the heart of magick through the bowl of water and the cone (Crowley, 1929, pp. 60–61) stands as one of the clearest accounts of the relationship between the aspirant and the angel ever written. His dealings with the Thing in the garden (Crowley, 1929, pp. 65–67) and his subsequent dealings with Douglas (Crowley, 1929, pp. 155–156) show us clearly the nature of healing and redemption, and his application of the way of the Tao to the path of magick offers an approach to the deepest in us that is unparalleled.

Ultimately, we are called to step beyond even Simon Iff (as we have seen in the previous chapter) because with the transfigured Cyril Grey we step into the place of unity–multiplicity. This place, which Ernest Butler would have described as being united with the living Christ, and Tom Oloman as "face beholds face" is both the end and the beginning, not just of this book but of our lives and our searching.

In 1909 Crowley wrote a short paper called "The Soldier and the Hunchback" (Crowley, 1909, pp. 113–137) that, in a way, encapsulates the deep structure of the path we have been following. The soldier is the exclamation mark "!" and represents the experience of direct revelation, while the hunchback is the question mark "?" and represents the sceptical spirit of enquiry that continually deconstructs the known. Like Ramana Maharshi or Han Shan, Crowley invites us to enter the spirit of the deconstructive enquiry, examining the nature of thought and existence as he considers Descartes theorem: "I think therefore I am". The continued process of enquiry dissolves form as we address this—for example, as we consider "I think" we consider both the nature of "I" and "thought", treating every answer as another step in the enquiry until finally we arrive at a place where thought and enquiry become exhausted. So, too, for the enquiry into "I am" though, now, the enquiry is into what is meant by the word "am". As we persist in the way of doubt and enquiry here, again, we arrive at the place of exhaustion and surrender, which then creates a similar enquiry into the nature of "I". From this place we learn to apply our awareness in a different way and become available to the experience of revelation, described here as *samadhi*, the experience of union. Each moment of *samadhi* or "!", as it embodies within us, arouses thought, feeling, and sensation, which is then inquired into via the work of "?". At length, this alteration of doubt and enquiry, *samadhi* and revelation, unifies so that our nature becomes transparent to the moment of revelation and in that moment of embodiment there is no residue that is attached to. This is the state that Maharshi calls *sahaja samadhi* or "spontaneous and continuous awareness" and is the fruition of the teaching of Oscar Eckenstein, unifying with the moving and still aspects of mind, heart, and body, and the ultimate demonstration of Allan Bennett's heart-mind steam engine with all parts working in unison.

In the spirit of returning to the beginning I want to end with the practice of the salutes to the sun. It was the first practice ever given to me and one that I have often not regarded as deeply as I should. The path that we have been studying in this book is one that takes us from believing ourselves to be in exile, in a fragmented world that does not care or even notice us, to knowing ourselves to be a shining star within the infinite field of life, connected to each star and upheld by the serpent that is the energy of life itself. Our task, therefore, is, like any star, to be a generative centre of life, maximising the possibilities of life within our sphere.

The salutes of the sun are a simple practice whose initial function is just to get us to stop in the midst of the cycle of the day and orient our attention to the source of light and warmth, reaching through it to the spiritual reality it represents. The morning prayer to Ra Harakhty takes us into the work of the Neophyte, the new plant whose task it is to grow, developing root and branch and leaves. The noon prayer, which orients us to Hathor and the fullness of the expression of light, reminds us of the practice of the Adept in mastering the Mass of the Holy Ghost and the quest for the Knowledge and Conversation of the Holy Guardian Angel. The sunset prayer to Atum takes us into the deep transition of the Babe of the Abyss as all mastery is abandoned into the fading of the light and the descent into the inner world of the *duat*. The midnight prayer to Khephera takes us into the unfailing process of self-generation, in which love, will, and awareness participate in the mystery of the sorrow that is joy, the change that is stability, and the selflessness that is Self.

There is for us, like Cyril, a further step to take: the deeper truth of the salutes of the sun is that it does not rise or set; it is we who are the turning earth that produces that illusion. The sun, like the angel, is the constant presence, the gravitational centre, and as we step from the peripheral position into the centre point the world inverts; we enter the alchemical fusion of will and love arising out of the centre point that is the union of Nuit and Hadit. This takes us into the lived experience of the final verse of *The Book of the Heart Girt with the Serpent*: surrounded on all sides by the presence of the angel appearing like the thunderbolt, the pylon door, a snake, a phallus, and the woman of the stars. What this means in practice is that the current of love and will radiates through us in different modes and tones into the vessel of quicksilver that is the universe. We shift from being the receiver of light to being the source of light—Ipsissimus, our very own self, and, as such, our experience is not one of light but of night for we are within the body of Nuit—the field of stars. We are a star and our experience is the opposite of radiance, for all our light, life, and power is freely given through the simple act of being. It is this final step that Shakespeare describes in *The Tempest* when Prospero, the Magus, renounces his magick:

> [T]his rough magic
> I here abjure […]
>> I'll break my staff,
> Bury it certain fathoms in the earth,
> And deeper than did ever plummet sound
> I'll drown my book. (*The Tempest*, V: i)

This surrender even of the profound understanding of the Master of the Temple and the creative will of the Magus, symbolised by the drowning of the book and the breaking of the staff, takes us into Cyril's sense of identity with Douglas and the simplicity and mystery of the *yechidah*.

The new way of operating from this place is indicated in the epilogue of the play:

> Now my charms are all o'erthrown,
> And what strength I have's mine own,
> Which is most faint. Now, 'tis true,
> I must be here confined by you [...]
> In this bare island by your spell,
> But release me from my bands
> With the help of your good hands.
> Gentle breath of yours my sails
> Must fill, or else my project fails,
> Which was to please. Now I want
> Spirits to enforce, art to enchant,
> And my ending is despair,
> Unless I be relieved by prayer,
> Which pierces so that it assaults
> Mercy itself and frees all faults.
> As you from crimes would pardoned be,
> Let your indulgence set me free. (*The Tempest*, Epilogue)

The "faint strength" is our simple sense of being; in this speech Prospero, having acted a role of power and mystery, now speaks directly to the audience coming from behind all the illusions into direct relationship and colloquy. He enters into the experience of union in which both actor and audience are freed through the simplicity of their unity, just as King Lamus's release in *The Diary of a Drug Fiend* (Crowley, 1922, p. 356) is achieved when he enables Peter and Lou to fulfil their wills.

The effect of touching this sense of being, or locating ourselves at the centre of the sun, is that our environment and all that we come into contact with are stirred by the experience, just as the sun illuminates and warms whatever is touched by its beams. The experience at the centre is one of stillness, being unshakeable in the midst of movement, and entering into a larger and more potent sphere, just as actor and audience in *The Tempest* are freed into greater and fuller life.

Of course, we do not remain in this place for long; at first, perhaps, just for a moment as we cycle through the aspects of soul and the grades of Neophyte, Adept, and Master, but each time we rest here we increase our capacity to remain. In each iteration some of the veils which shroud us are removed, the underlying simplicity becomes accessible, and the practice of being the sun that illuminates All manifests more strongly.

It is that quality I saw in Tom Oloman and Ernest Butler, and which shines through Maharshi's, Han Shan's, and Crowley's writings. It is the end of the quest and the beginning. Here, there is only one prayer: *eheieh asher eheieh* (אהיה אשר אהיה), "I am that I am and I will be that which I will be", and, as the Korahites would say, "all my springs are in you" (Psalms 87: 7). Amen. Selah.

# APPENDIX

# Aleister Crowley Partial Bibliography

Crowley's works exist in numerous editions; those quoted in the reference list are the editions I personally possess and have referred to. Quotations from the Holy Books: *The Book of the Law*, *Liber LXV Cordis Cincti Serpente sub figurâ* אדנ (*The Book of the Heart Girt with the Serpent*) and *Liber Liberi vel Lapidis Lazuli* (*The Book of the Azure Stone*) are listed in the main text under chapter and verse as well as in the page numbers of the editions I have used.

The list below shows the first publications of some of his key works which give a timeline of his writing. Some of his works can be difficult to find but all can be accessed electronically through this website https://hermetic.com/crowley/index.

ΘΕΛΗΜΑ London A A 3 vols containing the Holy Books 1909.
*Book Four*. London: Wieland and Co. 1912.
*Eight Lectures on Yoga*. London: Ordo Templi Orientis 1939.
*Liber Aleph vel CXI. The Book of Wisdom or Folly*. West Point California: Thelema Publishing Company 1962.
*Little Essays Towards Truth*. London: Ordo Templi Orientis 1938.
*Magick in Theory and Practice*. Paris: Lecram Press 1929.

*Magick Without Tears*. Hampton, New Jersey: Thelema Publishing Company 1954.

*Moonchild*. London: Mandrake Press 1929.

*The Book of Lies which is also falsely called Breaks*. London: Wieland & Co. 1913.

*The Book of Thoth*. London: Ordo Templi Orientis 1944.

*The Blue Equinox. The Equinox III (I)*. Detroit: Universal Publishing Co. Spring 1919.

*The Diary of a Drug Fiend*. London: W. Collins Sons and Co. 1922.

*The Equinox Vol. I (1)*. London: Simpkin, Marshall, Hamilton, Kent & Co. Spring 1909.

*The Equinox. Vol. I (2)*. London: Simpkin, Marshall, Hamilton, Kent & Co. Autumn 1909.

*The Equinox. Vol. I (3)*. London: Simpkin, Marshall, Hamilton, Kent & Co. Spring 1910.

*The Equinox. Vol. I (4)*. London: Privately printed. Autumn 1910.

*The Equinox. Vol. I (5)*. London: Privately printed. Spring 1911.

*The Equinox. Vol. I (6)*. London: Wieland & Co. Autumn 1911.

*The Equinox. Vol. I (7)*. London: Wieland & Co. Spring 1912.

*The Equinox. Vol. I (8)*. London: Wieland & Co. Autumn 1912.

*The Equinox. Vol. I (9)*. London: Wieland & Co. Spring 1913.

*The Equinox. Vol. I (10)*. London: Wieland & Co. Autumn 1913.

*The Equinox of the Gods*. London: Ordo Templi Orientis 1936.

*The Spirit of Solitude: An Autohagiography* (Later renamed *The Confessions of Aleister Crowley*). London: Mandrake Press 1929.

*The Vision and the Voice*. Bartson, California: Thelema Publishing Company 1952.

# REFERENCES

Anon. (1944). *The Cloud of Unknowing*. New York: Early English Texts Society.

Bennett, A. (1911). The Training of the Mind, http://tinyurl.com/5n8kpt5d (hermetic.com). Accessed August 2023.

Bogdan, H. (Ed.) (2012). *Aleister Crowley and Western Esotericism*. New York: Oxford University Press.

Butler, W. E. (1959). *The Magician: His Training and Work*. London: Harper Collins.

Butler, W. E. (1962). *Apprenticed to Magic*. Wellingborough, UK: Aquarian Press, 1972.

Butler, W. E. (1964). *Magic and the Qabalah*. London: Harper Collins, 1978.

Butler, W. E. (1971). *Magic: Its Ritual, Power and Purpose*. Wellingborough, UK: Aquarian Press.

Butler, W. E. (2004). *Lords of Light: The Path of Initiation in the Western Mysteries*. Rochester, VT: Destiny Books.

Case, P. F. (1947). *The Tarot*. New York: Macoy.

Churton, T. (2011). *Aleister Crowley: The Biography*. London: Watkins.

Corbin, H. (1969). *Creative Imagination in the Sufism of Ibn Arabi*. Princeton, NJ: Princeton University Press.

Critchlow, K. (1980). *The Soul as Sphere and Androgyne*. Ipswich: Golgonooza Press.

Crowley, A. (1909a). *The Equinox. Vol. 1 (1)*. London: Wieland & Co.

Crowley, A. (1909b). The Soldier and the Hunchback: ! and ?. *The Equinox*. Vol. 1 (1): 113–135.

Crowley, A. (1912). *The Equinox. Vol. I (7)*. London: Wieland & Co.

Crowley, A. (1922). *Diary of a Drug Fiend*. New York: University Books, 1970.

Crowley, A. (1929). *Moonchild*. New York: Weiser, 1970.

Crowley, A. (1971). *The Confessions of Aleister Crowley: An Autohagiography*. London: Routledge, Kegan & Paul.

Crowley, A. (1972a). *Book Four*. Dallas, TX: Sangreal Foundation.

Crowley, A. (1972b). *The Vision and the Voice*. Dallas, TX: Sangreal Foundation.

Crowley, A. (1973). *Magick Without Tears*. Woodbury, MN: Llewelyn.

Crowley, A. (1981). *The Book of Lies*. San Francisco. Newburyport, MA: Red Wheel/Weiser.

Crowley, A. (1985). *Little Essays Towards Truth*. Northampton, UK: Sut Anubis.

Crowley, A. (1989). *Magick*. Bungay, UK: Guild Publishing.

Crowley, A. (1995). *Tao Te Ching*. Newburyport, MA: Samuel Weiser.

Crowley, A. (2004). *The Book of Thoth*. York Beach, ME: Weiser.

Crowley, A. (2005). *Liber Aleph*. York Beach, ME: Red Wheel/Weiser.

Crowley, A. (2015). *The Holy Books of Thelema*. Berkeley, CA: Conjoined Creation.

Evans, D. (2007). *Aleister Crowley and the Twentieth Century Synthesis of Magick*. Oxford: Hidden Publishing.

Fortune, D. (1976). *The Mystical Qabalah*. London: Ernest Benn.

Frazer, J. G. (1890). *The Golden Bough*. London: Macmillan.

Karenga, M. (2004). *Maat, The Moral Ideal in Ancient Egypt: A Study in Classical African Ethics*. New York: Routledge.

Key, A. (1965). Traces of the Worship of the Moon God Sin among the Early Israelites. *Journal of Biblical Literature*, 1 (84): 20–26.

Komjathy, L. (2023). *Dao De Jing*. Chicago: Illinois Square Inch Press.

Kushner, L. (2006). *Kabbalah: A Love Story*. New York: Morgan Road Books.

Layne, D. (2013). Philosophical Prayer in Proclus's Commentary on Plato's Timaeus. *Review of Metaphysics*, 67 (2): 345–368.

Levi, E. (2017). *The Doctrine and Ritual of High Magic*. New York: Penguin.

MacGregor-Mathers, S. L. (1976). *The Book of the Sacred Magic of Abra-Melin the Mage*. Wellingborough, UK: Thorsons.

Maharshi, R. (1959). *The Collected Works of Ramana Maharshi*. London: Rider & Co.

Majercik, R. (2013). *The Chaldean Oracles*. Chepstow, UK: The Prometheus Trust.

Mantyk, E., trans. (2021). *Sir Gawain and the Green Knight*. Mount Hope, NY: Classical Poets Society.

Matt, D., trans. (2009). *The Zohar*, volume 5. Stanford, CA: Stanford University Press.

Mistlberger, P. T. (2010). *Three Dangerous Magi*. Winchester, UK: O Books.

Moore, J. (2009). *Aleister Crowley: A Modern Master*. Oxford: Mandrake.

Nanananda, B. (1986). *Concept and Reality*. Kandy, Ceylon: Buddhist Publication Society.

Pine, R., trans. (2000). *The Collected Songs of Cold Mountain*. Port Townsend, WA: Copper Canyon Press.

Pine, R., trans. (2009). *Lao-Tzu's Taoteching*. Port Townsend, WA: Copper Canyon Press.

Pischikova, E., Griffin, K., & Budka, J. (eds.) (2014). *Thebes in the First Millennium BC*. Newcastle, UK: Cambridge Scholars.

Rautenbach, N. (2010). *YHWH loves the Gates of Zion*. Riga, Latvia: VDM Verlag Dr. Müller.

Rees, I. (1973). Meditation Diary. Unpublished.

Rees, I. (2022). *The Tree of Life and Death*. London: Aeon.

Regen, I., & Traunecker, C. (2013). The Funerary Palace of Padiamenope at Thebes, https://tinyurl.com/mrc9wsan (researchgate.net). Accessed March 2024.

Rilke, R. M. (2009). *Duino Elegies and The Sonnets to Orpheus*, translated by S. Mitchell. New York: Knopf Doubleday.

Rouzer, P., trans. (2016). *On Cold Mountain*. Seattle, WA: University of Washington Press.

Salaman, C. (2000). *The Way of Hermes*. Rochester, VT: Inner Traditions.

Symonds, J. (1973). *The Great Beast*. St Albans, UK: Mayflower Books.

Tanahashi, K., & Levitt, P. (2018). *The Complete Cold Mountain*. Boulder, CO: Shambhala Publications.

Verman, M. (1992). *The Books of Contemplation*. Albany, NY: State University of New York.

Waddell, N. (2017). *Complete Poison Blossoms from a Thicket of Thorn*. Berkeley, CA: Counterpoint Press.

Wallis Budge, E. A. (1969 [1904]). *The Gods of the Egyptians, Vol II*. New York: Dover Publications.

Watson, B., trans. (2013). *Chuang Tzu: Basic Writings*. New York: Columbia University.

# INDEX